Alfred Creigh

History of the Knights Templar of the State of Pennsylvania

Alfred Creigh

History of the Knights Templar of the State of Pennsylvania

ISBN/EAN: 9783337293161

Printed in Europe, USA, Canada, Australia, Japan

Cover: Foto ©ninafisch / pixelio.de

More available books at **www.hansebooks.com**

Sir, Geo. A. Haines 35

KNIGHTS TEMPLAR.

I.N.R.I.

To all Sir Knights of the Illustrious Order of the
Red Cross and of the Valiant and Magnanimous
Orders of Knights Templar and Knights of
Malta to whom these presents may come — Greeting

THIS IS TO CERTIFY that

Sir Knight _____

whose name appears on page _____ of Creigh's
History of Knights Templar is a member
of _____ Commandery No.
instituted in _____
and subordinate to the R.E. Grand Commandery
of Pennsylvania and as such we commend
him to the courteous and fraternal regard of
all valiant and magnanimous Knights wherever
dispersed around the Globe —

In testimony whereof we have
hereunto set our hands and
caused the seal of our Commandery
to be affixed this _____ day
of _____ A.D. 186
A.O. 7   A.O.E.P.

E.C.
Rec.

Alfred Creigh, Grand Recorder of K.T. of Penna.:

HISTORY

OF THE

KNIGHTS TEMPLAR

OF THE

STATE OF PENNSYLVANIA

FROM

FEBRUARY 14th, A.D. 1794: A. O. 676 TO NOVEMBER 13th, A.D. 1866:
A. O. 748. A. O. E. P. 69.

PREPARED AND ARRANGED FROM ORIGINAL PAPERS

TOGETHER WITH THE

CONSTITUTION, DECISIONS, RESOLUTIONS AND FORMS

OF THE

R. E. GRAND COMMANDERY OF PENNSYLVANIA.

"Old historic rolls I opened."

ALFRED CREIGH, LL.D.: K. T. 33°.,

HISTORIOGRAPHER OF KNIGHTS TEMPLAR OF PENNSYLVANIA AND OF THE
UNITED STATES; AUTHOR OF "MASONRY AND
ANTI-MASONRY," &c.

PHILADELPHIA
J. B. LIPPINCOTT & CO.
1867.

THIS VOLUME

IS

ffraternally anꝺ Courteously Dedicated

TO THE

RIGHT EMINENT, THE GRAND OFFICERS, THE SUBORDINATĒ
OFFICERS OF THE SUBORDINATE COMMANDERIES,
AND THE INDIVIDUAL SIR KNIGHTS,

COMPOSING THE

RIGHT EMINENT GRAND COMMANDERY

OF THE

STATE OF PENNSYLVANIA,

AS A

TESTIMONIAL

OF THE

HIGH ESTEEM IN WHICH THEY ARE COLLECTIVELY AND
INDIVIDUALLY REGARDED BY THE

AUTHOR.

PREFACE.

THE present work on the Templarism of Pennsylvania is purely historical; collected and arranged from scattered memorials and authentic papers, which from time to time were committed to and collected by the Author, from many worthy Sir Knights, who feel that Pennsylvania should be honored as the Keystone of the Templar Arch.

The lapse of time—the decease of the Sir Knights who inaugurated the Orders of Knighthood in this State—the destruction of the minutes by fire and the persecuting Spirit of Anti-masonry, were the originating causes which led to the destruction of many valuable papers; which, if now in existence, would explain and demonstrate those *essentials*, in which we are now in doubt and perplexity.

Every craftsman in the exercise of his particular art provides himself with the proper implements, necessary to carry to perfection the object he desires to attain—and however anxious I may feel, to place myself in the same position, the causes I have stated, prevent me from procuring the full basis upon which to erect a superstructure worthy of the Knighthood of Pennsylvania. It is my ardent desire however, that the descendants of those noble Sir Knights who have been enrolled under our Banners and whose names appear on these pages, and who may have in their possession any documents, pamphlets, diplomas, etc., etc., on the subject of Knighthood, will IMMEDIATELY forward the same to the Author, so that in the next edition of this work the Templarism of Pennsylvania may be perfected and finished. The Right Eminent Sir Benjamin Parke, Grand Commander of the Grand Commandery of Pennsylvania, in his annual address truly and prophetically said, that "when the history of Knighthood in the United States should be written, PENNSYLVANIA KNIGHTHOOD, like Pennsylvania Masonry, will stand the GRANDEST, the FIRMEST, if not the LOFTIEST column in the Union."

With the kindest feelings towards all our Sister Grand Commanderies—with the highest respect for those ancient Grand Encampments who labored for the introduction of Knighthood into their respective States—and who afterwards unitedly formed a general Grand body—we have the highest respect, esteem and veneration—and would not detract from their merits, in their noble efforts, to preserve and perpetuate Templarism. The work of their Fathers is worthy of all commendation, and they would be recreant to their duties as Templars did they not guard their altars and their fame with the most religious attachment and love. But in their zeal, they must not forget to honor the State of Pennsylvania, who by the organization of the FIRST Grand Encampment of Pennsylvania, breathed into Knighthood the breath of life, MAY 12, 1797—and in the infancy of the United States, arose to manhood. Although she bears upon her brow the manhood of seventy years—yet she has not the marks of old age, nor signs of decay, but all the vigor of youth; pressing forward to the attainment of those high and holy principles for which our Fathers inaugurated the Orders of Christian Knighthood —the God-like principles of defending innocent maidens— helpless orphans—destitute widows and the Christian Religion. In these high and holy efforts, to preserve the peace, purity and perpetuity of Christian Knighthood may the Sir Knights of Pennsylvania and those of our Sister jurisdiction be preeminently successful.

ALFRED CREIGH.

ELLENDALE VILLA, WASHINGTON, PA.,
SEPTEMBER 10, 1866.

INTRODUCTION.

THE first legitimate Encampments wherein the Order of the Temple was conferred, required two essential qualifications—*first* that the candidate had previously received the degrees of Freemasonry—*secondly* that he should present with his application a Royal Arch certificate, duly attested.

Many reasons have been assigned why these prerequisites were added. Among the many conflicting reasons given—we add those most generally adopted. These qualifications were added either out of gratitude to the Masonic fraternity to whom the Templars had been greatly indebted for protection in times of dire necessity—or because, secret societies were prohibited by parliamentary enactments, and the Encampments sought shelter under the Masonic Order as a higher grade of Freemasons. For these reasons we may conclude that Templarism was engrafted on the original system of Freemasonry.

Nearly half a century since an address on the interesting question of the incorporation of Knighthood with Freemasonry, was delivered before Boyle Commandery No. 242 of Roscommon, Ireland—and as but very few Sir Knights have access to so valuable a document—I give an extract therefrom, to demonstrate this Union.

Of the many historical records which treat of Freemasonry those which are considered genuine and bear inherent evidence of authenticity, fix the date of the *first connection* of Knights Templar with the Masonic fraternity at the middle of the twelfth century. It is unnecessary to refer to the history of Freemasonry in remote ages—it is sufficient for the present purpose to state that it can be collected from very creditable

11

sources of information on the subject, that Freemasonry which had declined for some time previous to the reign of Edwara the Confessor began to flourish under the immediate patronage of that monarch—and thence received the countenance and support of succeeding Sovereigns—and we find that in the time of Henry II. Gilbert de Clare, Earl of Pembroke, esteemed it an honor to hold the office of PRESIDENT of the Society of Freemasons as it was then named.

It is recorded that in this reign Knights Templar were *first initiated* into the mysteries of Freemasonry, from which period they gave it their patronage, and the Grand Master of the Temple was appointed to superintend the Lodges, by which appointment pre-eminence was confined to the Orders of Knighthood, over the Society of Freemasons. By this junction of the two Orders, Freemasonry assumed a more important character and higher position in the eyes of the world and continued to increase in general estimation down to the reign of Richard I. It is generally believed that it was at this period that the first connection was formally established with a *Masonic Lodge* and the *Knights Templar*. Before that event, individual Knights were initiated into Masonic mysteries and patronized the Society of Freemasons, but subsequently and after the suppression of the Order and their dispersion throughout Christendom, and after they had regained stability and freedom from persecution, this Order of Knighthood was conferred exclusively on those who had previously passed through the higher degrees of Freemasonry.

It does not appear however that the *Knights of Malta* joined the Masonic Society until the close of the fourteenth century, and at that time the two Orders of Chivalry, that of *St. John* and the *Templars* had been united and have continued in unbroken union to the present day.

It is important to notice that at the time the Templars and Freemasons became an associated body, the Knights Templar as an Order had no authority over the Grand Master of Free-masonry as such—nor had that officer in his capacity as head and President of the Grand Lodge of Freemasons any power to give Laws to the Knights Templar. We could neither grant a Warrant to hold an Encampment, nor prohibit the installation of a candidate chosen and approved of by the Knights—neither had the Grand Master or Commander and Councils of the Order receiving this privilege, independent of any constraint by the superintendent of Freemasonry ; for it must be held in mind, that at this early period of incorporation, the offices of Grand Master of Freemasons and Grand Master of the Order of Knighthood, were separate and distinct, as is found to be the case frequently at this day, nor is there any reason why these two offices should be necessarily united in the same person.

This state of friendly and mutual relationship between these two institutions continued for a long period, and we in vain look for any authenticated works of Masonic proceedings which show the precise time when the Order of Knights Templar, as now established and recognized in Ireland, placed themselves under the authority of the Grand Lodge of this part of the United Kingdom. But we have the fact, an admitted and indisputable fact, that almost every Lodge in Ireland has for a long series of years *held Encampments*—installed Knights —granted certificates—walked in public processions—displayed the Banner of the Order.

The only law which regulated their proceedings and which was universally binding and universally acknowledged was that "no Knights Templar Encampment or Royal Arch Chapter could be opened unless by members of a Lodge who held a Warrant of the *third* or Master Mason's degree of Freemasonry under the Grand Lodge of Ireland."

The Grand Lodge of Ireland held an Encampment in Dublin in 1818, at which delegates from several lodges attended for the purpose of taking the matter (Freemasonry and Knighthood) into consideration. The result of this meeting was the adoption of a resolution that "in future no Encampment could be considered legal, nor any Knight subsequently admitted and recognized as a member of the Order unless such Encampment was held under *a Warrant from the Grand Lodge.*"

Hence in Ireland the whole Masonic body is under one head —a Chapter must have a Lodge attached to it—and an Encampment, both a Chapter and Lodge.

2

Sir W. J. B. Mc Leod Moore, Provincial Grand Commander of the Grand Conclave of Canada—who is well versed in Masonic literature—and who received his Lodge and Chapter degrees forty years since under the warrant of Lodge, 333, of Aberdeen, Scotland—and the Encampment degrees twenty-four years since under the warrant of Lodge, 242, at Roscommon, Boyle County, Ireland—thus gives his views upon the Templarism of Scotland.

The present inquiry is to endeavor to show *when*, and explain the *cause* of this order of Knights Templar becoming amalgamated with the Masonic body and its peculiar rites transmitted and promulgated by them. On considering the various surmises and assertions of different authors who have pronounced upon the authenticity of each of their peculiar views the *only one* that appears the most feasible and which bears evidence of genuineness, is that the ancient order (of Templars) after their dispersion, were alone preserved from total annihilation by a remnant of the Knights seeking refuge in SCOTLAND.

History tells us that in the early part of the fourteenth century, by the persecution of Philip the Fair of France, the Order was suppressed and their possessions confiscated throughout Europe—as also in England by Edward II. at the instance of the Pope. But it is well authenticated that many of the Knights retired to Scotland, then a separate kingdom, where they obtained lands and revenues, and with the Knights Hospitalers of St. John of Jerusalem, afterwards called *Knights of Malta*, lived together on amicable terms. In that kingdom they continued to reside unmolested, and there is every reason to believe, became in some measure associated with the Masonic fraternity which was patronized by the Kings of Scotland.

In England, during the long disturbed state of the kingdom, Masonry had lain dormant, but found its way back from Scotland, where it had continued uninterrupted under the hereditary guardianship of Royalty. We have no old or authentic documents to show when the present Masonic Templar Order or descendants 'of "Templars of the Crusaders" was first formed in England. But we do know, that about the year 1560, the Preceptor of the combined Orders of the Hospitalers and the Temple in Scotland, who had with several of the Knights, Esquires, and serving Brethren, joined the Reformation and became Presbyterians, resigned to the Crown the whole of the property belonging to the Hospitalers and the Templars, and subsequently connected themselves with the Freemasons' Lodge, and being under no governing head, initiated whom they pleased.

From this the system of Masonic Templarism took its origin, spreading itself throughout England, Ireland, and finally into North America, forming separate and independent Chapters of the Order, when sufficient members could be assembled, never less, however, than *the original number of the founders,* viz.: NINE.

These Chapters became known by the name of *Encampments of Masonic Knights Templar and Knights of Malta.* It is much to be regretted that soon afterwards the Ancient Constitutions, Rituals, and Titles of the Officers underwent, in many particulars, various changes, much of Masonic-like matter having been introduced, and we find at the present time, that the different jurisdictions do not practice the same ceremonies alike.

But to return to the Reformation. When the Hospital and Temple lands were resigned to the Crown, the Templars who still adhered to the Roman Catholic Religion placed themselves under a new Grand Master, David Seton, and continued to preserve and transmit the *Ancient Ceremonies* and Principles of the Order, and although they subsequently admitted Protestants, it continued in the hands of the High Church Party until the close of the last century. Viscount Dundee, known as the famous "Claverhouse," held the office of Grand Master. He was killed at the battle of Killecrankie, with the Grand Cross of the Order on his person. Prince Charles Edward Stuart, the Pretender, was installed at Holyrood, Edinburgh, September 24, 1745, and became Grand Master. At his death, Oliphant, of Bachiltar, was elected Grand Master, who died in 1795. Alexander Deucher, of Edinburgh, succeeded, and in 1811 His Royal Highness, the Duke of Kent, became Protector of the Order, and appointed Deucher Grand Master for life. By these measures the Order was rescued from insignifi-

cance, and it continued to flourish in different parts of the
British Dominion holding its Conclave. In 1836, Grand Master Deuchar resigned, when Admiral Sir David Milne, K. C.
B., was elected. The present Grand Master, his Grace, the
Duke of Athol, now reigns over the Order in Scotland, both
Masonic and Chivalric; and although a distinction is made
between the two classes, the first is open to persons in general
of the necessary qualifications, but to enter the latter requires
the applicant to be a *Royal Arch Mason.*

In England, the Blue Lodges have long since ceased to permit their Charters to be used for Encampments. In June,
1791, the Masonic Knights Templar being animated by the
flourishing state of Symbolic Masonry under the protection of
his Royal Highness, the Prince of Wales, (afterwards King
George IV.), with a desire to revive their ancient Royal Religious and Military Order, they confederated and elected
Brother and Knight Companion, Thomas Dunckerly, of
Hampton Court Palace, in the County of Middlesex, Grand
Master of the Confraternity, under the patronage of His
Royal Highness, Prince Edward, (afterwards Duke of Kent),
and on the 24th of June, 1791, a Grand and Royal Conclave
was held, by which the ANCIENT STATUTES of the Order were
revived, re-enacted and unanimously approved.

On the 10th day of April, 1809, a Grand and Royal Conclave was held according to ancient form under the sanction
of H. R. H., the Duke of Kent, Royal Grand Patron, in the
presence of the Most Eminent Grand Master, Walter Rodwell
Wright, where the Statutes of the Order (passed June 24,
1791) were revised, and with sundry alterations, confirmed.

On the 6th of August, 1812, H. R. H., the Duke of Sussex, was installed Grand Master of the Order, and gave these
revised Statutes his sanction and approval. On the demise of
the Duke of Sussex, Sir Knight Colonel Kennys Tynte, of
Halswell, Somersetshire, was installed Grand Master on the
3d of April, 1846, who gave his sanction to another revisal of
the Statutes. After the death of Col. Tynte, in the autumn
of 1861, Sir William Stuart, of Oldenham Abbey, County of
Kent, was on the 10th of May, 1862, installed Most Eminent
Grand Master of the Masonic Order of the Temple, and

Grand Master of Malta, in England and Wales, and the Colonial dependencies of the British Crown.

The history of the Templar Order may be thus summarily expressed. It was established in 1118—suppressed in 1312 by the cruelty and avarice of Clement the V., and Philip the Fair, King of France—after which the Templars and Knights Hospitalers of St. John of Jerusalem were incorporated into one body. In 1291, they took up their residence in Cyprus, and afterwards went to Rhodes and took the name of *Knights of Rhodes*. In 1530, the Emperor Charles V., of Spain, conferred on them the Island of Malta—hence they received the name of *Knights of Malta of the Order of St. John of Jerusalem*. When residing on the Island of Malta, they established their Preceptories throughout Europe—as the history of Ireland, Scotland, and England, above given, amply and fully demonstrate—and from all of which three Grand Conclaves, the Knights of Pennsylvania may be said to trace their origin. The founders of our Order emigrated to America for the enjoyment of civil and religious liberty—and although they engaged in a war of seven years to accomplish their object, they triumphed and established the principles of Liberty, Fraternity, and Equality. These principles being acknowledged, and a Constitution adopted, our Fathers commenced the work of resuscitating those institutions, whose principles they loved and honored—among which was. the Ancient and Honorable Society of Free and Accepted Masons— with authority to confer the Orders of Knighthood. Masonic Templarism having been first established in Pennsylvania by the first Grand Encampment which met in Philadelphia on the 12th day of May, 1797—is entitled, therefore, to the high honor of having introduced the orders of Christian Knighthood into the United States—deriving her work from the English, Scottish, and Irish Rituals, the two former of which use the same Ritual since 1791, a copy of which is now in my possession, and clearly proves that the present Ritual as used is one manufactured from several rites. We look forward with *hope* to that day when the present Ritual will give place to the one used by our Fathers, pre-eminently teaching the Christianity of the New Testament and discarding the Red

2 *

Cross degree, as not only an interpolation, but having been surreptitiously taken from the Ineffable degrees of the Scottish Rite. In the name of Christianity we protest against the Red Cross being acknowledged as the first degree of the Order of Christian Knighthood.

Pennsylvania Templars, as well as those of every State of this widely extended Union can now trace their respective origin from the sketches embodied in these introductory remarks, intended to prove the regular descent from a common origin, an eternal union with Free Masonry, and having only in view the propagation and dissemination of the principles of the Gospel of the Redeemer of Mankind.

We have stated that it required a candidate for the Knights Templar Order to be a Royal Arch Mason. As a matter of curiosity, yet worthy of preservation, I shall give extracts from Templar certificates, issued at various times, from 1791 to 1851, on this interesting subject.

We, the Captain-General, etc., etc., of the General Assembly of Knights Templar and Knights of Malta, do certify that A. B. was by us dubbed a Knight of the Most Holy Invincible and Magnanimous Order of Knights Templar, the true and faithful Soldier of Jesus Christ, as also of the Order of St. John of Jerusalem, now Knights of Malta, etc., etc., held at Newry, under the sanction of Lodge 706, on the Registry of Ireland, *May* 11, 1791.

ORDER OF KNIGHTS TEMPLAR,	3789,
ORDER OF MALTA,	921,
AND OF ARK AND MARK MASONRY,	3798,
IN ROYAL ARCH MASONRY,	4138,
BOOK OF THE LAW FOUND,	2415.

We, the Captain-General, etc., etc., of the General Assembly of Sir Knights Templar and Knights of Malta, held under the sanction of Lodge 835, at Douglas Bridge, County of Tyrone, on Registry of Ireland, do certify that A. B. was dubbed a Knight of that Most Holy, Glorious, and Magnanimous Order of Sir Knights Templar and Knights of Malta, etc., etc., *June* 9, 1798.

The Chiefs of the Order, *May* 29, 1807, at Londonderry.

under the sanction of Lodge 235, on Registry of Ireland, dedicated to Moses and King Solomon in the Ancient and Sacred
Law, and to the faithful Soldier, St. John of Jerusalem, in
the Gospel dispensation, do certify that A. B., etc., etc.

March 13, 1811. We, the Grand Master, Senior Brethren,
etc., etc., of this Magnanimous and Invincible Order of High
Knights Templar and Knights of Malta, of Lodge 401, held
in Monaghan, and on the Registry of Ireland, dedicated to
Moses and King Solomon in the Ancient and Sacred Law, and
to that faithful Soldier, St. John of Jerusalem, in the Gospel
dispensation, do certify that A. B. was regularly dubbed, admitted, initiated, and confirmed in the rights, ceremonies, and
mysteries of that Most Holy, Noble, and Christian Order of
a High Knight Templar, (the true and faithful Soldier of
Jesus Christ), also Knight of Malta, etc.

September 4, 1818. We, the High Priest, Captain-General
and Grand Master of a Royal Arch and Knights Templar Encampment, held (this day) under the sanction of Lodge 730,
in the County of Londonderry, certifies that A. B. having
passed the Chair, and having been initiated into the degrees
of a Royal Arch, Excellent and Superexcellent Mason, and
consequently was afterwards by us dubbed a Knight of the
Most Ancient and Honorable Order of Sir Knights Templar,
Knights of Malta, or of Jerusalem, also a Knight of the Ark
and Mark, an Elesian Knight, Knight of the Red Cross, and
also the Mediterranean Pass, etc.

June 11, 1819. The Grand Master, Deputy Grand Master,
and Captain-General of the Magnanimous and Invincible
Order of High Knights Templar and of Malta, held under
the sanction of Lodge 446, in the Sixty-eighth Light Infantry
Regiment, and on the Registry of ENGLAND, certifies that A.
B. was admitted, initiated, and confirmed in all the rights,
titles, ceremonies, and mysteries of the Most Noble and Christian Order of High Knights Templar and of Malta.

May 3, 1851. We, the Captain-General of the General Assembly of Knights Templar, dedicated to Moses and King
Solomon in the Ancient Law and to the Holy St. John of
Jerusalem, in the Gospel dispensation, held under the sanction
of Lodge 194, County of Down, and Registry of Ireland, was

by us dubbed a Knight of the Most Holy, Glorious and Magnanimous, and Invincible Order of Knights Templar and
Knights of Malta, of Masonry, 5851, of Excellent, Superexcellent, and Royal Arch Masonry, 3351, and of Knights
Templar, 751.

To these forms of certificates used in Ireland and England,
I add the one used by Encampment No. 1, of Philadelphia.
This certificate is a copper-plate engraving 16 by 20 inches, in
which are two columns, surmounted by an Arch, and on the
arch the motto "*In hoc signo vinces.*" On the keystone of
the arch is the ark with the two cherubim, and above all, the
All Seeing Eye. The top of the left hand column is surmounted with the sun, level, trowel, and gauge; on the right
column the moon and stars, with the square, compasses, and
setting maul. Under the arch are tents and a triangular table
with lights thereupon, while seven steps are placed between
the two columns. The whole design is emblematical of the
union between Masonry and Knighthood.

The certificate reads thus:

We, the Chiefs of the Encampment No. 1, Philadelphia,
of the Most Sublime and Ancient Order of Knights Templar,
Free and Accepted Masters of Masonry, do hereby certify that
our well-beloved Brother, A. B., is with us a regular regis-
tered Knight Templar and Knight of Malta, and that he has
valiantly supported and maintained the great principles of our
Order, during his stay amongst us, to our great satisfaction.
Therefore, we do most cordially recommend him to all the
sublime and respectable Encampments in the Universe; hoping
they will cheer a Pilgrim on his way; and that this certificate
may not be of service to any other person, we have caused our
said Brother to set his name adjacent to the seal *Ne Varietur.*

In testimony of which, being assembled, we have delivered
unto him this certificate, under our hand and the seal of our
Encampment, No. 1, Philadelphia, June 24, 1794, at the East
End of the Universe, under the azure arch at high noon.

Attest:

G. H., *Recorder.*

A. B., E. G. M.
C. D., E. G.
E. F., E. C. G.

To the questions asked, why are these certificates, issued in Ireland, England and America inserted? I answer, it is another link in the chain of argument to elucidate the fact that the present degree of Knights of the Red Cross never had any connection with the Templar Order and Knights of Malta of St. John; but that it is an interpolation unworthy of the high character of the Christian Orders of Knighthood; an interpolation which should be frowned upon by all Sir Knights who revere the Cross and are looking forward to the Crown;—an interpolation which tells us of broken vows, violated faith, and perjured principles.

·

Knights Templar.

APPOINTMENT OF HISTORIOGRAPHER

AND THE ACTION OF THE GRAND COMMANDERY OF THE STATE OF PENNSYLVANIA THEREUPON.

In the Annual Address of June 22, 1860, of the R. E. Sir William Henry Allen, Grand Commander of the Grand Commandery of Knights Templar of Pennsylvania, he expressed his sentiments in these words:

Impressed with the importance of collecting and preserving the history of Masonic Knighthood in Pennsylvania, I appointed in August last (1859) our Grand Recorder, Sir Alfred Creigh, HISTORIOGRAPHER of the Grand Commandery of this State, and sent him a COMMISSION, handsomely engrossed on parchment. The ability and zeal of this officer have been illustrated by his activity in collecting and arranging a great number of documentary and traditional memorials which will prove of much interest and value to the Order. All this has been done, without any other compensation than the pleasure which these researches have afforded him and the hope of contributing to the honor of Pennsylvania Knighthood.

The Commission issued by the R. E. Grand Commander Allen reads as follows:

COMMISSION.

OFFICE OF THE RIGHT EMINENT GRAND COMMANDER
OF THE GRAND COMMANDERY OF KNIGHTS TEMPLAR
OF THE STATE OF PENNSYLVANIA.

*To all true and courteous Knights, to whom these Presents
may come, Greeting:—*

HEALTH,   UNION,   FRATERNITY.

Whereas, It is the duty and interest of the Knights of
Pennsylvania, to collect and preserve the history of the
Order.

And whereas, It is believed that much valuable information may be gathered from the records of the First
Grand Encampment of Knights Templar in the United
States, which was organized in the City of Philadelphia
on the 12th day of May, in the year of our Lord one
thousand seven hundred and ninety-seven.

And whereas, It is desirable to commission a learned
and distinguished Sir Knight to trace the history of
Masonic Knighthood in the State of Pennsylvania, and
to collect, arrange, and preserve the written and printed
memorials thereof, and promoting the good, well-being,
and perpetuation of Templar Masonry.

Therefore, Now know ye, that I, WILLIAM HENRY
ALLEN, Right Eminent Grand Commander of the Grand
Commandery of Knights Templar of the State of Penn-
sylvania, by virtue of the authority in me vested by the
Constitution, do hereby appoint our illustrious Knight

SIR ALFRED CREIGH,

Eminent Grand Recorder of our Grand Commandery
aforesaid, to the honorable and responsible office of

HISTORIOGRAPHER

of the Grand Commandery of Knights Templar of the

State of Pennsylvania, commending him to the knightly regard and courteous attention of all the Subordinate Commanderies under our jurisdiction, and of all true and magnanimous Sir Knights as worthy of their confidence; and courteously recommend each and every of them to furnish him with all such written or printed documents as will aid him in the discharge of his duties as HIS-TORIOGRAPHER OF PENNSYLVANIA KNIGHTHOOD.

Given under my hand and the seal of our Grand Commandery at Philadelphia, this twenty-fifth day of August, in the year of our Lord one thousand eight hundred and fifty-nine, and of our Order seven hundred and forty-one.

:|: WILLIAM HENRY ALLEN,
R. E. Grand Commander.

On the 23d of June, 1860, the Historiographer made a partial report of his labors, with the view of eliciting information, and of procuring the written and printed memorials of the Knighthood of Pennsylvania.

The Grand Commandery feeling a deep interest in her own history thus far reported on, on the recommendation of Sir Wm. Lilly, passed a resolution, That a vote of thanks be and the same is hereby unanimously tendered to E. Sir Alfred Creigh, for his deep research, untiring zeal, and unwearied perseverance, in collecting and arranging the history of Knighthood in this State since May 12, 1797. The partial report made at that time was referred to the Committee on the doings of the Grand Officers, consisting of Sir Knights Edmund H. Turner, Thomas D. Wattson, and H. D. Lowe.

The Committee reported that they approved most cordially both the propriety of making such an appointment and the selection of Sir Alfred Creigh for that position,

3   B

and recommended that when the work now in the course of preparation by him shall be published, this Grand Commandery shall purchase such a number of copies as shall be alike honorable to the Grand Commandery, and due to the zeal of the author.

The civil war raging—and many of our active Sir Knights engaged in the defense of Constitutional Liberty, it was deemed prudent, that no further action should be taken by the Grand Commandery, until peace should return. Consequently on the 14th of June, 1864, the question of the History of Knights Templar in Pennsylvania was again brought before the Grand Commandery by the R. E. Sir H. Stanley Goodwin, Grand Commander. In his Annual Address he says:

During the year 1859, the very Eminent Sir Knight Alfred Creigh, LL. D., our Grand Recorder, was appointed Historiographer of this Grand Commandery. This appointment was a very important one, and in my opinion, very judiciously made; for the Eminent Sir Knight has for very many years, as you all are aware, devoted much of his time and attention to the history of Masonry, and of our order in this State. I would suggest, if it meets your views, that he be called on to report the progress he has made in the work assigned him, and that you take such action as may seem to you right and proper to rescue our early history from oblivion.

In reply to this suggestion and the wish of the Grand Commandery as expressed through the Committee on the Doings of the Grand Officers, the Historiographer submitted the following report:—

Officers and Members of the Grand Commandery of Pennsylvania :

In the Annual Address of 1864, of the R. E. Sir H. Stanley Goodwin, Grand Commander, reference was made to the labors of the Historiographer, recommending that a report be made and measures taken, to rescue from oblivion the History of Knights Templar in this State. These views were also concurred in by the Committee to whom was referred the address of Grand Commander Goodwin. To comply, therefore, with the universal desire expressed, not only by your R. E. Grand Commander, your Committee, and the Sir Knights of this and other jurisdictions, I avail myself of the present opportunity to report how far I have progressed in the laborious duties assigned me.

Six years since, I received a commission from the then R. E. Sir Wm. H. Allen, LL. D., Grand Commander, to write the History of Knights Templar in Pennsylvania, since which period I have been collecting and arranging documentary and traditional memorials, which I have procured from various sources, from the year 1794, and three years prior to the organization of the first Grand Encampment in the United States until the present time.

I have classified the whole into four divisions, embracing—1st. The introduction of Knighthood into Pennsylvania, from the year 1794 to 1797, when the degrees were conferred under a Blue Lodge Warrant. 2d. The history of the first Grand Encampment organized May 12th, 1797, and its subordinates. 3d. The History of the Pennsylvania Grand Encampment, and its Subordinates in New York City; Wilmington, Delaware, and Baltimore, Maryland, instituted February 16, 1814, and—4th. The full history of the Third, or present Grand Encampment or Commandery, constituted April 14, 1854, with the history of its Subordinates, which will necessarily embrace the Union of the two Grand Encampments of this State, which was consummated February 12, 1857. To these divisions will be added many interesting Templar facts and documents, which can only be obtained from the *manuscripts* now in my possession, procured from the Grand Conclave of England, through Sir Kt. Col. W. J. B. Moore, Prov. Gr. Com. of Canada.

In an examination of the whole subject, the *Rituals of the Order* were also examined into—and from information and authentic copies now in my possession, and subject to the inspection of this Grand Commandery, I am free to confess that many radical changes have been made, which destroys the beauty of the rituals and the teachings of Templarism. These rituals date as far back as 1794, when Templarism was introduced into Pennsylvania

These innovations were introduced by Thos. S. Webb, who received these degrees in Philadelphia prior to 1802, and is styled the Father of American Masonry. By what authority he changed the work and ritual, we have not the means of knowing, except to build up for himself the reputation of a learned Mason. We desire not to detract from his great Masonic abilities, but we do contend that as Pennsylvania gave birth to the *first* Grand Encampment in the United States, deriving her work, her ritual, and her teachings from the Grand Conclave of England, we should be the first to *put ourselves right* upon the record, and endeavor by her influence to re-introduce the work in its original purity. It would not be proper at this time, in a document prepared for publication, to enumerate the discrepancies and errors—suffice it to say, that the ritual as now used for the Knights of Malta, was prepared in Massachusetts a few years since, and from what we can learn from distinguished Templars, was only intended to fill the vacuum of historical and scriptural truths, until we could come in possession of the true and original work. I have procured a certified copy, through the Grand Registrar of the Grand Conclave of England and Wales, which, when perused, will clearly define the innovations, and make plain our teachings in accordance with truth, the Scriptures, and Templar history.

Again: In England the degree of Past Eminent Commander is conferred as an honorary distinction, like our degrees of P. M., P. H. P., etc., which is beautiful, historical, and worthy of being incorporated among our regular degrees as a reward of merit.

The task, however laborious, is not yet completed. Before giving it to the Templar world, an examination should be had among the archives of the papers of the R. W. Grand Lodge of Pennsylvania, and other institutions—and for the accomplishment of this end, a resolution should be passed, asking permission of the Grand Lodge for this purpose; also, a seal should be purchased for the use of the Historiographer, which usually appertains to the office, so that the correspondence may have more official authority in communicating with other parties for the benefit of Templars and procuring historical and Templar facts.

The Grand Commandery, through their Committee, Sir Knights Edmund H. Turner, Rev. J. R. Dimm, and

J. M. Scott, offered the following resolution, which was unanimously adopted:

That this Grand Commandery owes a debt of gratitude to the Eminent Sir Alfred Creigh for the pre-eminent success with which he, by great exertion, is rescuing from oblivion, the records of Templarism in Pennsylvania, and therefore we offer the following resolution: That this Grand Commandery will co-operate with Sir *Knight Alfred Creigh in his labors, so far as it may be in our power to aid him in his distinguished work.

On the 12th day of June, 1866, the Historiographer made his final report to the R. E. Grand Commandery of Knights Templar of Pennsylvania.

To the R. E. Grand Commander, Officers and Sir Knights, of the Grand Commandery of Knights Templar of Pennsylvania :

The history of Templarism in Pennsylvania is one of peculiar interest to every Sir Knight of the Order, whether enrolled under *our* Banner—or waging war in sister jurisdictions in defence of innocent maidens, helpless orphans, destitute widows, and the Christian Religion. To Pennsylvania, and *Pennsylvania alone,* are we indebted for the FIRST Grand Encampment which was ever constituted in the United States; she therefore has no competitor for the honor, the glory, and the immortality which is emblazoned upon her Templar history, and the 12th *day of May,* 1797, when the Convention met in Philadelphia, composed of delegates from Nos. 1 and 2 of Philadelphia, No. 3 of Harrisburg, and No. 4 of Carlisle, (whose respective organizations took place from 1793 to 1797), should be held as sacred as the 4th of July, 1776, the *one* having given birth to the Orders of Christian Knighthood, and the other to our political existence. It required sober thought, sound judgment, mature reflection, discriminating mind, and far seeing perception in the Sir Knights composing that Convention, as they were about to inaugurate a system of Christian Ethics, which would have an influence for weal or for woe upon the dissemination of the principles of Christian Knighthood. The idea was happily conceived, and the Sir Knights who

3 *

risked their Masonic and Templar reputation upon its success, have rendered the name of Pennsylvania eternal in the annals of Templarism. Let us, therefore, as the descendants of an honored and illustrious ancestry, render that day immortal by printing upon all documents issued by this Grand body the Latin words *Anno Equitum Ordinis Pennsylvaniæ*, instead of the words Anno Ordinis, which is a general term and applies to any order or religious association—hence it would be written A. E. O. P. 69. Other State Grand Commanderies date their origin from the constituting of their first Grand body, and to me it appears reasonable and just that we should do the same, so that instead of issuing to the Templar world our present Annual Proceedings, with the 13th Annual Conclave thereupon, it should read the 69th. *Justice* to the Founders of our Order, *Right*, sanctified by usage, nay, *Gratitude*, demands the immediate action of this Grand Body, upon this important question.

In order that we may have some light upon a question of so much importance, it shall be my pleasure as well as my duty to demonstrate to you that the fire of Templarism, which was lighted upon our Altar in Philadelphia as early as February 14, 1794, which is the oldest record in her possession, has never been extinguished, not even in the persecuting days of Antimasonry, although, it is true, the light shone dimly, and its rays were occasionally obscured, yet amid all the unhallowed and unholy convulsions of the human heart, baptized as they were with the feelings of jealousy, envy, hatred, religious and political bigotry, yet when our altars were assailed, the principles of our Order were kept pure in faithful breasts, and the light of the altar erected in their individual Templar hearts was preserved intact—and after the unholy fires of persecution had ceased, the Templarism of Pennsylvania came forth conservative in its character, pure in its development, undestroyed and unsuppressed. To demonstrate this, let facts be submitted for your inspection and approval.

It is beyond dispute, and settled by all masonic writers as well as antimasonic historians that the *first* Grand Encampment of Knights Templar of the United States was instituted May 12, 1797, in Philadelphia, although the Constitution was not adopted until the 19th of the same month. This Grand Body at its organization had four Subordinates; Nos. 1 and 2 in Philadelphia, No. 3 in Harrisburg, and No. 4, in Carlisle.

In 1860, Colonel John Johnston, then residing in Cincinnati, but lately deceased, wrote me some time since that in 1797 he was admitted to the K. T. degree in Carlisle, in No. 4, and that the Commander's name was Robert Leyburn, and that in 1799 he removed to Philadelphia, and visited the Encampments in that city. This testimony therefore establishes the existence of these four Subordinates prior to 1797; but we find from the published By-Laws of Nos. 1 and 2 of Philadelphia, that on the 27th of December, 1812, these two Subordinates united as No. 1, and from this Encampment, and also No. 2 of Pittsburg was formed a second Grand Encampment on the 16th of February, 1814, with the addition of Delegates from Rising Sun Encampment No. 1 of New York, Washington Encampment No. 1 of Wilmington, Delaware, and Baltimore Encampment No. 1 of Baltimore, Maryland. The style of the second Grand Encampment was the "Pennsylvania Grand Encampment with Masonic jurisdiction thereunto belonging." This second Grand Encampment existed until the 10th of June, 1824, or at least its Grand Master Sir Anthony Fannen exercised his authority as such, for on that day he issued a Dispensation to the Officers of St. John's Encampment No. 4, which was instituted June 8, 1819, "to dub and make John E. Schwarz a Sir Knight of our most illustrious Order of Knights Templar." This No. 4 is still in existence, and of which we will treat hereafter more particularly, as being more intimately connected with the Templarism of Pennsylvania than any of our Subordinates.

The original No. 1 of 1794, kept up a complete and unbroken organization until June 13, 1824, although No. 2 was merged into it on December 27, 1812. We now retrace our steps to St. John's No. 4, and we find, that after the Parent body had ceased in 1824, she still continued to exist, recognizing as her superior the source of all masonic authority within our State, the R. W. Grand Lodge of Pennsylvania. It was upon this rock that the delegates of the Pennsylvania Grand Encampment of 1814, and the delegates of the New England States, which assembled in Convention on the 16th of June, 1816, in Philadelphia, split; and the Pennsylvania Grand Encampment charged the other delegates with *seceding* from the Convention, while the New England delegates, (consisting of Sir Knights Webb, Fowle, and Snow), reported that the reasons why Pennsylvania would not enter into the Union for a General Grand Encampment, were: First, "that the Encampments in Pennsylvania avow themselves as being in subordination to and under the Grand Lodge of Master Masons;" and second, "their unwillingness to the arrangement or order of succession in conferring the degrees," as practiced by the New England States, especially objecting to the Mark and the Excellent Master as unnecessary and not belonging to the system of Masonry." The delegates of the New England States then adjourned to meet on the 20th of June, 1816, in New York, and *there* formed the present General Grand Encampment of Knights Templar of the United States.

After the disagreement, the Pennsylvania Grand Encampment still preserved her existence until 1824, after which those in other States, which acknowledged her authority, through the antimasonic persecution, ceased to exist, or became members of their State Grand bodies, and thereby recognized the General Grand Encampment of the United States. This was particularly the case with Rising Sun Encampment of New York, which afterwards became Columbia Encampment No. 1, and is still in existence, thereby giving another argument in favor of the light which emanated from our Pennsylvania Templar altar, and which has never yet become extinct.

After the Second Pennsylvania Grand Encampment had ceased in 1824, it was natural, that St. John's Encampment No. 4, (the only one in existence in Pennsylvania), should look up to the R. W. Grand Lodge of Pennsylvania for its countenance and support, and the principles which she maintained in 1797 and 1816 were carried out in 1824, and continued in St. John's No. 4 until February 12, 1857. In May, 1852, St. John's No. 4, Philadelphia No. 5, Union No. 6, and De Molay of Reading, established a Grand Encampment under the authority of the Grand Lodge of Pennsylvania, but the Grand Lodge on the 16th of February, 1857, resolved that they had no authority over the degrees of Knighthood, but that its legitimate sphere was the primitive degrees of ancient Craft Masonry; a union therefore was effected, and both Grand Encampments of Pennsylvania since 1857, acknowledge as their legal head the Grand Encampment of Knights Templar of the United States.

Thus we have demonstrated that from 1794 to 1824, Templarism was preserved in No. 1, and from 1819 to 1847, (the date of the introduction of Templarism into Pennsylvania by the G. G. E. of the United States), St. John's Encampment, No. 4, kept it alive upon its altar, and to this very day we turn our eyes to the altar of St. John's No. 4, as pilgrims to their shrine at Mecca, consecrated by the teachings of nearly half a century, with Sir Knights jealous and envious of their ancient altar, their land-marks, their glory, their long list of good and true Sir Knights, and the heritage of their fathers. We give these facts to con-vince the most prejudiced that *beyond the possibility* of a doubt, the position we *first* assumed, that we are entitled to use the phrase A. E. O. P. to all our Templar documents, is both true and con-sistent. If we are the most ancient in the United States, and who can doubt it? we are certainly entitled to all the honors which antiquity can give us. We detract not from the merits of others, and we trust we have *none* of that spirit within us; but if in the respective organizations of sister Jurisdictions they cannot place upon their brow the mark of manhood, we shall ever treat them as loving and dutiful children, but never, never will we permit any State Grand Encampment to detract from our antiquity or our merits, and build their hopes and their fortune upon our ruins. With all her faults, with all her errors, we love the noble old Keystone State, which has perpetuated Masonry for one hun-dred and thirty-three years entire and continuous, and Templar-ism for sixty-nine years unbroken, entire and uninterrupted.

We have been *forced* to make these remarks from the fact that the M. E. Sir William Sewall Gardner, Grand Master of the Grand Encampment of Knights Templar of Massachusetts and Rhode Island, in his address of May 5, 1865, uses the following language:

"We have then for our gratification, not only the fact, which is now universally conceded, that this Grand Encampment (Massa-chusetts and Rhode Island) is the oldest Grand body of Masonic Knighthood upon this Continent, but also that it has furnished the ritual which is now used in all the bodies, both Grand and Subordinate, in the United States."

I trust, Sir Knights, I am not deviating from my duty as his-toriographer of this the most ancient Grand body of Knighthood in America, when I say that in all the relations of life, as an ac-complished and Christian gentleman, a true and courteous Knight, faithful to his friend and devoted to the interests of his State, Sir W. S. Gardner has no superior. The highest eulogium I can possibly pronounce upon so distinguished a Sir Knight is, that God made him in his own image and endowed him with the highest mental faculties, and we feel honored when we hail him

as our brother; but sometimes State pride, local interests and a
desire of immortalizing our own State, warps our better judgment
and, unfortunately, we publish our thoughts (intended *only* for our
asylums) to the world. By this test let us examine the address
and decide whether "the Grand Encampment of Massachusetts
and Rhode Island is the oldest Grand Body of Masonic Knighthood in the United States."

The M. E. Gardner says, "On the 6th of May, 1805, Sir Thomas
Smith Webb of Providence, Sir Henry Fowle of Boston, Sir
Jonathan Gage of Newburyport, with other Templar Masons,
assembled in the Masonic Hall at Providence, and *opened* this
Grand Encampment,"—eight years after the Pennsylvania Grand
Encampment had been opened.

Again, "This Grand Encampment was the germ of Templar
Masonry as now organized in the United States," (eleven years
after our Grand Encampment), "and the ritual as adopted here,
has been taken as the true Templar work throughout the jurisdiction of the Grand Encampment of the United States. I am
aware (he adds) that in Pennsylvania there was a Grand Encampment in the early part of this century, and that it professed to
confer the Order of the Temple. It is impossible to tell what its
ritual was; but there is evidence tending to show that it was entirely different from that taught by this Grand Body."

As Sir Thomas Smith Webb appears to be the moving spirit in
this matter, the head and front, the centre and circumference, the
Alpha and Omega of this, "the oldest Grand Body of Masonic
Knighthood upon this Continent," under what State organization,
pray, did he receive his degrees of Knighthood, and where did
he vow that he would never permit innovations to be made upon
our landmarks, rites, ceremonies, and customs? Let Massachusetts and Rhode Island reply. Sir James Salsbury, of Providence, says: "I am informed that Thomas S. Webb received the
Orders of Knighthood in Philadelphia;" and the Rev. Paul Dean,
in his eulogy on Webb, says: "Brother Webb aided in organizing a Chapter and Encampment in Albany, and the degrees of
the York Rite were worked from E. A. through all the degrees
of Symbolic, Capitular, and Chivalric Masonry, up to Knight of
Malta. But Webb had taken all *these degrees* previous to his
removal—he received them in Philadelphia."

Webb, therefore, must have received the degrees in Philadelphia prior to 1802, for in that year we find him at the head of the

St. John's Encampment of Providence, Rhode Island, and *three* years PRIOR to the organization of the Grand Encampment of Massachusetts, which claims to be the oldest Grand Body of Masonic Knighthood on the Continent. Will the learned Sir Knight inform us how and by what authority St. John's Encampment of Providence, Rhode Island, was instituted?

Take the entire history of Knighthood in Pennsylvania, from the 14th of February, 1794, to the present time, the reception of Thomas Smith Webb in Philadelphia prior to 1802, the testimony of Sir James Salsbury and that of Rev. Paul Dean—and it will not do in this enlightened age to endeavor to ignore and blot out the history of Knighthood in Pennsylvania, and upon our ruins erect a Grand Encampment, because, forsooth, it happens to be located at the HUB of the Universe. It will not do to present so naked and bald a proposition, unsupported by facts and reasoning, as the learned Sir Knight would have us believe, and ask us to subscribe to a doctrine and principle at variance with the plainest facts and most reliable historic Masonic truths.

Thus far, with regard to the claim of antiquity of the Grand Encampment of Massachusetts and Rhode Island, whereby we have demonstrated that all honor is due to the Keystone State, not only for its introduction into the United States, but for having preserved upon our Templar altars the fire which was lighted on the 14th of February, 1794, the rays of which have penetrated, through the instrumentality of the Grand Encampment and State Grand Commanderies, into every State of our glorious Union and many of the Territories, destined eventually to extend throughout the length and breadth of America.

With regard to the second assertion, that "the Grand Encampment of Massachusetts and Rhode Island has furnished the *ritual* which is now used in all the bodies, both Grand and Subordinate, within the United States," IS TRUE, and it is equally true that that Prince of impostors, innovations and new fangled theories, not understanding the great and glorious principles of our Order, and on purpose to secure to himself a name not only at the "hub of the Universe," but elsewhere, resorted, in conjunction with Sir Knights Fowle and Snow, to establish Ancient York Masonry as Americanized, which we will demonstrate by New England testimony. Unfortunately for the Ancient Rituals of our Order, they succeeded, but it was at the expense of broken vows, of violated faith, of perjured principles. Do you ask the proof? P. G. Master Fowle, in his autobiography, gives an account of a meeting of Webb, Snow, and himself, making a visit to Philadelphia, on 11th of June, 1816, (being appointed delegates,) and met with the Knights Templar of Philadelphia in Convention to effect a coalition of all Grand Encampments in the United States under one general Grand Encampment; but they found the Knights of Philadelphia averse to a coalition, because they were under the *control of the Grand Lodge,* and several of the members were candidates for office in the Grand Lodge, and dare do nothing which would curtail her revenue, lest they should not be elected to office, and as it respected the Orders of Knighthood, they were ignorant as mules. He adds: "Finding them (the Philadelphia Grand Encampment) incorrigible, the committee gave them up and prepared for their return."

Unwilling that so slanderous a document as the autobiography of Sir Snow should go to the Masonic world, as a reflection upon our Templar fathers who have passed into the spirit world, and to preserve their memories in our hearts, for their devotion to our principles and our Order, I am forced to pronounce his declarations as the raving of a garrulous old man, who, jealous of the notoriety of Webb, as well as himself and Sir Snow, wished to place a feather in his own cap, and ask the Masonic world to pronounce them a worthy trio, not in deeds of noble daring, but in the infamy of interpolating the ancient rituals of the Order, and surreptitiously using some of the degrees of the Ancient and Accepted Rite, and from these manufacturing the Order of Knight of the Red Cross. If sacrificing truth, principle and honor could gain for them such a distinction, they have truly earned it. But before we decide, let us investigate the case.

Webb, in his report to the Grand Encampment of Massachusetts and Rhode Island, on the 25th of June, 1817, says, "that after several days spent in deliberation, they found that the *mode of array* and system of work differed in many points so essentially from what is customary in the Encampments *hitherto in connection* with this Grand Encampment, that they could not feel justified in making concessions, such as were required by the delegates from Pennsylvania particularly." Among the reasons were, subordination to the Grand Lodge and their unwillingness to incorporate the Mark Master and Most Excellent Master.

We have now given you Mr. Fowle and Mr. Webb's testimony; let me quote from the records: June 11, 1816, the Pennsylvania

Grand Encampment appointed a committee to report upon the establishment of a General Grand Encampment, and they gave it as *their unanimous opinion* that the establishment of a General Grand Encampment for the United States would greatly tend to promote union, and order, and strength amongst Knights Templar; and they appointed Sir Knights McCorkle, Hamilton, Edes and Ireland delegates, clothed with full powers to carry the same into effect.   Is it not therefore false that the Pennsylvania Grand Encampment was averse to a union ?   Had proper terms been proposed, a union would have been effected, but not at the expense of violated obligations.   The Pennsylvania delegates met in Convention with the delegates from the Grand Encampments of New England and New York, and in their report they state, "that it was impossible to carry their designs into execution without making a sacrifice upon the part of this Grand Encampment and its subordinate Encampments, which was considered to be *unwarranted by every principle of Masonry*, which was made a *sine qua non* by the delegates from New England, who having SECEDED from the Convention, it was of consequence dissolved."

We now have given the facts, indisputable facts that the *seceders* went to New York, and then and there organized the General Grand Encampment.   Pennsylvania, however, true to her teachings, true to primitive masonry which is based upon the Old Testament, would not consent that the old work which she had received from the hands of her fathers, should become interpolated or amended, and therefore regarded the Webb Work as a New England heresy, requiring the degree of Mark and M. E. Master as a prerequisite for all Knights Templar.   One principal reason why Pennsylvania refused to acknowledge the work of Webb and his associates, was that they had in the Mark degree connected two events, which transpired at a distance of ten hundred and twenty-five years from each other, one happening in the time of King Solomon, at the erection of the Temple, and the other during the mission of our Saviour while on earth, the one under the Jewish, the other under the Christian dispensation.

But another inseparable objection was the degree of Knights of the Red Cross, formed, fashioned, manufactured for New England and its dependencies, and our illustrious Brother has well said that the Grand Encampment of Massachusetts and Rhode Island has furnished the ritual which is now used in all the (Templar) Orders in the United States.   Let us examine into the character of the Red

4

Cross Order, and see if it is not as foreign to the Orders of Christian Knighthood as the parable of Christ is to the building of the Temple in the Mark degree. And while upon this part of the subject, it will be proper to remark that the same inconsistency is inaugurated by Webb in introducing Pagan and Jewish ceremonies in the Christian Orders of Knighthood as was engrafted by him and his associates into the Royal Arch. In this sublime degree we have the Divine call of Moses, the erection of the Tabernacle in the wilderness, the sack of Jerusalem, the carrying away of the captives into Babylonish captivity, the proclamation of freedom, the journey back, the various incidents of the reconstruction of the Temple, occupying ten hundred and twenty-five years, being a perfect and complete medley, calculated to mystify the masonic student in his inquiries after truth; hence we agree with the Provincial Grand Commander of Knighthood in Canada, where he says "we question the purity of Webb's teaching, not only in the Orders of Knighthood but in the degrees of Masonry proper."

Let us for a moment examine into the history and ritual of this degree of Knight of the Red Cross. The times and circumstances demand it of us as intelligent Sir Knights, although, Pennsylvania Sir Knights, in the autobiography of Snow, have been characterized "as ignorant as mules." In Scotland and Ireland the right is not insisted upon as a pass to the Templar Order. In Canada, by permission of the Grand Conclave of England and Wales, they impart as much information as will secure the admittance of their members into the Encampments in the United States. They regard the Red Cross as only a continuation of the Royal Arch degree commemorating the dangers encountered by the Jews in building the second Temple, and consequently is of Jewish and Pagan Origin, and has no connection whatever with the Christian Orders of Knighthood, as based upon the birth, life, death, resurrection and ascension of our Saviour.

Do you ask me then from whence is the degree of Knight of the Red Cross derived? I reply, it was manufactured by Webb and his associates from the Knight of the East or Sword, Knight of the East, and Knight of the East and West, degrees of the Ancient and Accepted Scottish Rite.

The testimony of the learned Colonel Moore, P. G. C., of Canada, is important on this point; he says: I have carefully examined the rituals of the Red Cross, used in the United States, as also that of the Knights of the Sword, East, East and West, as given in the Templar Encampments of Ireland, and in the Royal Chapter of Scotland, being the same degree as that of the fifteenth of the Ancient Scottish Rite, and sixth of the French. But he adds, the third point of the Knight of the Sword must not be confounded with the seventeenth of the Ancient and Accepted Rite, bearing the same name, and consider that the ritual used in Ireland and Scotland (the one best adapted for us) *it being the original from which that of the Red Cross of the United States is taken.* In the Red Cross of the United States there are inconsistencies and inaccuracies, and it has been much altered from the original.

CITY OF OTTAWA, CANADA WEST, *June* 20, 1862.

To all True and Courteous Knights, Greeting :—

Be it known to all concerned, that the Supreme Grand Master and Grand Conclave of Knights Templar of England and Wales, on my representation to them that to gain admittance to Encampments or Commanderies in the United States, Fratres of the Order required the preceding degree called RED CROSS, known in Scotland and Ireland by the name of Babylonish Pass or Knights of the Sword; East, East and West have authorized me to use my own discretion in conferring the degree under my Patent as Provincial Grand Commander for Canada. By virtue of such authority I hereby grant you very Eminent Sir Knight Frater Samuel D. Fowler, Deputy Grand Chancellor of Knights Templar of Canada, this, my Dispensation to confer the degree on such Knights Templar as your own judgment may direct.

Given under my hand and seal at the City of Ottawa, this 20th day of June, 1862.   W. J. McLEOD MOORE,
Provincial Grand Commander for Canada.

(I have been furnished with a copy of the Ritual above alluded to).

A learned Sir Knight of Massachusetts, writes me April 19, 1865, that our Red Cross was taken from the "Irish Knights of the East and Sword;" nay, he further adds: "Our Templar Ritual was made by Fowle and Gleason ; Webb devoted his attention mostly to the Chapter degrees; Fowle was a very able man naturally, but had little education; Gleason was graduated at Harvard University and was a refined scholar."

From the same source I learn from my valued correspondent, that he himself does not know where the General Grand Encampment obtained the Rituals for the Orders of the Red Cross and of the Templar; but, he adds, I have no doubt they were obtained from Henry Fowle, deceased.* The Maltese Ritual *originated* in Boston Encampment, at Boston. About twenty years ago this ritual was adopted by our Grand Encampment, and has been used by our subordinates ever since. I think, indeed know, it was made arbitrarily, and that *it was not taken from any other Ritual.*

I am satisfied, says my learned correspondent, that the English Ritual was not in the possession of the Boston Encampment, and that, if it had been, the work would have been different from what it now is. The Ritual then prepared was more to fill up a vacuum and supply a want than for any other purpose.

Ten years since, when the Grand Encampment met at Hartford, Connecticut, the Maltese Order was stricken out through the influence of Sir Robert Morris, and we *speak that* we do know, when we say that the reason for so doing was, that Sir Morris might present one of his own, for the why and the wherefore it will not become us to say.

To the arguments already given, and to demonstrate beyond the possibility of a doubt that the English Templar work was originally used in Pennsylvania, and continued as the Ritual until about the year 1828, I shall produce conclusive evidence.

In the old Ritual of the Cross of Christ Encampment of Portsmouth, London, chartered in 1791, and confirmed under the Grand Mastership of Sir Thomas Dunckerly, among the emblems explained to the candidate, were those of the Lamb, the Cock, and the Dove; and to *this very day* these emblems are used. The old Ritual of 1791 uses these words:

At the corners of the triangle you find a Lamb, a Cock, and a Dove, sacred emblems (*symbols*) of the Order. (*The first is*) the Paschal Lamb slain from the foundation of the world. The Dove, the Almighty Comforter which descended in a bodily form (*shape*) on Christ at his Baptism, whereby his Divine Mission was indicated to St. John the Baptist. (*And*) the Cock (*is*) the Monitor of the Order, for as his crowing heralds the morn, (*so*) let it even at that still hour call to our minds (*remembrance*) our duties as Knights Templar, and admonish (remind) us always (thus early) to ask assistance to perform them (*inviolably*) throughout every (*the*) coming day, and may we ever welcome it (the same) as a friendly warning (caution); but never cause (*and not have oc-*

* Who died in Boston in 1837, aged 71 years

casion) to fear it as the periodical memento (*monitor*) of a broken vow.

The words in *parentheses* and *italicized*, is the language now used, showing no material change, except in the language for seventy-five consecutive years.

That these same emblems were used in Philadelphia Encampment No. 1, we shall now give the proof. This Encampment was organized in 1794, but on the 17th of May, 1820, a Committee was appointed to purchase new furniture, regalia, etc., etc., in lieu of that now used. Among the articles enumerated and purchased by the Committee, were the appropriate Cloaks, a Trumpet, and the emblems of the Dove, the Lamb, and the Cock.

In 1827, when Trinity Encampment, at Harrisburg, ordered these emblems, and Sir John De Pui writes to the Grand Recorder at Philadelphia, "The hour glass you sent us was only a minute glass. The Lamb, the Cock, and the Dove, are too small, they will answer for the present, but the Crucifix we are well pleased with."

On the 17th of May, 1820, Sir J. D. Ferguson, Rev. Abner Kneeland and others, resigned their membership because new regulations and certain forms were introduced, as well as the dispensing with appropriate emblems, all of which they cannot conscientiously reconcile with that standard which they have heretofore taken as the Rule and Guide of their faith. These Sir Knights regarded their Ritual, their emblems, their forms as sacred and inviolable, and believing that their Encampment had not the authority to change, modify, and alter the same, they withdrew from the Order.

At what time the General Grand Encampment dispensed with these emblems and the use of the Trumpet, etc., etc., I have not the means of ascertaining; but that changes have been made, I have now fully demonstrated.

Thus, Sir Knights of Pennsylvania, you will perceive that a discussion of vast and great importance has been unceremoniously thrust upon us. It may be that as a kind Providence put it into the hearts of our fathers sixty-nine years ago to establish the First Grand Encampment, so He intends that we shall be the humble instruments of bringing light out of darkness, and harmony out of chaos. We have proven that the Ritual of the Orders of Knighthood, as practiced, and taught, and enforced, is *not the old* Templar work of England, which our fathers brought

4 *

with them, some of whom came to this country as early as 1784, in possession of the Templar degrees, and which did not embrace that strange, heterogeneous Order, Knight of the Red Cross, composed of Jewish and Pagan ceremonies, mixed together and thrown in by way of *ballast* to keep steady the Orders of Christian Knighthood! To demonstrate the impracticability of the Red Cross Degree, in the Order of Christian Knighthood, may I not with great truthfulness say, that the Jew and Mahomedan, who takes the Royal Arch Degree, can with equal propriety receive the Red Cross Degree. We have the acknowledgment of one of Massachusetts' most distinguished officers. We have the action of the General Grand Encampment of the United States in 1856, wherein in Art. 4, Sec. 2 of the Constitution, it reads: The rule of succession in conferring the Orders of Knighthood shall be as follows: *First*, Knight of Red Cross; *Second*, Knights Templar; thereby ignoring the Order of Knight of Malta. We have the testimony of the lamented Hubbard in his address in 1856, that the "intercalary degrees" were formerly unknown to our Order as essential to the obtainment of the Order of Knight Templar. We have the testimony of Past Grand Master French in 1862, stating that a material change was ordered in the conferring of the Order of Knights of Malta, and he said I can see no reason why the regular work in conferring of that Order should not be adopted, as it is in some, if not *all of those in Massachusetts*—that on September 4, 1862, it was enjoined by the Grand Encampment of the United States upon all State Grand Bodies and Subordinate Bodies under the jurisdiction of this Grand Body, to use the Ritual, a copy of which is in the possession of the M. E. Grand Master, being the same which is in use in the *jurisdiction of Massachusetts*.

In the Freemason's Magazine of December, 1865, published by that distinguished Mason, Sir Charles W. Moore, whose name of itself is sufficient authority in everything pertaining to Masonry, uses the following significant language:

" In 1797 the Chapter (St. Andrew's) united in the organization of a Grand Chapter for the Northern States. In the record of this year we find the following:

" Voted that the Knights of the Red Cross by Bro. Benjamin Hurd, Sr., be and they are hereby permitted to make their records in the books of this Chapter."

Sir Moore says, at this time the degree of RED CROSS HAD NO

CONNECTION WITH THE ORDER OF THE TEMPLE, and was conferred like that of the Templars as an honorary degree."

Hence it is self-evident that our rituals have been tampered with, altered, changed, modified, to suit the whim and caprice of Individual Sir Knights. As Pennsylvania Knights, therefore, let us make a united and decided effort to restore the old Ritual of the Order, the Ritual which was in use before the establishment of the Grand Encampment of Pennsylvania, in 1797; and the Ritual used by the Baldwin Encampment at Bristol; of Antiquity Encampment at Bath; the Observance Encampment at London; which Encampments existed from time immemorial, in the latter of which the Dukes of Kent and Sussex received the Orders of Knighthood; it being the same Ritual used by the Duke of Kent on the 24th of June, 1791, and by his successor, the Duke of Sussex, 6th of August, 1812, and by his successor, the present Grand Commander, Wm. Stuart, since May 10, 1862. This old Ritual discards the Knight of the Red Cross, and confers 1st. *Knights Templar;* 2d. *Knights of St. Paul or Mediterranean Pass;* 3d. *Knights of Malta;* and upon those who have been elected E. Commanders the degree of *Past Commander.* Of the correctness and authenticity of these degrees, we have a certified copy transmitted from the Grand Conclave of England and Wales, to Sir Col. W. J. B. M'Leod Moore, Prov. Grand Commander of Canada, with a Patent dated 11th of May, 1865, conferring upon your Historiographer the title of Past Deputy Provincial Grand Commander and Grand Prior, "with full power and authority to perform and exercise all and every the duties and functions vested in me (him) by such rank, and for so doing this Patent shall be sufficient authority."

The question therefore recurs, what will the G. C. of Pennsylvania do? We answer unhesitatingly and boldly, that it is our imperative duty to return to the ancient work and not remove the Landmarks of our fathers. We cannot but proclaim these truths to the Templar world, which we have enunciated, when an attack is made upon us and the work of our fathers. We ask all Templars, and all State Grand Commanderies to assist us in the glorious work of restoring Templarism to its original Ritual, as that practiced by the Grand Conclave of England and Wales, and which has legitimately descended to them through the Encampments at Bristol, Bath and London, and now in our possession. When this change is effected the whole Templar world will then be united as a powerful family, bound together by the same

Ritual, the same Landmarks, the same Principles, acknowledging
and worshiping the same Redeemer, and having inscribed upon
our ancient and venerated banner the glorious living and dying
sentiment of every Sir Knight,

Non nobis Domine! Non nobis sed Nomini tuo da Gloriam!

To assist the Masonic student in his inquiries after truth, and
in order that he may have facts before him which cannot be con-
troverted, I have carefully prepared a full statement of all the
Subordinate Commanderies holding Charters from and by authority of the Grand Encampment of Knights Templar of Pennsylvania and Masonic jurisdiction thereunto belonging, since 1794.

Whole No. since 1794.	Present No.	Name and Location.	Date of Dispensation.	Date of Charter.
1		Philadelphia,		Feb. 14, 1794
2		Philadelphia,		1795
3		Harrisburg,		1795
4		Carlisle,		1796
5		Pittsburg,	Feb. 2, 1814,	May 2, 1814
6		Baltimore, Maryland,	1790,	May 2, 1814
7		Rising Sun, New York,	1808,	May 3, 1814
8		Washington, Wilmington, Del.,		May 17, 1814
9		Philadelphia,		Mar. 18, 1816
10	4	St. John's, Philadelphia,		June 8, 1819
11		Wivanda, Towanda,		July 20, 1826
12		Holy and Undivided Trinity, Harrisburg,	Nov. 22, 1826,	
13	1	Pittsburg,	May 13, 1847,	Sept. 16, 1847
14	2	Philadelphia,		May 25, 1849
15	3	Jacques de Molay, Washington,	Sept. 12, 1849,	Oct. 24, 1850
16	5	Hubbard, Waynesburg,	Nov. 10, 1851,	Sept. 12, 1856
17	7	St. Omer's (Uniontown,) Brownsville,		Sept. 16, 1853
18	9	De Molay, Reading,		Feb. 7, 1854
19	8	St. John's, Carlisle,		June 13, 1854
20		Keystone, Philadelphia,	April 23, 1855,	
21	6	Union, Philadelphia,		May 10, 1855
22	10	Blumenthal, (Mountain,) Altoona,	Sept. 18, 1855,	June 11, 1856
23	11	Parke, Harrisburg,	Dec. 15, 1855,	June 11, 1856
24	12	Crusade, Bloomsburg,	March 5, 1856,	June 11, 1856
25	13	Columbia, Lancaster,	April 10, 1856,	June 11, 1856
26	14	Palestine, Carbondale,	May 1, 1856,	June 11, 1856
27	15	Jerusalem, Pottstown,	May 5, 1856,	June 11, 1856
28	16	Northern, Towanda,	Oct. 3, 1857,	June 22, 1858
29	17	Cœur de Lion, Scranton,	April 22, 1858,	June 22, 1858
30	18	Kedron, Greensburg,	Mar. 19, 1860,	June 23, 1860

Whole No. since 1794.	Present No.	Name and Location.	Date of Dispensation.	Date of Charter.
31	19	Hugh de Payens, Easton,	April 12, 1860,	June 23, 1860
32	20	Allen, Allentown,	April 21, 1860,	June 23, 1860
33	21	York, York,	Jan. 19, 1865,	June 14, 1865
34	22	Baldwin II., Williamsport,		June 13, 1866

All of which is respectfully and courteously submitted.

ALFRED CREIGH,

Historiographer.

On motion of P. E. C. Sir William Lilly,

Resolved, That so much of the able report of the *Historiographer,* as relates to the true work of the Knights Templar and appendant Order, be and the same is hereby referred to the Past Grand Commanders with the request, that they report upon the whole subject at this Grand Conclave.

Before the close of the Grand Conclave of 1866, the Past Grand Commanders submitted the following report:

To the R. E. Grand Commander, Officers and Sir Knights of the Grand Commandery of Pennsylvania:

We, the Committee to whom was referred the report of the HISTORIOGRAPHER of the Grand Commandery of Pennsylvania, beg leave to report:

That we believe the History of Knight Templarism in Pennsylvania, as set forth by Sir Knight Alfred Creigh, to be a valuable acquisition to the records of this Grand Commandery. The able manner in which the subject is treated, and the important facts therein set forth, all show the great fund of information possessed by our Grand Recorder, creditable alike to his skill and zeal as a Templar, and we beg leave to offer the following resolutions:

Resolved, That the thanks of this Grand Commandery be unanimously voted to Sir Knight Alfred Creigh for his untiring zeal and the great ability manifested by him in the discharge of his duties as Historiographer of the Grand Commandery of Pennsylvania.

Resolved, That a copy of the above be engrossed on parchment, signed by the Grand Officers and presented to Sir Knight Alfred Creigh.

Resolved, That the exemplification of the English Templar

work as cited by Sir Knight Alfred Creigh before this Grand Body, would materially add to the interest of Templarism.

Respectfully submitted.

H. STANLEY GOODWIN,
E. H. TURNER,
C. F. KNAPP,
. *Committee.*

On motion of Sir J. M. Whitby,

The report was received and adopted and the committee discharged.

Resolved, That the resolutions as reported by the committee, be unanimously adopted.

On motion of D. G. C. Sir J. L. Hutchinson,

Resolved, That the Right Eminent Grand Commander Sir Robert Pitcairn, be authorized to subscribe for two hundred copies of the History of the Knights Templar of Pennsylvania, as prepared by Sir Alfred Creigh, and draw on the Treasurer for the amount.

PRIOR to the year 1797, FOUR Encampments were instituted in Pennsylvania; *two* in Philadelphia, the *third*
in Harrisburg, and the *fourth* in Carlisle. The Right
Worshipful Grand Lodge of Pennsylvania from its organization, until the 16th day of February, 1857, believed that the General Regulations of Ancient York Masons authorized the conferring of the Orders of Christian
Knighthood, under the sanction of a Charter or Warrant
of a Lodge. But at the Grand Communication referred
to, they resolved "That Ancient Masonry consists of but
three degrees, viz.: E. A., F. C., and M. M., including the
degree of the Holy Royal Arch, and this Grand Lodge
claims no jurisdiction beyond the limits of Ancient Masonry." By this action, Templarism, as a component
part of Masonry, and in accordance with *Masonic usage*
in Pennsylvania, were forever divorced, which happily
eventuated in the union of all the Subordinate Commanderies in Pennsylvania, under the Right Eminent
Grand Commandery of Pennsylvania, which acknow-
ledges as its Supreme head the Grand Encampment of
Knights Templar of the United States.

The Convention, however, which met on the 12*th day*
of May, 1797, was composed of sixteen representatives;
four from each of the Encampments, who met to deliberate upon the expediency of organizing a Grand Encampment, as none had previously existed in America.
After mature deliberation, and anticipating the glorious
results which would necessarily ensue from having a

47

controlling head, whereby a more perfect union could be effected, the Convention on the 19th day of May, 1797, adopted a Constitution to govern the Knights Templar of Pennsylvania. Thus in the very infancy of our Republic, Pennsylvania inaugurated the system of each State having within its limits a Grand Encampment, and thereby demonstrating to the world the undeniable fact, that as civilization advances, and new States are formed, Masonry and Templarism go hand in hand, with the early settlers, and amid their trials, privations, and dangers, prove to them a guardian angel.

Pennsylvania, at the date of the organization of the Grand Encampment, (1797), could only boast of a constitutional existence of ten years, yet she had already established, besides her many Lodges and Chapters, two Encampments in Philadelphia, one in Harrisburg, and one in Carlisle. It is a matter of deep regret to the Fraternity, that in the destruction of the Masonic Hall, by fire in 1803, all our Templar records were destroyed, and no vestige remained except the rolls of the members of Encampments Nos. 1 and 2. These two Encampments effected a union in 1812. We shall give their membership in 1812, with the date of their respectively receiving the Orders of Knighthood: No. 1 is perfect in this respect, as far as the individual membership was concerned at that time, but the members of No. 2, when merged into No. 1, gave the date of their admission, December 27, 1812, instead of the date they respectively received the Order of Knights Templar.

With these prefatory remarks, we proceed to give all the information we could procure concerning Philadelphia Encampment No. 1, Philadelphia Encampment No. 2, Harrisburg Encampment No. 3, and Carlisle Encampment No. 4, premising their history with the remark, that these several Encampments were organized under the authority of the Charter of a Lodge of Master Masons, which gave full authority and power to admit and make Masons according to the ancient customs and constitutions of the Royal Craft in all ages.

A CHARTER therefore may be defined to be an instrument printed or written upon parchment, and signed by some noble *Grand Master*, his *Deputy* and *Grand Wardens* and *Grand Secretary*, sealed with the Grand Lodge seal, constituting particular persons as *Master* and *Wardens*, with full power to congregate and hold a LODGE at such a place, and therein "make and admit Freemasons, according to the most ancient and honorable custom of the Royal Craft, in all ages and nations, throughout the known world, with full power and authority to nominate and choose their successors."

Under this authority the Master of a Lodge " had the right and authority of *calling his Lodge* or congregating the members into a Chapter at pleasure, upon the application of any of the Brethren, and upon any emergency and occurrence which in his judgment may require their meeting."

The original Masonic Charter used in Pennsylvania read as follows—and under which, the degrees of Ancient Craft Masonry and the Orders of Knighthood were conferred.

To all whom it may concern:

The Grand Lodge of the Most Ancient and Honorable Fraternity of Free and Accepted Masons (according to the old Constitutions, revised by His Royal Highness, Prince Edwin, at York, in the kingdom of England, in the year of the Christian Era 926, and in the year of Masonry 4926), in ample form assembled at Philadelphia SEND GREETING:

Whereas, The Right Worshipful Grand Lodge of Eng-

5   C

land, did by a Grand Warrant, under the hands of the
Right Honorable Thomas Erskine, Earl Kelly, Viscount
Fenton, Lord Baron of Pitton Weem, etc., etc., in Great
Britain, Grand Master of Masons; the Right Worshipful
William Osborne, D. Grand Master; the R. W. M.
William Dickey, Senior Grand Warden; the R. W.
James Gibson, Esq., Junior Grand Warden, and the seal
of the Grand Lodge, bearing date June 20, 1764, A. M.
5764, nominate, constitute and appoint the Right Worshipful William Ball to be Grand Master; the R. W.
Captain Blaithwate Jones, ¯Deputy Grand Master; the
R. W. M. David Hall, S. G. Warden; the R. W. M.
Hugh Lenox, J. G. Warden of a Provincial Grand Lodge
to be held at Philadelphia, for the Province of Pennsylvania, granting to them and their successors in office,
duly elected and lawfully installed, with the consent of
the Members of the said Grand Lodge, full power and
authority to grant Warrants and Dispensations for holding Lodges, to regulate all matters appertaining to
Masonry, and to do and perform all and every other act
and thing which could be usually done and performed
by other Grand Lodges, as by the said above in part
recited Grand Warrant, reference being thereto had,
may more fully and at large appear.

And whereas, The Right Worshipful William Adcock,
Esq., Grand Master, the Right Worshipful Mr. Alexander Rutherford, Deputy Grand Master, the Right
Worshipful Jonathan Bayard Smith, Esq., Senior Grand
Warden, the Right Worshipful Mr. Joseph Dean, Junior
Grand Warden, legal successors of the above named
Grand Officers, as by the Grand Lodge Books may appear, together with the Officers and Representatives of a
number of regular Lodges, under the jurisdiction, duly
appointed and specially authorized, as also by and with
the advice and consent of several other Lodges, by their

letters expressed, did at a Grand Quarterly Communication, held in the Grand Lodge room, in the City of Philadelphia, on the 25th day of September, A. D. 1786, after mature and serious deliberation, unanimously

Resolve, "That it is improper the Grand Lodge of Pennsylvania should remain any longer under the authority of any foreign Grand Lodge," and the said Grand Lodge did thereupon close *sine die*.

And whereas, All the Grand Officers of the said late Provincial Grand Lodge, together with the Officers and Representatives of a number of Lodges of the Commonwealth of Pennsylvania, did, on the said 25th day of September, 1786, meet in the room of the late Provincial Grand Lodge, and according to the powers and authorities to them entrusted, form themselves into a Grand Convention of Masons to deliberate on the proper methods of forming a Grand Lodge totally independent from all foreign jurisdiction.

And whereas, The said Grand Convention did then and there unanimously resolve, that the Lodges under the jurisdiction of the Grand Lodge of Pennsylvania aforesaid, lately held as a Provincial Grand Lodge, under the authority of the Grand Lodge of England, should, and they then did, form themselves into a Grand Lodge to be called "THE GRAND LODGE OF PENNSYLVANIA AND MASONIC JURISDICTION THERETO BELONGING," to be held in the said City of Philadelphia, as by the Records and Proceedings of the said Convention, remaining among the Archives of the Grand Lodge aforesaid, may more fully appear.

And whereas, By a warrant bearing date —— *under the hands of* —— —— *Grand Master*, —— —— *D. Grand Master*, —— —— *G. Senior Warden*, —— —— *G. Junior Warden, and the Seal of the late Grand Lodge of Pennsylvania, the following Brethren to wit :* —— *Mas-*

ter, —— Senior Warden, —— Junior Warden, with their lawful Assistants, were authorized and appointed to hold a Lodge of Free and Accepted Masons at ——, number ——. And the said Lodge when duly congregated, to admit, enter, and make Masons, according to the ancient and honorable custom of the Royal Craft in all ages and nations throughout the known world. And also with the further right, privilege, and authority, to nominate, choose, and instal their successors, and them to invest in the like power, authority, and dignity, to nominate, choose, and instal their successors forever, as by the said warrant, reference being had, may appear.

And whereas, The said Warrant hath been surrendered up to Us, the Grand Lodge of Pennsylvania and Masonic jurisdiction thereunto belonging, by the present Officers and Brethren of the said Lodge, praying that the same may be renewed under the authority of this Grand Lodge.*

Now know ye, That we, "The Grand Lodge of Pennsylvania and Masonic jurisdiction thereunto belonging," by virtue of the powers and authorities in us vested, by the said Grand Convention, do hereby renew and confirm to our trusty and well-beloved Brethren, to wit: the Worshipful —— Master, —— Senior Warden, and —— Junior Warden, and the other regular members of the said Lodge, No. —, of Ancient York Masons, and to their true and lawful successors forever, all the Masonic rights, privileges, authority, jurisdiction, and pre-eminence, which by their said original warrant, herein beforementioned, and in part recited, they are or may be in any manner or way entitled to hold and enjoy. *Provided*

---

* The two sentences above in italics were inserted in Charters which had procured them prior to the 25th day of September, 1786; but as an historical fact, I have deemed it proper to insert the above sentences, so that the Masonic Student can more readily understand the difference.

always, That the abovenamed Brethren and members of the said Lodge and their successors, continue at all times to pay due respect and obedience to this Right Worshipful Grand Lodge, agreeably to the rules and ordinances, lawfully made, or to be made, for the benefit of Masonry and the advancement of our Royal Craft; otherwise this Warrant to be of no force or virtue.

Given in open Grand Lodge, under the hands of our Right Worshipful Grand Officers, and the seal of our Grand Lodge at Philadelphia, this —— day of —— A. D. 1787, and of Masonry, 5787.

—— ——, *Grand Secretary.*

PHILADELPHIA ENCAMPMENT, No. 1.*

NAME.	DATE OF KNIGHTING.
Baker, George A.,	June 10, 1796.
Black, Thomas,	January 18, 1811.
Coit, Gabriel,	August 21, 1812.
Cook, David,	October 16, 1812.
Dillon, John,	October 19, 1810.
De Silver, Robert,	August 16, 1811.
Ford, Edward,	November 20, 1812.
Glenn, John,	July 20, 1810.
Gunderlach, C. H.,	December 19, 1811.
Humes, James,	July 20, 1810.
Keyser, Adam,	September 20, 1811.
McCorkle, William,	December 18, 1812.
Milnor, Rev. James,	March 16, 1809.
Porter, John, Jr.,	June 21, 1811.

* See page 82 for a continuation of No. 1, which is its history after the union with No. 2.

5 *

NAME.	DATE OF KNIGHTING.
Sloan, Hugh,	February 21, 1806.
Smith, Robert,	December 21, 1810.
Stinger, John,	April 17, 1812.
Thompson, John A.,	February 14, 1794.
Tearney, Hugh,	November 12, 1800.
Thompson, James,	March 12, 1812.
Wilson, Andrew,	July 11, 1794.
Walter, John J.,	December 19, 1811.

PHILADELPHIA ENCAMPMENT, No. 2.

NAME.	DATE OF KNIGHTING.
Aston, James,	November 12, 1800.
Brobston, Joseph,	November 12, 1800.
Black, Samuel,	April 19, 1811.
Burns, William,	December 27, 1812.
Bailey, Francis,	
Ferrier, James,	
Gray, George,	
Irving, David,	September 11, 1795.
Macoy, James,	
Mackey, John,	
McDevitt, James,	
Nielson, William,	
Nielson, Andrew,	
O'Brien, John,	
Quinn, Daniel,	
Reed, George,	
Shallens, Frederick,	
Scott, Andrew,	
Wisdom, John,	

ENCAMPMENT, No. 3.

This Encampment was located in Harrisburg, Dauphin County, Pennsylvania, and was one of the original Encampments which sent delegates to organize the Grand Encampment of 1797. The records of this Encampment were forwarded to the Archives of the Grand Lodge, but by the destruction of the Masonic Hall by fire, they were destroyed, hence no record of it exists, to give us even the names of those who were Knighted, or its Officers; neither can the memory of the oldest Mason in Harrisburg point out sufficiently clear those who had been honored with the Order of Christian Knighthood.

ENCAMPMENT, No. 4.

This Encampment was established in Carlisle, Cumberland County, Pennsylvania, in 1796, by authority and with the sanction of Lodge No. 56, which was instituted on the 29th day of October, 1792. I cannot better subserve the interests of Templarism than by publishing a letter to me from the distinguished Sir Knight, Col. John Johnston, (now deceased), formerly of Piqua, Ohio, who resided in Carlisle until about 1797, and was then appointed as Indian Agent by the President of the United States, and continued in the discharge of the onerous duties of his office for about thirty-one years. His letter reads thus:—

CINCINNATI, OHIO, *February* 11, 1860.

SIR ALFRED CREIGH—My dear friend: Your letter of the 30th January, addressed to me at Dayton, reached

me in this city a few days ago, in answer to which I have
to state that owing to my advanced years, now EIGHTY-
FIVE, impaired health and the loss of memory will prevent me from furnishing you all the information you
desire.

I can afford very little information on the subject of
the Templars' Lodge or *Encampment at Carlisle, Pennsylvania.* I was admitted to the Knights Templar degree
in that town in 1797. My certificate for that and the
Royal Arch were, with many of my papers lost in the
war of 1812.

The Commander of the Temple was named ROBERT
LEYBURN, who kept a Tavern on the Main street, leading south or east below the residence of General Irvine,
and on the same side of the street. Both the Royal
Arch and Templar degree was conferred on me there.
Not residing in Carlisle, I never was more than twice or
thrice within the Lodge.

During my residence in Philadelphia, I was occasionally in THE ENCAMPMENTS, but not a member, was a
regular and active member of a Blue Lodge, and Secretary at the time of Washington's death. My removal
from Philadelphia with Congress to Washington, cut off
my connection with Masonry in Pennsylvania. My
residence at the Federal City being of a temporary character I did not connect myself with the Craft in Washington City; and thereafter for thirty-one years in succession, in the service of the United States, in the wilds
of the Northwest, I had not been within the walls of a
Lodge. I regret not being able to assist you more and
better in your researches. There is probably not a man
living now but myself, who belonged to the Templars
sixty-two years ago, nor is there a single individual in

this large city, now alive, who was here in the time of General Wayne, sixty-seven years ago, but myself.

I am my dear friend and Sir Knight,

Most affectionately and fraternally yours,

JOHN JOHNSTON.

Sir Robert Leyburn, the Commander of the Temple spoken of by Col. Johnston received the Orders of Knighthood and emigrated to America in 1784. He settled in Carlisle the same year. He was a very prominent Mason, and devoted his time to the prosperity of Lodge No. 56. Through his influence I find the following entry in a MS. book in my possession, demonstrating the fact that our funds are generally devoted to benevolent objects.

Robert Leyburn, Dr.

To his subscription on behalf of the Free Masons' Lodge, No. 56, to build Dickinson College, April, 1799, ... £22 10

Cr. October 3, 1799. By cash, . . . £22 10

Among the Masons of Carlisle who were acknowledged as Templars, were Robert Taylor, John Underwood, John Gibson, (the father of Chief Justice Gibson, who filled the office of Grand Master of the Grand Lodge of Pennsylvania), Robert Porter and William Porter. Other Knights Templar resided there and were connected with No. 3, but we cannot find anything positive, but only traditionary evidence on the subject.

C *

GRAND CONVENTION OF KNIGHTS TEMPLAR
OF 1814.

At a Grand Convention of Knights Templar, convened by appointment, in the Masonic Hall, in the City of Philadelphia, on Tuesday, the 15*th day of February*, *A. D.* 1814, for the purpose of forming a Grand Encampment of Knights Templar in Pennsylvania, with jurisdiction belonging thereto, and also over all such Encampments in other States, as may agree to come under the jurisdiction of the same.

Sir Knight John Sellars, of the Borough of Wilmington, in the State of Delaware, was called to the Chair, and Sir Knight Henry S. Keatinge, of the City of Baltimore, in the State of Maryland, was appointed Secretary.

Whereupon, on motion made and seconded,

Resolved, That the Delegates and Proxies from the several Encampments, to be represented in this Grand Convention, from the respective States, be called over; when the following named Sir Knights produced their credentials, under the seals of their respective Encampments, as Delegates and Proxies, and were accordingly admitted to take their seats in this Grand Convention, to wit:

Delegates from *Encampment No.* 1, Philadelphia—Sir William McCorkle, Sir Alphonso C. Ireland, Sir Nathaniel Dillhorn.

Proxies from *Encampment No.* 2, Pittsburg—Sir Thomas Black, Sir James Humes.

Delegate from *Rising Sun Encampment No.* 1, New York City—Sir James McDonald.

Proxies from *Rising Sun Encampment No.* 1, New York City—Sir Thomas Armstrong, Sir Anthony Fannen.

Delegates from *Washington Encampment No.* 1, Wil-

mington, Delaware—Sir John Sellars, Sir Archibald
Hamilton, Sir John W. Patterson.

Delegate from *Encampment No.* 1, Baltimore, Maryland—Sir Henry S. Keatinge.

The Grand Convention being thus duly organized,
proceeded to the formation of a Constitution for the
Grand Encampment about to be formed; and after
several meetings and adjournments from time to time, on
Wednesday evening, *February* 16, 1814, adopted, rati-
fied, and signed the Constitution.

The Grand Convention then proceeded to the election
of officers for the Pennsylvania Grand Encampment.

FEBRUARY 14, 1814, A. O. 696, A. O. E. P. 17.

M. E. Sir William McCorkle, of Philadelphia, G. G. M.
M. E. Sir Archibald Hamilton, of Wilmington, G. G.
M. E. Sir Peter Dob, of New York, G. C. G.
R. E. Sir Henry S. Keatinge, of Baltimore, G. St. B.
R. E. Sir John Sellars, of Wilmington, G. Ch.
R. E. Sir George A. Baker, of Philadelphia, G. Rec.
R. E. Sir Nathaniel Dillhorn, of Philadelphia, G. Treas.
R. E. Sir James Humes, of Philadelphia, G. Sw. B.

The Grand Officers were then installed by P. E. G. M.
Sir James McDonald, of New York, according to ancient
usage.

With regard to *Charters of Recognition*, the Constitution of the "PENNSYLVANIA GRAND ENCAMPMENT OF
KNIGHTS TEMPLAR with jurisdiction thereunto belonging," Article 1, Section 6, provided that "Any Encampment *heretofore formed*, may upon application to this
Grand Encampment, receive a *Charter of Recognition*,
upon paying into the hands of the Grand Treasurer the
sum of fifteen dollars for the use of the Grand Funds,
and five dollars to the Grand Recorder, provided the

application for the Charter be made at any time before
the second Friday of June, 1815. Under this provision
of the Constitution, *Charters of Recognition* were granted
to Philadelphia Encampment No. 1, Pittsburg Encampment No. 2, Rising Sun Encampment No. 1, of New
York, Washington Encampment No. 1, of Wilmington,
Delaware, and Encampment No. 1, of Baltimore, Maryland.

The Charter of Recognition was couched in the following language:

We, The Most Eminent Sir William McCorkle, General
Grand Master of the Pennsylvania Grand Encampment
of Knights Templar and the Appendant Orders—

To all whom it may concern, Greeting:

Whereas, By the Constitution of the said Pennsylvania
Grand Encampment of Knights Templar and the Appendant Orders, it is provided that the several Encampments which were represented in the Grand Convention
at the establishing of the said Grand Encampment,
should be furnished with Charters of Recognition, etc.,
as by the said Constitution reference being thereunto had
will fully appear.

And whereas, An Encampment of Knights Templar
held in the —— of —— in the State of —— was represented in the said Convention, and by their petition they
have prayed us to grant them a Charter of Recognition
conformably to the said Constitution.

Now know ye, That we, the Most Eminent Sir William
McCorkle, General Grand Master aforesaid, in virtue of
the powers and authorities in *Us* vested, *Do* by these
presents recognize Sir Knights —— —— Grand Master,
—— —— Generalissimo, —— —— Captain General,
and the other officers and present members of the said
Encampment as a legal Encampment under the jurisdic-

tion of our said Grand Encampment, to be held in the —— of —— in the State of —— and to be called and known by the name of —— Encampment of Knights Templar, No. — with full and adequate powers to confer the Orders of *Knights of Malta* and *Knights of the Red Cross*, with continuance to their successors in office and members, forever. *Provided, nevertheless,* That the said Sir Knights —— —— Grand Master, —— —— Generalissimo, and —— —— Captain General, and the other officers and their successors and members pay due respect to our said Grand Encampment and the regulations thereof, otherwise this Charter of Recognition to be of no force or effect.

Given under our hand and seal of our Grand Encampment at the City of Philadelphia in the Commonwealth of Pennsylvania, this 17th day of May, in the year of our Lord 1814, and of our Order 696.

Attest : WM. McCORKLE,
  GEORGE A. BAKER, *General Grand Master.*
    Grand Recorder.

PENNSYLVANIA GRAND ENCAMPMENT OF 1814.

JUNE 10, 1815, A. O. 697, A. O. E. P. 18.

M. E. Sir William McCorkle, of Philadelphia, G. G. M.
M. E. Sir Archibald Hamilton, of Wilmington, G. G.
M. E. Sir Peter Dob, of New York, G. C. G.
R. E. Sir Henry S. Keatinge, of Baltimore, G. St. B.
R. E. Sir John Sellars, of Wilmington, G. Ch.
R. E. Sir George A. Baker, of Philadelphia, G. R.
R. E. Sir Nathaniel Dillhorn, of Philadelphia, G. T.
R. E. Sir James Humes, of Philadelphia, G. Sw. B.

JUNE 9, 1816, A. O. 698, A. O. E. P. 19.

M. E. Sir Joseph Barnes, G. G. M.
M. E. Sir Archibald Hamilton, G. G.
M. E. Sir Peter Dob, G. C. G.
R. E. Sir Henry S. Keatinge, G. St. B.
R. E. Sir John Sellars, G. Ch.
R. E. Sir Thomas Hennessy, G. R.
R. E. Sir Nathaniel Dillhorn, G. T.
R. E. Sir James Humes, G. Sw. B.

JUNE 8, 1817, A. O. 699, A. O. E. P. 20.

M. E. Sir Archibald Hamilton, G. G. M.
M. E. Sir Peter Dob, G. G.
M. E. Sir Samuel Maverick, of New York, G. C. G.
R. E. Sir Henry S. Keatinge, G. St. B.
R. E. Sir John Sellars, G. Ch.
R. E. Sir George A. Baker, G. R.
R. E. Sir Nathaniel Dillhorn, G. T.
R. E. Sir James Humes, G. Sw. B.

JUNE 7, 1818, A. O. 700, A. O. E. P. 21.

M. E. Sir William McCorkle, of Philadelphia, G. G. M.
M. E. Sir Peter Dob, G. G.
M. E. Sir Henry S. Keatinge, G. C. G.
R. E. Sir Archibald Hamilton, G. St. B.
R. E. Sir Thomas Hennessy, G. Ch.
R. E. Sir George A. Baker, G. R.
R. E. Sir Nathaniel Dillhorn, G. T.
R. E. Sir James Humes, G. Sw. B.

JUNE 6, 1819, A. O. 701, A. O. E. P. 22.

M. E. Sir Alphonso C. Ireland, of Philadelphia, G. G. M.
M. E. Sir Peter Dob, G. G.

M. E. Sir Henry S. Keatinge, G. C. G.

R. E. Sir John Sellars, G. St. B.

R. E. Sir Nathaniel Dillhorn, G. Ch.

R. E. Sir Robert Ferris, of Philadelphia, G. R.

R. E. Sir Anthony Fannen, of Philadelphia, G. T.

R. E. Sir James Humes, G. Sw. B.

JUNE 21, 1820, A. O. 702, A. O. E. P. 23.

M. E. Sir Bayse Newcomb, of Philadelphia, G. G. M.

M. E. Sir Henry S. Keatinge, G. G.

M. E. Sir John Sellars, G. C. G.

R. E. Sir Anthony Fannen, G. St. B.

R. E. Sir Robert Ferris, G. Ch.

R. E. Sir George A. Baker, G. R.

R. E. Sir Thomas P. McMahon, G. T.

R. E. Sir Archibald Hamilton, G. Sw. B.

JUNE 20, 1821, A. O. 703, A. O. E. P. 24.

M. E. Sir S. P. Barbier, of Philadelphia, G. G. M.

M. E. Sir Bayse Newcomb, G. G.

M. E. Sir Archibald Hamilton, G. C. G.

R. E. Sir Anthony Fannen, G. St. B.

R. E. Sir Robert Ferris, G. Ch.

R. E. Sir George A. Baker, G. R.

R. E. Sir Thomas P. McMahon, G. T.

R. E. Sir Henry S. Keatinge, G. Sw. B.

JUNE 19, 1822, A. O. 704, A. O. E. P. 25.

M. E. Sir S. P. Barbier, of Philadelphia, G. G. M.

M. E. Sir John Sellars, G. G.

M. E. Sir Bayse Newcomb, G. C. G.

R. E. Sir Henry S. Keatinge, G. St. B.

R. E. Sir George A. Baker, G. Ch.

R. E. Sir Emmor T. Weaver, G. R.

R. E. Sir Thomas P. McMahon, G. T.
R. E. Sir James Humes, G. Sw. B.

JUNE 18, 1823, A. O. 705, A. O. E. P. 26.

M. E. Sir Anthony Fannen, of Philadelphia, G. G. M.
M. E. Sir John Sellars, G. G.   .
M. E. Sir Robert Ferris, G. C. G.
R. E. Sir S. P. Barbier, G. St. B.
R. E. Sir Alphonso C. Ireland, G. Ch.
R. E. Sir John L. Baker, G. R.
R. E. Sir Bayse Newcomb, G. T.
R. E. Sir James Humes, G. Sw. B.

The Pennsylvania Grand Encampment closed its
labors as a Grand Encampment June 10, 1824.

LETTERS AND REPORTS.

NEW YORK, *April* 8, 1814.

To the R. E. Sir George A. Baker, Grand Recorder of the Grand Encampment of the State of Pennsylvania.

The Petition of a Committee appointed by Rising Sun Encampment, held in the City of New York, on the 8th day of April, 1814, for the express purpose of applying for a Warrant to the regular authority for and in behalf of said Encampment. We therefore pray for a Constitutional Warrant or Charter, to empower us to confer the orders of the Red Cross, Knights Templar and Knights of Malta, on worthy Royal Arch Masons, as directed by said Grand Encampment, and that said Warrant shall include Sir Knight Elias Dob, as E. Grand Master ; Sir Knight John Benson, Generalissimo, and Sir Knight William Lee, as Captain General ; with such other officers as you may think proper to include with their successors elect, and a competent number of Sir Knights to open an Encampment to be hereafter known and designated by the name of *Rising Sun Encampment, No. 1, of the City of New York*, under the Grand Encampment, and in duty bound we will ever pray.

M. HUGHES,
ARCHIBALD BULL, } *Committee.*
JAMES MCDONALD,

PITTSBURG, *April* 12, 1814.

WILLIAM McCORKLE, ESQ.—Sir and Brother: At the request of the Knights of Pittsburg Encampment, I enclose an application for a Charter, accompanied by the Constitutional fee. It affords me much real pleasure to contemplate the advantages likely to result from the establishment of a Grand Encampment, and nothing shall be wanting on my part, or that of our Encampment, to render our ancient and illustrious order respectable in the eyes of the world. I feel much gratified by the honor conferred on me, by naming me one of the officers, and if I can possibly make it convenient, I will meet you in June, but my situation at present is such, that I dare not be too sanguine; but at all events rest satisfied of the warmest wishes and most cordial coöperation of,   Yours respectfully,

MAGNUS M. MURRAY.

WILMINGTON, DELAWARE, *May* 13, 1814.

WILLIAM McCORKLE, G. G. MASTER.—Dear Sir Knight: Yours of the 27th ult., I duly received, and in answer thereto, am happy to inform you that our Encampment have unanimously resolved to apply to the Pennsylvania Grand Encampment for a *Charter of Recognition*, agreeably to the Constitution of the said Grand Encampment, as you will perceive by the enclosed extract from the minutes of our proceedings. This application would have been made much sooner but we find it difficult to get our members together at this season, the evenings being so short, as to make it late before we can get through the business—and a number of our members objecting to stay late from home, they are prevented on that account from attending.

You will find from the enclosed extracts also, that we have had an election for officers under the Constitution,

which was considered absolutely necessary before application was made for a Charter, as the officers of our Encampment were not known to the Constitution, and if it
had been granted to them, it would have contained
officers totally different from those established in Convention, whereas now it will be strictly conformable to the
Constitution.   Yours sincerely,

A. HAMILTON.

NEW YORK, *June* 6, 1814.

SIR KNIGHT GEORGE A. BAKER, GRAND RECORDER.
—It is with pleasure I inform you that Rising Sun Encampment, No. 1, is in a flourishing condition, and it
would afford me greater satisfaction to have it in my
power to enclose you a complete list of the members
composing this Encampment. But Sir, on account of
having only one meeting, and that, on the night of installation, renders it completely out of my power to
comply with my wishes. I am in hopes, however, in a
few weeks to forward you such a return of members as
will cause the Rising Sun Encampment, No. 1, to rank
with the first in the United States. I remain with sentiments of respect and esteem, yours, etc.,   .

THOMAS DURRY,
Rec. K. T. Encamp't., No. 1.

BALTIMORE, *February* 19, 1815.

DEAR AND RESPECTED SIR KNIGHT.—In answer to
your request of November 29, 1814, I can only say that
the same should have been complied with before this
time. Owing to the commotion of this city with the
enemy being at the door, the Encampment did not
meet regular until a few weeks ago, when we resumed
our labors. Have the goodness to give my respects to
the General Grand Master, and assure him this Encamp-

ment, No. 1 of Maryland, will always be ready to promote the good of the Grand Encampment of this Illustrious Order. With my best wishes for yourself, I am dear Sir Knight, yours respectfully,

PHILIP P. ECKEL.

To George A. Baker, Gr. Rec.

At the annual meeting of the Pennsylvania Grand Encampment, held in the City of Philadelphia, June 11, 1816, the following report was read and accepted:

The Committee appointed by the Pennsylvania Grand Encampment of Knights Templar to confer with Delegates from the New England Grand Encampment of Knights Templar, and on the general interests of the Order, respectfully report: That they have had a full conference with them, as also with a Delegate from a Grand Encampment in New York, and give it as their unanimous opinion, that the establishment of a General Grand Encampment for the United States would greatly tend to promote UNION, ORDER, AND STRENGTH amongst Knights Templar.

They therefore beg leave to recommend to this Grand Encampment to appoint Delegates clothed with FULL powers to carry the same into effect.

WM. MCCORKLE,
A. HAMILTON,
BENJAMIN EDES.

The Pennsylvania Grand Encampment appointed the following Committee to carry out their views as expressed by the above report, viz.: Sir Knights William Mc-Corkle, A. Hamilton, Benjamin Edes, and Alphonso C. Ireland, being authorized to convene the Grand Encampment for the purpose of ratifying or rejecting any proposal for a Union.

On the 14th of June, 1816, a special meeting of the

Pennsylvania Grand Encampment was held to receive the report of the Committee, which being read, was accepted. The report read as follows:

The Delegates appointed at an extra meeting of the Pennsylvania Grand Encampment of Knights Templar to confer with Delegates from the Grand Encampments of New England and New York, upon the subject of forming and establishing a General Grand Encampment of Knights Templar, and the Appendant Orders for the United States of America, beg leave to report: That they have met the Delegates from New England and New York, and after exchanging their powers, they proceeded to deliberate upon the object of their meeting, and having spent some time therein, these Delegates discovered that it was impossible to carry their designs into execution, without making a sacrifice upon the part of this Grand Encampment and its Subordinate Encampments, which was considered to be unwarranted by every principle of Masonry; which was made a *sine qua non* with the Delegates from New England, who having seceded from the Convention, it was of consequence dissolved.

WILLIAM McCORKLE,
A. HAMILTON,
BENJAMIN EDES,
ALPHONSO C. IRELAND.

The difficulties which existed between the New England and New York Encampments on the one hand, and those of the Pennsylvania Grand Encampment on the other hand were: *First,* That the Encampments belonging to the latter, recognized themselves as in subordination to the R. W. Grand Lodges of their respective States. *Second,* That the Degrees of Mark and Most Excellent Masters were unnecessarily engrafted on Ancient Craft Masonry, and did not belong to Ancient Masonry. Under this state of affairs the Convention dissolved, each body pertinaciously holding fast to their peculiar views.

On the 24th of June, 1824, the Grand Encampment closed its labors, and we find that the General Grand Encampment subsequently took possession of the State of Pennsylvania, according to the terms of the Constitution, in which it claimed the right of establishing Encampments in States and Territories where no Grand Encampment existed. Accordingly, on the 22d of November, 1826, the M. E. Dewitt Clinton, General Grand Master of the General Grand Encampment of the United States, issued a Dispensation for an Encampment to be located at Harrisburg, Dauphin County, Pennsylvania, by the name of Holy and Undivided Trinity Encampment, which was legally and constitutionally instituted, with the Rev. Gregory T. Bedell, as its first Grand Master.

On the 23d of February, 1827, St. John's Encampment No. 4, adopted a resolution appointing Sir Knights N. Fowle, T. S. Manning, and John Norton, to select and report such name as they may think proper for heading a petition for a Warrant from the General Grand Encampment of the United States at New York for their future and better work.

On the 25th of May, 1827, the Committee were discharged, and on the 12th of June following, Sir Knights N. Fowle, C. Felt, and John Norton, were appointed to confer with the proper officers of the General Grand Encampment of the United States respecting the recognition as an Encampment by them.

In the meantime, however, (viz.: on the 25th of May, 1827), Rev. Gregory T. Bedell had not only been elected a member of St. John's No. 4, but its Grand Master.

He addressed the following letter to the Sir Knights of St. John's No. 4, of Philadelphia, dated November 23, 1827.

SIR KNIGHTS: Since I had the pleasure of meeting you in Encampment a difficulty has been thrown in my way, which compels me as a matter of conscience to resign my situation as Master. It has been stated to me by a worthy Brother Sir Knight, that according to a strict and literal interpretation of my obligation, I have committed an error in permitting myself to be elected Master of an Encampment, not formally acknowledging the jurisdiction of the General Grand Encampment. This difficulty is of a technical character, but as it concerns a solemn obligation, is nevertheless of such importance as to require my resignation. This difficulty I call of a technical character, for I am aware that virtually your Encampment is acknowledged by the General Grand Encampment, but still so long as this recognition has not been the subject of a special act on the part of the Grand Encampment, I feel as it were more safe in me to avoid any act which might look like a violation of any obligation. As this matter has been suggested to me, I cannot plead ignorance, and therefore must request that while I tender you my grateful acknowledgments for the honor already conferred, you permit me to retire, as nothing can alter the feeling of my mind, that I might be doing wrong by remaining. With these views I place in your hands the CHARTER, and also some papers with which I was entrusted. Yours, etc.,

G. T. BEDELL.

The Anti-masonic excitement which had begun to extend itself into Pennsylvania at this time, caused all the departments of Masonry (consisting of Lodges, Chapters, Councils, and Encampments) to become lukewarm in their high and holy mission, several of which suspended ' their labors. But after the excitement had passed away, and the different Orders were purified, by lopping off unsound members, and refusing to reinstate those who from unworthy motives had abused and spoken evil of the Order and violated their obligations, Masonry and Templarism resumed their sway, and the General Grand Encampment of the United States claimed jurisdiction over the State of Pennsylvania, and began to establish Encampments at Pittsburg, Washington, and Uniontown, from which was organized the present Grand Commandery, by a warrant from the M. E. William B. Hubbard.

GRAND ENCAMPMENT OF THE STATE OF VIRGINIA, }
RICHMOND, VIRGINIA, *July* 20, 1819.   }

To the M. E. Grand Master, Generalissimo and Captain - General of the Grand Encampment of Pennsylvania.

SIR KNIGHTS: The Grand Encampment of the State of Virginia being desirous to establish a correspondence with all worthy Knights Templar, and more particularly with the Grand Encampment at Philadelphia, have appointed us whose names are hereunto subscribed, a Corresponding Committee to carry that praiseworthy object into effect.

On the 24th of March, 1816, A. L. 5816, A. O. 698, a Convention of Knights Templar took place in Masons' Hall, in the City of Richmond, and within the jurisdiction of the Grand Lodge of Virginia, and formed themselves into an Encampment called the *St. John's Rising Star Encampment of Virginia*, under the guidance of many worthy Sir Knights from Europe and other places. Since which time many brave Sir Knights have been enrolled on our list who are willing to guard the passes leading to the Holy Temple, thereby promoting that benign religion of the Prince of Peace, whose standard we bear and whose divine principles we wish to inculcate.

The Encampment being aware that our Southern and Western Brethren in the United States are thirsting for light and knowledge, are willing, in conjunction with the Grand Encampment of Pennsylvania, to spread the glorious light of Zion and plant the standard of our Order in the earth's remotest bounds.

Let us hear from you as soon as convenient; until then, may the light of Him who became the head of the corner, guide and preserve you. With sentiments of respect and brotherly love, we subscribe ourselves,

Yours, etc.,

JOHN MOODY, *Chairman,*
CHARLES Z. ABRAHAM,
CALEB COOK,
JOHN W. ROBINSON,
L. CONVERT,
THOMAS H. MCVEE,
HENRY ANDERSON,
THOMAS B. CONWAY,
THOMAS CUSHING,
WILLIAM MARSH, *Recorder.*

RICHMOND, VA., *July* 20, 1819.

TO ALL KNIGHTS TEMPLAR.—Greeting: Know ye, That from the special trust and confidence reposed in our well beloved Brother, Sir John Moody, a member of Saint John's Rising Star Encampment of the State of Virginia, I have hereby, with the consent of the said Encampment, given full power and authority to Sir John Moody to negotiate with all the Encampments North of this City, and more particularly with the Grand Encampment of Philadelphia, thereby establishing that

7   D

brotherly union and good faith which should at all
times be cultivated between all who wish to walk in the
steps of our Great Preceptor. I have the honor to subscribe myself for and in behalf of the Encampment, courteously yours,   CHARLES Z. ABRAHAM,
    Test. Wm. Marsh, Recorder.   *E. G. Master.*

RICHMOND, VA., *November* 10, 1819.

SIR KNIGHT: When I left you in Philadelphia, you
promised to answer the letter of correspondence I delivered to you from the Encampment of this place. On
my return here, I reported to them my proceedings on
that subject with Sir Knight Baker and yourself, in
writing, which is filed in their archives.

The Encampment here say, they are ready to send on
and *comply with your terms,* but are waiting anxiously for
the above answer, as without that document they are not
certain of their being welcome guests with you. Really,
Sir, I feel myself rather uneasy, as they all here (I ven-
ture to say) believe I represented them to you, fairly and
candidly—as to myself, I saw your engagements daily,
while I waited on you. I will thank you very kindly, if
there is impediment in the way to tell me of it and it
shall be removed. I have no view on earth but the prosperity of the order. May Him who governs all, bless
and preserve you. I am, courteously yours,
                                        JOHN MOODY.
To Sir Kt. Alphonso C. Ireland, Esq.

RICHMOND, VA., *November* 11, 1819.

To GEORGE A. BAKER, ESQ., GRAND SECRETARY:
On my return home, this Encampment of Knights Templar convened, to hear the report of my proceedings under
their authority. Your friend, Sir Knight Ireland, promised me an answer should be returned to the Letter of

Correspondence left with him, which letter I think was friendly and polite. The Encampment here believe I represented fairly and honorably their situation and desire, and are therefore of opinion that they are at least entitled to a polite answer. Their officers tell me they are prepared to send on the requisites and comply with your terms, although the times here are very severe. No answer has come to hand.

This evening we have a meeting a mile from my home, which I cannot attend. The last mail I wrote to Sir Knight Ireland of this nature, but fearing an accident to him, I have taken this liberty with you, hoping that you will set all things right. I am, with the greatest respect and esteem, courteously yours,   JOHN MOODY.

PHILADELPHIA, *January* 16, 1820.

SIR KNIGHT JOHN MOODY: The several communications you handed me the Grand Officers have had under consideration, but nothing can be done until the meeting of the Grand Encampment. The annual meeting will be held on the second Friday in June next, when the papers will be laid before them and their decision will be *immediately* communicated to you. You will recollect that Sir Knight Baker and myself informed you when you were in this city, that we believed nothing could be done until the meeting of the Grand Encampment. If you contemplate petitioning for a WARRANT, it must be sent previous to the meeting of the Grand Encampment. The Constitution and By-Laws which you received when here, will tell you what is necessary to be done on your part to enable you to obtain one.

Courteously and Knightly yours,
ALPHONSO C. IRELAND.

HAVANA, *February* 28, 1820.

To the Most Eminent the Grand Master of Knights Templar of the Grand Encampment of the State of Pennsylvania.

MOST RESPECTFULLY GREETING: I, the undersigned, a regular Sir Knight of the Temple, Knight of the Red Cross and Malta, have been duly authorized by four more Sir Knights from Ireland, residing with myself at this place, to solicit and most humbly to request of you a dispensation and power to give and grant the degrees of Knights Templar, Red Cross and Malta, to so many worthy Royal Arch Masons as are sufficient to open a regular Encampment of Sir Knights Templar, provided, that they do no further work until they have received a regular Warrant from the Grand Encampment of Pennsylvania.

We are well aware that five Sir Knights were not able to do so without having obtained such power or Dispensation, and how far it will answer to obtain it from you, time must show. Permit me on behalf of the other four Sir Knights (who are not known in America), to assure you that it would greatly redound to the honor and advancement of Masonry, as it will then convince some, that it only tends to the advancement of Christianity.

Should you as we sincerely hope, deem it expedient to grant us our prayer, you are then requested to enclose it, directed to me, and send it to the Worshipful Brother Lewis, Grand Treasurer of the Grand Lodge of Pennsylvania, who will pay the expenses attending it, and forward it to Brother Pedro Gracias, Corresponding Secretary of this place. Permit me to subscribe myself M. E. G. M., your obedient and affectionate Brother,

JACOB BURNS,

Of Encampment No. 1 of Philadelphia.

To Alphonso C. Ireland, G. G. M.

CITY OF AUGUSTA, GEORGIA, *May* 1, 1823. A. O. 706.

MOST EMINENT SIR PHILIP WINNEMORE: I have the pleasure to inform you, that an Encampment of Knights Templar and the appendant Orders has been established in the City of Augusta, under the jurisdiction and by virtue of the authority of the General Grand Encampment of the United States, and on behalf of our Encampment I crave from your Grand Encampment, that friendly and social intercourse between our respective members individually, and between our Encampment by written correspondence which characterizes our Illustrious and Magnanimous Order. You have herewith an impress from our seal and the signatures of our officers, and I beg you may reciprocate with us. I salute you fraternally,   L. CUMMINGS, RECORDER.

JAMES C. WINTER, G. C.

DAVID CLARKE, G.

JOHN P. ANDREWS, C. G.

OFFICE OF THE GRAND MASTER OF THE GENERAL ⎫
GRAND ENCAMPMENT OF THE UNITED STATES, ⎬
COLUMBUS, OHIO, *February* 18, 1854. ⎭

To ALL TRUE AND COURTEOUS KNIGHTS: *Know ye,* That whereas there are now established and existing three Commanderies in the State of Pennsylvania, holding their authority from, in, and working under our jurisdiction, to wit: Pittsburg Encampment No. 1, Jacques de Molay Encampment No. 2, and St. Omers Encampment No. 3; *And whereas,* on behalf of those several Encampments, it has been duly certified unto me, that they are desirous to form, hold and maintain, a GRAND ENCAMPMENT, in and for the said State of Pennsylvania, subordinate to the General Grand Encampment of the United States of America:

Therefore, I, William B. Hubbard, General Grand

7 *

Master of the aforesaid General Grand Encampment, being satisfied that the aforesaid request is reasonable and proper, by virtue of the high powers in me vested, and in accordance with the Constitution and Rules of our Order, do hereby authorize and empower the aforesaid Encampments Nos. 1, 2, and 3, in due order, to meet at such time and place as they may agree upon and FORM a State Grand Encampment in and for the State of Pennsylvania, subordinate to our General Grand Encampment. The said State Grand Encampment, when so formed, making due return and report to me of all their official doings and proceedings in the premises, and making a like return to our Illustrious Grand Recorder. And for all of their doings in accordance with the rules and usages of our Order, in forming such State Grand Encampment, this shall be their WARRANT.

Given under my hand and private seal at the City of Columbus the day and year above written.

:|: WILLIAM B. HUBBARD, [L. S.]

PROVIDENCE, R. I., *November* 27, 1857.

SIR KNIGHT B. B. FRENCH, GRAND RECORDER—Dear Sir : With a view to obtain as well as to give information, I will state what I have in my possession, beginning with the formation of St. John's Encampment of Providence, R. I.

The first record I can find is August 23, 1802, and alludes to a previous meeting of which I can find no record. At this meeting the Encampment was formed and established, and Thomas S. Webb was elected Grand Master, and was elected to that office annually until 1813.

A Grand Convention of Knights Templar was held in Providence on the 6th of May, 1805. They appointed a Committee and adjourned to the 13th, and the Committee reported as follows: "Constitution of the Grand Encampment of Rhode Island and jurisdiction thereunto belonging." At this meeting Providence Encampment of Knights Templar, Newbury Encampment of Knights Templar, and Boston Encampment of Knights of the Red Cross were represented. Thomas S. Webb, of Providence was elected G. M., N. Fowle, of Boston, G., and J. Gage, of Newburyport, C. G. This Constitution may be found in Webb's Monitor for 1806.

At the Annual Assembly of the Grand Encampment holden at Boston in the month of May, 1806, it was deemed expedient to extend the jurisdiction of the Grand Encampment to any State or Territory wherein there is no regularly established Grand Encampment, and for this and other purposes a number of alterations and amendments were made in the Constitution. The Constitution as altered and amended is in the following words: "Constitution of the United States Grand Encampment of Knights Templar and the Appendant Orders." At this meeting, Massachusetts, Rhode Island, Maine, and New York, were represented. Thomas S. Webb, of Providence, was elected G. G. M., N. Fowle, of Boston, G. G., Jonathan Gage, of Newburyport, G. C. G., Ezra Ames, of Albany, G. S. W., Sterry Foster, of Portland, G. S. B.

Article 1, Sect. 3 of the Constitution read as follows: The jurisdiction of this Grand Encampment shall extend to any State or Territory wherein there is not a Grand Encampment regularly established. Is not this the commencement of the General Grand Encampment? This Constitution may be found in Webb's Monitor of 1816. At the Annual Assembly at Boston in 1812, the same Officers were elected as in 1806, and the same States represented, with the addition of Maryland, I think.

In 1816, this same United States Grand Encampment

met at New York, and altered the Constitution to that
of General Grand Encampment of Knights Templar
and the Appendant Orders for the United States of
America. De Witt Clinton was elected General Grand
Master. Thomas S. Webb, of Providence, (not of Boston, as the publisher of Webb's Monitor of 1821 has it),
was elected Deputy G. G. Master, the same States represented and the same principal officers elected as in 1812.

Thus we find Webb in 1802 at the head of St. John's
Encampment of Providence. In 1805 we find him at
the head of the Grand Encampment of Knights Templar. In 1806, and also in 1812, we find him at the
head of the United States Grand Encampment. In 1816
we find him D. D. G. M. of the G. G. E. of the U. S.
Webb died in 1819.

I claim for Webb that he was the originator of 1st.
St. John's Encampment of Providence; 2d. Of the
Grand Encampment of Massachusetts and Rhode Island;
and 3d. Of the United States Grand Encampment, now
the G. G. Encampment of the United States.

The Charter of St. John's Encampment is dated in
October, 1805, and is No. 1 the first from us.

Truly and fraternally yours,

JAMES SALSBURY.

PROVIDENCE, R. I., *January* 28, 1860.

ALFRED CREIGH, GRAND RECORDER.—Eminent Sir
Knight: Yours of the 23d came duly to hand, inquiring
for information in regard to the history of Knighthood
in the United States. In answer, will say that I can give
but little information in addition to what you will find
in Webb's Monitors of 1805 and 1816, and my letter to
Sir B. B. French, of November 27, 1857, (see foregoing
letter).

I am informed, but cannot now give my author, that

Thomas S. Webb received the orders of Knighthood in Philadelphia.

The records of the United States Grand Encampment from 1806 to 1816, are in possession of the Grand Encampment of Massachusetts and Rhode Island.   I was not sure in regard to Maryland being represented in the United States Grand Encampment in 1812.   My copy says, " with the addition of Maryland I think."   I am, respectfully and truly yours,   JAMES SALSBURY.

In the Masonic Review, published by Sir C. Moore, of Cincinnati, Ohio, Vol. 23, June, 1860, are these words :

" Brother Webb aided in organizing a Chapter_ and Encampment in Albany, and the degrees of the York Rite were worked from Entered Apprentice through all the degrees of Symbolic, Capitular, and Chivalric Masonry, up to Knights of Malta.   But Brother Webb had taken all these degrees previous to his removal."

The Rev. Paul Dean, in his Eulogy on Thomas S. Webb, says he received the orders of Knighthood in Philadelphia.

D *

ENCAMPMENTS.

PHILADELPHIA ENCAMPMENT, NO. 1.

Philadelphia Encampment, No. 1, was constituted in the City of Philadelphia on *December* 27, 1812, by the union of No. 1 and No. 2. These two bodies had existed for about the last sixteen years, but the members of both Encampments believed they could accomplish more good by a common union, and thereby cement the bonds of their fraternity, whereby they could participate in those glorious rights and privileges, which their ancestors had enjoyed. Hence the union was happily consummated, and in the year 1814, No. 1, commissioned as Delegates to form the Pennsylvania Grand Encampment, Sir Knights William McCorkle, Alphonso C. Ireland and Nathaniel Dillhorn, which event being accomplished, they received a CHARTER of Recognition on the 2d *day of May*, 1814.

LIST OF OFFICERS FROM DECEMBER 27, 1812, TO JUNE 13, 1823.

DECEMBER 27, 1812, A. O. 694, A. O. E. P. 15.

Sir Thomas Black, M. E. H. P.
Sir Andrew Scott, G. M.
Sir James Humes, C. G.
Sir Francis Bailey, G. S. W.
Sir John Glenn, G. J. W.

Sir Samuel Black, G. St. B.
Sir George Reed, G. Sw. B.
Sir Joseph Brobston, T.
Sir James Thompson, R.
Sir George Gray, O. G.

These officers continued in office until they received a Charter from the Pennsylvania Grand Encampment, having elected on the 13th of April, 1814, a list of officers whose names are inserted in their petition and confirmed by the Grand Encampment.

APRIL 13, 1814, A. O. 696, A. O. E. P. 17.

Sir John Glenn, E. G. M.
Sir Samuel Black, G.
Sir Anthony Fannen, C. G.
Sir Alphonso C. Ireland, St. B.
Sir Charles Snyder, Her.
Sir Daniel Marshall, Ch.
Sir M. J. Littleboy, Sw. B.
Sir James Thompson, R.
Sir George Reed, T.

MAY 20, 1814, A. O. 696, A. O. E. P. 17.

Sir Alphonso C. Ireland, E. G. M.
Sir Samuel Black, G.
Sir Daniel Marshall, C. G.
Sir Patrick Reed, St. B.
Sir Thomas Black, Ch.
Sir James Hamill, Her.
Sir John Conrad, R.
Sir James Thompson, T.
Sir Robert Harris, Sw. B.

MAY 19, 1815, A. O. 697, A. O. E. P. 18.

Sir Samuel Black, E. G. M.
Sir Anthony Fannen, G.
Sir Nathan Buncker, C. G.
Sir Patrick Reid, St. B.
Sir John L. Baker, Her.
Sir Thomas Black, Ch.
Sir James Thompson, R.
Sir John Conrad, T.
Sir John Glenn, Mar.
Sir Gabriel Coit, Sw. B.

MAY 17, 1816, A. O. 698, A. O. E. P. 19.

Sir John L. Baker, E. G. M.
Sir Patrick Reid, G.
Sir G. W. Bartram, C. G.
Sir Ebenezer Osborn, St. B.
Sir Robert Shanes, Her.
Sir James Ferris, Ch.
Sir John H. Star, R.
Sir Samuel Black, T.
Sir John Stinger, Mar.
Sir William Farr, Sw. B.

JUNE 13, 1817, A. O. 699, A. O. E. P. 20.

Sir Patrick Reid, E. G. M.
Sir Ebenezer Osborn, G.
Sir John Glenn, C. G.
Sir Robert Hill, St. B.
Sir Frederick Nice, Her.
Sir S. P. Barbier, Ch.
Sir George Howarth, R.
Sir Samuel Black, T.

Sir John Young, Mar.
Sir James Ferris, Sw. B.

JUNE 12. 1818, A. O. 700, A. O. E. P. 2

Sir Ebenezer Osborn, E. G. M.
Sir George A. Baker, G.
Sir Anthony Fannen, C. G.
Sir John Glenn, St. B.
Sir Robert Hill, Her.
Sir S. P. Barbier, Ch.
Sir George Howarth, R.
Sir Samuel Black, T.
Sir John Young, Mar.
Sir James Ferris, Sw. B.

MAY 21, 1819, A. O. 701, A. O. E. P. 22

Sir George A. Baker, E. G. M.
Sir James Ferris, G.
Sir John Young, C. G.
Sir Anthony Fannen, St. B.
Sir John Johnston, Her.
Sir John Glenn, Ch.
Sir Elisha L. Antrim, R.
Sir Samuel Black, T.
Sir James Kearnes, Mar.
Sir James Ferris, Sw. B.

MAY 19, 1820, A. O. 702, A. O. E. P. 23.

Sir Anthony Fannen, E. G. M.
Sir John Young, G.
Sir John Diamond, C. G.
Sir John Johnston, St. B.
Sir George Howarth, Her.
Sir John Glenn, Ch.

Sir Elisha L. Antrim, R.
Sir Daniel Creath, T.
Sir James Kearnes, Mar.
Sir Andrew McAffee, Sw. B.

MAY 18, 1821, A. O. 703, A. O. E. P. 24.

Sir John Young, E. G. M.
Sir John Diamond, G.
Sir John Johnston, C. G.
Sir James Kearns, St. B.
Sir Ferdinand Deviling, Her.
Sir John Glenn, Ch.
Sir Emmor T. Weaver, R.
Sir Daniel Creath, T.
Sir Andrew McAffee, Mar.
Sir William Smyth, Sw. B.

MAY 17, 1822, A. O. 704, A. O. E. P. 25.

Sir John Diamond, G. G. M.
Sir John Johnston, G.
Sir James Kearns, C. G.
Sir Ferdinand Deviling, St. B.
Sir John Glenn, Her.
Sir A. McAffee, Ch.
Sir Emmor T. Weaver, R.
Sir Ebenezer Osborn, T.
Sir Daniel Creath, Mar.
Sir William Smyth, Sw. B.

JUNE 13, 1823, A. O. 705, A. O. E. O. 26.

Sir John Johnston, G. G. M.
Sir James Kearns, G.
Sir Robert Hunter, C. G.
Sir Ferdinand Deviling, St. B.

Sir John Glenn, Her.
Sir A. McAffee, Ch.
Sir Emmor T. Weaver, R.
Sir Ebenezer Osborn, T.
Sir Daniel Creath, Mar.
Sir William Smyth, Sw. B.

MEMBERS.

NAME.	DATE OF KNIGHTING.
Aston, James,*	November 12, 1800.
Alexander, William,	January 15, 1813.
Allibone, Thomas, (No. 3),	September 15, 1815.
Antrim, Elisha L.,	May 1, 1819.
Baker, George A.,	June 10, 1796.
Brobston, Joseph,	November 12, 1800.
Black, Thomas, (No. 3),	January 18, 1811.
Black, Samuel,*	April 19, 1811.
Burns, Jacob,*	December 27, 1812.
Bailey, Francis, (No. 2),*	December 27, 1812.
Bussier, Daniel,	August 20, 1813.
Britton, Hugh,	July 15, 1814.
Buncker, Nathaniel,	January 21, 1815.
Baker, J. L.,	February 17, 1815.
Barnes, Joseph, (No. 3),	September 15, 1815.
Bartram, G. W.,	November 17, 1815.
Baker, George A. Jr.,	April 18, 1817.
Badger, Samuel,	May 17, 1816.
Barbier, S. P., (No. 4),	August 16, 1816.
Bravo, Jacob,	July 20, 1819.
Coit, Gabriel,	August 21, 1812.
Cook, David,	October 16, 1812.
Conrad, John,	January 21, 1814.
Caster, Daniel,	April 21, 1815.

* Those members marked with * were admitted from No 2, at the union of the two Encampments, December 27, 1812.

NAME.	DATE OF KNIGHTING.
Cash, Jacob,	March 21, 1817.
Creath, Daniel,	March 19, 1820.
Dillon, John,	October 19, 1810.
De Silver, Robert, (No. 3),	August 16, 1811.
Dillhorn, Nathaniel, (No. 3),	May 21, 1813.
Durborrow, Samuel, (No. 3),	December 16, 1814.
Diamond, John,	May 19, 1820.
Devilling, Ferdinand,	June 18, 1820.
Ford, Edward,	November 20, 1812.
Ferrier, James,*	December 27, 1812.
Fallen, James,	January 15, 1813.
Fannen, Anthony,	May 21, 1813.
Ferris, James,	July 15, 1814.
Farr, William,	February 17, 1815.
Fullen, John,	June 14, 1816.
Freeman, Henry,	July 19, 1816.
Glenn, John,	July 20, 1810.
Gundelach, C. H., (No. 3),	December 19, 1811.
Gray, George,*	December 27, 1812.
Humes, James,	July 20, 1810.
Hammill, James,	April 16, 1813.
Harris, Robert, Jr.,	March 19, 1813.
Hill, Robert,	October 20, 1815.
Hennessy, Thomas, (No. 3),	October 20, 1815.
Howarth, George,	August 16, 1816.
Hunter, Robert,	May 1, 1823.
Irving, David,	September 11, 1795.
Ireland, Alphonso C., (No. 3),	March 19, 1813.
Jones, Joseph,	February 18, 1814.
Johnston, John,	May 19, 1820.
Keyser, Adam,	September 20, 1811.
Kearns, James,	May 19, 1820.
Littleboy, M. J.,	April 13, 1814.
Levering, Benjamin,	February 17, 1815.

NAME.	DATE OF KNIGHTING.
Le Blanc, Lewis,	December 20, 1816.
Macoy, James,*	December 27, 1812.
Mackey, John,*	December 27, 1812.
McDevitt, James,*	December 27, 1812.
McCorkle, William,	December 18, 1822.
Marshall, Daniel,	June 18, 1813.
Milnor, Robert, (No. 3),	June 17, 1814.
Mitchell, William,	April 18, 1817.
McAffee, Andrew,	May 19, 1820.
Nielson, William,*	December 27, 1812.
Nielson, Andrew,*	December 27, 1812.
Nice, Frederick,	May 17, 1816.
Norris, Robert, Jr.,	January 16, 1817.
O'Brien, John,*	December 27, 1812.
Osborn, Ebenezer,	March 19, 1813.
Porter, John, Jr., (No. 3),	June 21, 1811.
Quinn, Daniel,*	December 27, 1812.
Reed, George,*	December 27, 1812.
Reid, Patrick,	April 15, 1814.
Russell, George,	May 17, 1820.
Sloan, Hugh,	February 21, 1806.
Scott, Andrew,* (No. 2),	December 27, 1812.
Smith, Robert,	December 21, 1810.
Shallens, Frederic,	December 27, 1812.
Stinger, John,	April 17, 1812.
Schnider, Charles,	April 16, 1813.
Slater, Anthony,	March 18, 1814.
Shanes, Robert,	July 15, 1814.
Snyder, Daniel,	February 17, 1815.
Schott, John P., (No. 3),	August 8, 1815.
Starr, John H.,	March 15, 1816.
Stevenson, Thomas,	March 17, 1816.
Smyth, William,	May 18, 1821.
Thompson, John A.,	February 14, 1794.

8 *

NAME.	DATE OF KNIGHTING.
Tearney, Hugh,	November 12, 1800.
Thompson, James,	March 12, 1812.
Thomas, A.,	March 21, 1817.
Wilson, Andrew,	July 11, 1794.
Walter, John J.,	December 19, 1811.
Wisdom, John,*	December 27, 1812.
Weiss, Adam,	March 15, 1816.
Weaver, Emmor T.,	May 16, 1820.
Yearnall, Nathan,	February 20, 1815.
Young, Andrew,	March 15, 1816.
Young, John,	December 20, 1816.

PITTSBURG ENCAMPMENT, No. 2.

Pittsburg Encampment No. 2 assisted in the formation of the Pennsylvania Grand Encampment on the 15th of February, 1814, and was represented by Sir Knights Thomas Black and James Humes.

On the 2d of February, 1814, "the undersigned Knights of the Temple, residing in the Borough of Pittsburg, being desirous of participating in those glorious rights and privileges enjoyed by our valiant ancestors from *time immemorial*, have resolved to form an Encampment in this Borough, for that purpose being duly authorized and commanded to do so by the sublime Warrant under which we work." The Warrant alluded to was the Warrant or Charter of Lodge No. 45, which authorized "said Lodge when duly congregated, to admit, enter, and make Masons, according to the ancient and honorable custom of the Royal Craft in all ages and nations throughout the world."

The application for a CHARTER OF RECOGNITION was signed by

SIR FRANCIS BAILEY, H. P.
SIR ANDREW SCOTT, G. M.
SIR MAGNUS M. MURRAY, C. G.
SIR JESSE HAMILTON, S. G. W.
SIR ROBERT HENDERSON, J. G. W.
SIR GEORGE MILTENBERGER, T.
SIR HENRY BAIRD, R.
SIR COL. MCALLISTER, G. SW. B.,

and the following Sir Knights, viz.: John Gorman, Joseph Davis, John Hanshaw, William Porter, John Tate, William Steele, Lewis Peters, William Jack, Asa B. Shepherd, G. M. Ward, Christian Carson Febiger, John S. Swearingen, Henry Bailey, Daniel Keller, Anthon' Beelen, and George Anshultz, Jr.

The Charter was granted May 2, 1814.

MAY 21, 1814, A. O. 696, A. O. E. P. 17.

Sir Francis Bailey, E. G. M.
Sir Andrew Scott, G.
Sir Magnus M. Murray, C. G.
Sir Henry Bailey, R.
Sir Christian Carson Febiger, T.
Sir George Stewart, St. B.
Sir William Porter, Her.
Sir Robert Henderson, Ch.
Sir Col. McAllister, Sw. B.
Sir Philip Comma, O. G.

MAY 20, 1815, A. O. 697, A. O. E. P. 18.

Sir Francis Bailey, E. G. M.
Sir Andrew Scott, G.

Sir William Porter, C. G.
Sir Jesse Hamilton, R.
Sir George Miltenberger, T.
Sir George Stewart, St. B.
Sir Henry Bailey, Her.
Sir Robert Henderson, Ch.
Sir Col. McAllister, Sw. B.
Sir Philip Comma, O. G.

On the 26th of June, 1815, Sir Knight Andrew Scott, Generalissimo, returned the Charter to the Pennsylvania Grand Encampment through the Grand Recorder, Sir George A. Baker, and paid off their indebtedness to the Grand Encampment.

MEMBERS.

NAME.	DATE OF KNIGHTING.
Anshultz, George,	February 2, 1814.
Bailey, Francis,	February 2, 1814.
Bailey, Henry,	February 2, 1814.
Baird, Henry,	February 2, 1814.
Beelen, Anthony,	February 2, 1814.
Comma, Philip,	February 2, 1814.
De Lacy, John, knighted by dispensation,	September 15, 1815.
Davis, Joseph,	February 2, 1814.
Febiger, Charles Carson,	February 2, 1814.
Gorman, John,	February 2, 1814.
Henderson, Robert,	March 13, 1811.
Hamilton, Jesse,	February 2, 1814.
Hanshaw, John,	February 2, 1814.
Jack, William,	February 2, 1814.
Keller, Daniel,	February 2, 1814.
Murray, Magnus M.,	February 2, 1814.
Miltenberger, George,	February 2, 1814.

NAME.	DATE OF KNIGHTING.
McAllister, Col.	February 2, 1814.
Porter, William,	February 2, 1814.
Peters, Lewis,	February 2, 1814.
Scott, Andrew,	February 2, 1814.
Steele, William,	February 2, 1814.
Stewart, George,	February 2, 1814.
Smith, Andrew,	February 2, 1814.
Shepherd, Asa B.,	February 2, 1814.
Swearingen, John S.,	February 2, 1814.
Tate, John,	February 2, 1814.
Ward, G. M.	February 2, 1814.

RISING SUN ENCAMPMENT, NO. 1.

The Grand Encampment of New York was constituted by the Sovereign Grand Consistory of the Chiefs of ex- alted Masonry, for the United States of America, on the 1st day of June, 1814. Prior to this organization, how- ever, it appears that *four* Encampments existed in the State of New York, for in the history of the Proceedings of the Grand Encampment of New York, at page 45 we read that " it being stated that at the formation of this Grand Encampment, Numbers 1, 2, 3 and 4, of the Sub- ordinate Encampments, were left unemployed and held in reserve for certain Encampments previously established under the OLD SYSTEM, provided they should cause peti- tions to be duly presented therefor."

It appears No. 2, (Temple Encampment at Albany), applied and received a Charter, but Nos. 1, 2, 4, did not, and in December, 1823, by resolution, they forfeited their right to obtaining a Charter from the Grand Encampment. Under the *Old System*, No. 1, was Rising Sun Encampment at New York City. No. 2, Temple Encampment at Albany.

Rising Sun Encampment, No. 1, subsequently became Columbian Commandery, No. 1. This Encampment was the oldest Encampment in New York, and by reference to the Commercial Advertiser of New York, dated 30th December, 1799, I find the following interesting order :

The Knights Templar are requested to attend to-morrow morning, at 10 o'clock, in the French Church in Pine Street, in full dress, with crape round the arm and sword, in order to join in the funeral procession, in honor of the memory of our late worthy Grand Master, Lieut.-General George Washington. By order of Sir J. M.

Wm. Richardson, Scribe, Dec. 30, 1799.   G. M.

The Grand Master's initials are only added to the notice, but it may be inferred that it was James McDonald, who was the prominent Knight Templar. But a question arises here, was General Washington a K. T.? If so, where did he receive his degrees? The notice gives him the position of having been a Grand Master (Eminent Commander) of a Commandery.

Rising Sun Encampment was therefore instituted prior to 1808, but received a Charter of Recognition from the Pennsylvania Grand Encampment, May 3, 1814, and afterwards from the Grand Encampment of the State of New York. We are only in possession of the officers from 1808.

OFFICERS OF RISING SUN ENCAMPMENT.

James McDonald, M. E. Grand Master in 1808—1810.
Thomas Lownds, M. E. Grand Master in 1810—1811.
Stephen B. Beckman, M. E. Grand Master in 1811—1813.
Michael Hughes, M. E. Grand Master in 1813—1814.
Elias Dob, M. E. Grand Master in 1814—1817.

Samuel Maverick, M. E. Grand Master in 1817—1820.
George Howard, M. E. Grand Master in 1820—1822.
Gerrit Morgan, M. E. Grand Master in 1822—1823.
Oliver M. Lownds, M. E. Grand Master in 1823.
R. B. Atterbury, M. E. Grand Master in 1862.
John Costello, M. E. Grand Master in 1862—1863.
Titus M. Evans, M. E. Grand Master in 1863—1864.
Henry C. Banks, M. E. Grand Master in 1864—1865.
A. W. Budlong, M. E. Grand Master in 1865—1866.
James A. Reed, M. E. Grand Master in 1866.

Rising Sun ENCAMPMENT, No. 1, of the City of New York, was represented in the Convention of Knights Templar, which met in Philadelphia on the 15th day of February, 1814, for the purpose of organizing a Grand Encampment of Knights Templar in Pennsylvania, "with jurisdiction belonging thereto." The Delegates from Rising Sun Encampment of New York, were Sir Knights James McDonald, Thomas Armstrong and Anthony Fannen, who, with the representatives from Pennsylvania, Delaware, and Maryland, adopted a Constitution on the 15th and 16th days of February, 1814, to form a more perfect union, and named it the " PENNSYLVANIA GRAND ENCAMPMENT OF KNIGHTS TEMPLAR, with jurisdiction thereunto belonging." The CHARTER of Recognition was granted May 3, 1814, to Sir Knights Elias Dob, John Benson, William Lee, Artemus Brookins, James Chadwell, John McMullan, John Ossman, M. Hughes, Thomas Durry, Lewis Weaver, Stephen Beekman, Archibald Bull, Charles D. Bevoise, James McDonald and John McMillen. These Charter members had received the Orders of Knighthood prior to 1814.

OFFICERS OF RISING SUN ENCAMPMENT, NO. 1.
FROM MAY 3, 1814, TO MAY 15, 1817.

MAY 3, 1814, A. O. 696, A. O. E. P. 17.

Sir Elias Dob, E. G. M.
Sir John Benson, G.
Sir William Lee, C. G.
Sir Artemus Brookins, Ch.
Sir James Chadwell, Her.
Sir John McMullan, St. B.
Sir John Ossman, Sw. B.
Sir M. Hughes, Tr.
Sir Thomas Durry, R.
Sir Lewis Weaver, Sen.

MAY 17, 1815, A. O. 697, A. O. E. P. 18.

Sir Elias Dob, E. G. M.
Sir Charles D. Bevoise, G.
Sir John McMillen, C. G.
Sir Artemus Brookins, Ch.
Sir William F. Noble, Her.
Sir John Chadwell, St. B.
Sir John Gasner, Sw. B.
Sir M. Hughes, W.
Sir John W. Brimsmead, R.
Sir John McDonnell, Mar.

MAY 16, 1816, A. O. 698, A. O E. P. 19.

Sir Elias Dob, E. G. M.
Sir Charles D. Bevoise, G.
Sir John McMullan, C. G.
Sir Artemus Brookins, Ch.
Sir William F. Noble, Her.
Sir John Chadwell, St. B.

Sir John Gasner, Sw. B.
Sir M. Hughes, W.
Sir John W. Brimsmead, R.
Sir John McDonnell, M.

MAY 15, 1817, A. O. 699, A. O. E. P. 20.

Sir Samuel Maverick, E. G. M.
Sir Thomas Durry, G.
Sir Alexander Sibbald, C. G.
Sir Artemus Brookins, Ch.
Sir William F. Noble, Her.
Sir John Chadwell, St. B.
Sir John Gasner, Sw. B.
Sir M. Hughes, T.
Sir John W. Brimsmead, R.
Sir John McDonnell, M.

We have been furnished with the following, from Sir
Knight J. A. Reed, M. D., the present E. C. of Columbia
Commandery, (originally Rising Sun Encampment, No.
1), which demonstrates the existence of Rising Sun En-
campment. The extract is from the N. Y. Dispatch of
October 7, 1866.

MASONRY IN MARBLE.

We are indebted to our much esteemed Bro. R. W.
Wm. Sinclair, whose eye is as quick to detect Masonic
traces as his heart is to respond in sympathy to the calls
of the worthy and needy, for the following literal copy
of inscription upon a tomb-stone in St. Paul's church-
yard, in this city. Fifty years ago! What other society
then in being can show as little variableness in its landmarks, or marble-marks, as ours? All who were connected with our companion are gone to dust, but here we

9   E

find in the face of the hard marble the traces of Brotherly
Love, and it will be as admirable and as admired a hundred years hence.   Such is Masonry!

RISING SUN CHAPTER, No. 16, R. A. M.

AND

RISING SUN ENCAMPMENT, No. 1, K. T.

HAVE CONJOINTLY ERECTED THIS STONE

IN COMMEMORATION OF THEIR RESPECT

FOR THE AFFECTIONS AND VIRTUES

THAT ONCE GLOWED IN THE HEART

AND ANIMATED THE SOUL

OF THEIR DECEASED

COMPANION AND SIR KNIGHT

THOMAS FREEBORN.

HE DIED THE 3D DAY OF MAY, 1815,

AGED 43 YEARS, 3 MONTHS AND 22 DAYS.

——

IN THE VARIOUS EXCELLENCIES

THAT FLOWED FROM THE RELATIONS

OF HUSBAND, PARENT AND FRIEND,

HE HAS NOT BEEN SURPASSED,

SELDOM EQUALLED,

AND HAS LEFT TO THE BROTHERHOOD, HIS EXAMPLE

FOR THEIR IMITATION.

NAME.	DATE OF KNIGHTING.
Beekman, Stephen, Charter Member,	April 8, 1814.
Benson, John, Charter Member,	April 8, 1814.
Brookins, Artemus, Charter Member,	April 8, 1814.
Bull, Archibald, Charter Member,	April 8, 1814.
Bevoise, Charles D., Charter Member,	April 8, 1814.
Butler, John,	June 9, 1815.
Brimsmead, John W.,	June 9, 1815.

NAME.	DATE OF KNIGHTING.
Burnis, Enos,	June 9, 1815.
Beemas, Elijah,	March 24, 1815.
Boylin, William,	June 10, 1817,
Chadwell, James,	April 8, 1814.
Chardwell, James,	June 7, 1815.
Cauldwell, Mark,	June 7, 1815.
Carmichael, Daniel,	June 7, 1815.
Champlin, Robert,	June 7, 1815.
Carney, Patrick,	June 7, 1815.
Dob, Elias, Charter Member,	April 8, 1814.
Durry, Thomas, Charter Member,	April 8, 1814.
Dob, Peter,	June 9, 1815.
Freeborn, Thomas,	June 9, 1813.
Frash, Daniel,	June 9, 1815.
Fleming, William,	June 9, 1815.
Gastner, John,	May 16, 1865.
Hughes, Michael, Charter Member,	April 8, 1814.
Harrison, William,	April 8, 1815.
Hall, Charles,	June 9, 1815.
Hardcastle, John,	June 9, 1815.
Kipp, David,	June 9, 1815.
Keenan, Dennis,	June 9, 1815.
Lee, William, Charter Member,	April 8, 1814.
McDonald, James, Charter Member,	April 8, 1814.
McMullan, John, Charter Member,	April 8, 1814.
McMillen, John, Charter Member,	April 8, 1814.
McDonald, John,	March 24, 1815.
McEnee, Thomas,	June 10, 1815.
McEnee, David,	June 10, 1815.
McCausland, John,	June 10, 1815.
McComb, John,	June 10, 1815.
McEnee, Hugh,	June 10, 1815.
Morris, Edward,	June 10, 1815.
McFarland, Henry,	March 24, 1815.

NAME.	DATE OF KNIGHTING.
McKaig, Jacob,	June 6, 1815.
Maverick, Samuel,	December 6, 1816.
McKenny, William,	December 6, 1816.
Noble, William F.,	May 16, 1815.
Ossman, John, Charter Member,	April 8, 1814.
Oliver, John,	June 9, 1815.
Pryor, John,	June 9, 1815.
Richardson, William,	Decemb'r 16, 1799.
Shellcross, Stephen,	March 24, 1815.
Smith, John,	May 16, 1815.
Sibbald, Alexander,	June 6, 1815.
Tuttle, Stephen F.,	May 16, 1815.
Weaver, Lewis, Charter Member,	April 8, 1814.
Whilley, Hugh,	June 9, 1815.
Wood, Francis,	June 9, 1815.

WASHINGTON ENCAMPMENT, No. 1, DELAWARE.

This Encampment was located in the City of Wilmington, Delaware, and commissioned Sir Knights John Sellars, Archibald Hamilton, and John W. Patterson, as their delegates to the Convention which assembled in Philadelphia, February 15, 1814, to organize the Pennsylvania Grand Encampment.

A CHARTER OF RECOGNITION was issued *May* 17, 1814, to the following petitioners: Sir Knights Archibald Hamilton, John Sellars, John W. Patterson, John Gordon, George Reid, Sr., George Reid, Jr., John Ramman, John Springer, Thomas Stockton, Amon Thomas, and Nicholas G. Williamson.

OFFICERS OF WASHINGTON ENCAMPMENT, No. 1,
SINCE MAY 17, 1814 to JUNE 5, 1821, INCLUSIVE.

MAY 13, 1814, A. O. 696, A. O. E. P. 17.

Sir Archibald Hamilton, E. G. M.
Sir John W. Patterson, G.
Sir John Sellars, C. G.
Sir John Hedrick, St. B.
Sir Thomas G. Cable, Her.
Sir. John Springer, Chan.
Sir William B. Weaver, R.
Sir James Cochran, T.
Sir John Adams, Mar.
Sir James McKean, Sw. B.

MAY 8, 1815, A. O. 697, A. O. E. P. 18.

Sir Archibald Hamilton, E. G. M.
Sir John W. Patterson, G.
Sir John Hedrick, C. G.
Sir Thomas G. Cable, St. B.
Sir John Springer, Her.
Sir Benjamin Chandler, Ch.
Sir William B. Weaver, R.
Sir James Cochran, T.
Sir John Adams, Mar.
Sir James McKean, Sw. B.

MAY 13, 1816, A. O. 698, A. O. E. P. 19.

Sir Archibald Hamilton, E. G. M.
Sir John W. Patterson, G.
Sir John Hedrick, C. G.
Sir Thomas G. Cable, St. B.
Sir John Springer, Her.
Sir Benjamin Chandler, Ch.

9 *

Sir William B. Weaver, R.
Sir James Cochran, T.
Sir John Adams, Mar.
Sir James McKean, Sw. B.

MAY 12, 1817, A. O. 699, A. O. E. P. 20

Sir John Sellars, E. G. M.
Sir John W. Patterson, G.
Sir John Mountain, C. G.
Sir Thomas G. Cable, St. B.
Sir John Springer, Her.
Sir Benjamin Chandler, Ch.
Sir William B. Weaver, R.
Sir James Cochran, T.
Sir John Adams, Mar.
Sir James McKean, Sw. B.

MAY 11, 1818, A. O. 700, A. O. E. P. 21.

Sir John W. Patterson, E. G. M.
Sir John Mountain, G.
Sir Thomas G. Cable, C. G.
Sir John Springer, St. B.
Sir Benjamin Chandler, Her.
Sir John Hedrick, Ch.
Sir William B. Weaver, R.
Sir James Cochran, T.
Sir John Adams, Mar.
Sir James McKean, Sw. B.

MAY 10, 1819, A. O. 701, A. O. E. P. 22.

Sir John Mountain, E. G. M.
Sir Thomas G. Cable, G.
Sir Joseph Seeds, C. G.
Sir James McKean, St. B.

Sir Benjamin Chandler, H.
Sir John Springer, Ch.
Sir John McClung, R.
Sir James Cochran, T.
Sir David T. Jones, Mar.
Sir Alexander Wilson, Sw. B.

MAY 20, 1820, A. O. 702, A. O. E. P. 23.

Sir John Mountain, E. G. M.
Sir Thomas G. Cable, G.
Sir Joseph Seeds, C. G.
Sir Alexander Wilson, St. B.
Sir Benjamin Chandler, H.
Sir John Springer, Ch.
Sir John McClung, R.
Sir James Cochran, T.
Sir John Adams, Mar.
Sir Thomas A. Sterret, Sw. B.

MAY 19, 1821, A. O. 703, A. O. E. P. 24.

E. Benjamin H. Springer, E. G. M.
E. John Adams, G.
E. Joseph Seeds, C. G.
E. John Gordon, St. B.
E. James McKean, Her.
E. John McClung, Ch.
E. Frederick Leonard, Rec.
E. James Cochran, T.
E. John D. Wood, Mar.
E. Benjamin Chandler, Sw. B.

MAY 18, 1822, A. O. 704, A. O. E. P. 25.

Sir Benjamin Springer, E. G. M.
Sir John Adams, G.

Sir Josiah F. Clement, C. G.
Sir John Gordon, St. B.
Sir Joseph Seeds, Her.
Sir James McKean, Ch.
Sir Frederick Leonard, R.
Sir James Cochran, T.
Sir John D. Wood, Mar.
Sir Benjamin Chandler, Sw. B.

The only remaining document with regard to the officers is in these words:

I, Josiah F. Clements, Grand Master of the Washington Encampment, No. 1, holden in Wilmington, Delaware, do by these presents, constitute and appoint my beloved Sir Knight, John McClung, my proxy to represent me and the Encampment aforesaid, in the Pennsylvania Grand Encampment of Knights Templar, at their next meeting in the City of Philadelphia, hereby conferring on my said Proxy, all the powers vested in me by virtue of my said office.

Given under my hand this 10th day of June, 1823.

JOSIAH F. CLEMENT, E. G. M.

NAME.	DATE OF KNIGHTING.
Adams, John,	June 10, 1816.
Bolden, Levi,	June 7, 1814.
Baileys, Samuel,	April 14, 1817.
Cochran, James,	June 10, 1814.
Cable, Thomas G.,	June 10, 1814.
Chandler, Benjamin,	June 10, 1814.
Chesnut, Jarred,	June 10, 1814.
Chesnut, David,	June 10, 1814.
Connally, Dominick,	December 17, 1816.
Clement, Josiah F.,	May 10, 1821.
Dupont, Victor,	June 10, 1814.

NAME.	DATE OF KNIGHTING.
Day, Joseph, Sen.,	June 10, 1814.
Day, Joseph, Jr.,	June 10, 1815.
Gordon, John, Charter Member,	May 11, 1812.
Guy, Samuel,	June 10, 1814.
Hamilton, Alex'der, Charter Member,	May 17, 1812.
Harvey, William W.,	June 10, 1814.
Harvey, Andrew,	June 10, 1814.
Hedrick, John,	June 10, 1814.
Huffington, Edward,	August 10, 1815.
Jones, David T.,	July 10, 1817.
Leonard, Frederick,	June 10, 1814.
Milnor, William,	June 10, 1814.
McKean, James,	February 20, 1815.
McClarry, Richard,	June 10, 1815.
Mountain, John,	July 8, 1816.
Montgomery, William,	July 10, 1816.
McClung, John,	April 14, 1817.
Nielson, Jno., (Trinity En. Harrisb'g.),	June 10, 1815.
Patterson, John W., Charter Mem.,	April 11, 1812.
Pecon, Leon,	July 10, 1817.
Reid, George, Sen., Charter Member,	December 28, 1813.
Reid, George, Jr., Charter Member,	December 28, 1813.
Ramman, John, Charter Member,	November 29, 1813.
Robinson, Joseph,	June 10, 1814.
Rambeau, John,	June 10, 1814.
Sellars, John, Charter Member,	June 10, 1812.
Springer, John, Charter Member,	March 14, 1814.
Stockton, Thomas, Charter Member,	March 14, 1814.
Stevenson, Isaac,	May 8, 1815.
Seeds, Joseph,	May 8, 1815.
Springer, Benjamin H.,	November 13, 1815.
Smyth, William,	February 12, 1816.
Sterret, Thomas A.,	April 8, 1816.
Thomas, Amon, Charter Member,	April 22, 1813.

E *

NAME.	DATE OF KNIGHTING.
Williamson, Nicholas G., Ch. Mem.,	April 4, 1812.
Weatherby, Edmund,	June 10, 1814.
Weaver, William B.,	May 8, 1815.
Wright, Ebenezer,	June 10, 1815.
Wilson, Alexander,	February 12, 1816.
Weeks, William,	April 14, 1817.
Wood, John D.,	May 4, 1812.
Yearnall, Isaac,	May 8, 1815.

ENCAMPMENT NO. 1. BALTIMORE, MARYLAND.

ENCAMPMENT No. 1, was located in Baltimore, Maryland, and claims to have conferred the Order of Knighthood as early as 1790, by traditionary evidence.

The Petitioners for a CHARTER of Recognition, made application to the Pennsylvania Grand Encampment, their Encampment having been represented in the Convention which formed the Constitution of the Grand Body on the 15th February, 1814, by Sir Knight Henry S. Keatinge.

The Charter was granted *May* 2, 1814, to Sir Knights Philip P. Eckel, Peter Galt, Adam Denmead, Henry S. Keatinge, Thomas Boyle, Samuel Cole, Archibald Dobbin, John L. Wampler, James Vinson, J. A. Smith, Josias A. Smith, L. B. Barnes, William Cook, Nathaniel Chittenden, George Keyser, Thomas Kirk, L. L. Rosseau, Thomas Ring, James Sellars, Henry Starr, Jacob Small, Walter Theeker, F. M. Wills, George Woelper, Tobias Watkins.

OFFICERS OF ENCAMPMENT NO. 1, OF BALTIMORE,
FROM ITS ORGANIZATION.

MAY 2, 1814, A. O. 696, A. O. E. P. 17.

Sir Philip P. Eckel, E. G. M.
Sir Peter Galt, G.
Sir Adam Denmead, C. G.
Sir Henry S. Keatinge, St. B.
Sir Thomas Boyle, Her.
Sir Samuel Cole, Ch.
Sir Archibald Dobbin, R.
Sir John L. Wampler, T.
Sir James Vinson, Mar.
Sir J. A. Smith, Sw. B.

MAY 3, 1815, A. O. 697, A. O. E. P. 18.

Sir Philip P. Eckel, E. G. M.
Sir Peter Galt, G.
Sir Adam Denmead, C. G.
Sir Henry S. Keatinge, St. B.
Sir Thomas Boyle, Her.
Sir Samuel Cole, Ch.
Sir Archibald Dobbin, R.
Sir John L. Wampler, T.
Sir James Vinson, Mar.
Sir J. A. Smith, Sw. B.

MAY 5, 1816, A. O. 698, A. O. E. P. 19.

Sir Adam Denmead, E. G. M.
Sir Henry S. Keatinge, G.
Sir Benjamin Edes, C. G.
Sir Archibald Dobbin, St. B.
Sir Henry Starr, Her.
Sir Samuel Cole, Ch.

Sir George Keyser, R.
Sir John L. Wampler, T.
Sir E. Simpkins, Mar.
Sir James Hammersly, Sw. B.

MEMBERS.

NAME.	DATE OF KNIGHTING.
Asmith, Josias, Charter Member,*	May 2, 1814.
Barnes, L. P., Charter Member,*	May 2, 1814.
Boyle, Thomas, Charter Member,*	May 2, 1814.
Biney, Thomas,	June 14, 1816.
Beastor, Henry,	June 14, 1816.
Cook, William, Charter Member,*	May 2, 1814.
Cole, Samuel, Charter Member,*	May 2, 1814.
Chittenden, Nathaniel, Char. Mem.,*	May 2, 1814.
Denmead, Adam, Charter Member,*	May 2, 1814.
Dobbin, Archibald, Charter Mem.,*	May 2, 1814.
Eckel, Philip P., Charter Member,*	May 2, 1814.
Edes, Benjamin,	June 1, 1815.
Frank, John,	June 14, 1816.
Galt, Peter, Charter Member,*	May 2, 1814.
Hammersly, James,	June 14, 1816.
Keatinge, Henry S., Charter Mem.,*	May 2, 1814.
Keyser, George, Charter Member,*	May 2, 1814.
Kirk, Thomas, Charter Member,*	May 2, 1814.
Pancake, Isaac,	June 14, 1816.
Rosseau, L. L., Charter Member,	May 2, 1814.
Ring, Thomas, Charter Member,*	May 2, 1814.
Sellars, James, Charter Member,*	May 2, 1814.
Starr, Henry, Charter Member,*	May 2, 1814.
Small, Jacob, Charter Member,*	May 2, 1814.
Smith, J. A., Charter Member,*	May 2, 1814.

* The Charter Members marked with * denotes their *Admission* on May 2, 1814, although they had previously received the Orders of Knighthood.

NAME.	DATE OF KNIGHTING.
Simpkins, Elias,	June 1, 1815.
Thecker, Walter, Charter Member,*	May 2, 1814.
Travers, S.,	June 14, 1816.
Vinson, James, Charter Member,*	May 2, 1814.
Wampler, John L., Charter Mem.,*	May 2, 1814.
Wills, F. W., Charter Member,*	May 2, 1814.
Woelper, George, Charter Member,*	May 2, 1814.
Watkins, Tobias, Charter Member,*	May 2, 1814.

Upon an examination of the Archives of Encampment No. 1, of Knights Templar of Baltimore, Maryland, the following endorsement is upon the Charter issued by the Pennsylvania Grand Encampment of 1814.

At a triennial meeting of the General Grand Encampment of the United States held in the City of Baltimore, on the 29th of November, 1832, it was ordained that the within Encampment of Knights Templar No. 1, should be received under the jurisdiction of the said General Grand Encampment of the United States on their conforming to the requirements of the Constitution of the General Grand Encampment aforesaid.

Now, therefore, we certify that the said Encampment No. 1, have given assent to the constitutional requirements, and by virtue of these presents are acknowledged, accredited, and received under the jurisdiction of the General Grand Encampment of the United States.

Dated at the City of Baltimore, 8th December, A. D. 1832.

JAMES M. ALLEN,
Deputy General Grand Master.

JAMES HERRING,
General Grand Recorder.

10

PHILADELPHIA ENCAMPMENT, No. 3.

On the 16th day of February, 1816, the following Sir
Knights, (formerly members of Encampment No. 1, of
the City of Philadelphia,) viz: Robert Milnor, N. Dillhorn, Thomas Hennessy, Joseph Barnes, C. H. Gundelach, Samuel Durborrow, John Porter, Jr., Robert De
Silver, John P. Schott, Thomas Allibone, Alphonso C.
Ireland, and Thomas Black, made application through
the M. E. William McCorkle, Grand Master for Encampment No. 3. The petitioners state that they believe
its establishment would contribute to the general prosperity and stability of the Order. This application was
recommended by No. 1, and accordingly a warrant for
its organization was issued February 16, 1816, which was
subsequently constituted March 27, 1816.

OFFICERS OF PHILADELPHIA ENCAMPMENT, No. 3,
FROM ITS ORGANIZATION, UNTIL

MARCH 27, 1816, A. O. 698, A. O. E. P. 19.

Sir Thomas Hennessy, E. G. M.
Sir Joseph Barnes, G.
Sir Robert Milnor, C. G.
Sir Samuel Durborrow, St. B.
Sir Thomas Allibone, Her.
Sir Thomas Black, Chan.
Sir C. H. Gundelach, Rec.
Sir John P. Schott, Tre.
Sir John Porter, Jr., Mar.
Sir Robert De Silver, Sw. B.

MAY 17, 1817, A. O. 699, A. O. E. P. 20.

Sir Joseph Barnes, E. G. M.
Sir Robert Milnor, G.

Sir Samuel Durborrow, C. G.
Sir John Porter, Jr., St. B.
Sir John P. Schott, Her.
Sir Thomas Black, Chan.
Sir C. H. Gundelach, Rec.
Sir Lambert Keating, Tr.
Sir Robert De Silver, Mar.
Sir William F. Seegar, Sw. B.

MAY 11, 1818, A. O. 700, A. O. E. P. 21.

Sir Thomas P. McMahon, E. G. M.
Sir Thomas Black, G.
Sir Thomas Pearson, C. G.
Sir M. H. Anthony, St. B.
Sir Charles A. Droz, Her.
Sir John P. Schott, Chan.
Sir Josiah S. Kay, Rec.
Sir C. H. Gundelach, T.
Sir Pearce Wood, Mar.
Sir Charles Mercier, Sw. B.

MAY 11, 1819, A. O. 701, A. O. E. P. 22

Sir John P. Schott, E. G. M.
Sir John Porter, Jr. G.
Sir Robert Ferris, C. G.
Sir Henry C. Carey, St. B.
Sir Charles A. Droz, Her.
Sir Thomas Black, Ch.
Sir Josiah S. Kay, Rec.
Sir C. H. Gundelach, Tr.
Sir Adam Hatfield, Mar.
Sir Charles Mercier, Sw. B.

MAY 9, 1820, A. O. 702, A. O. E. P. 23.

Sir Bayse Newcomb, E. G. M.
Sir Charles A. Droz, C.
Sir Samuel Webb, C. G.
Sir Adam Hatfield, St. B.
Sir Charles Mercier, Her.
Sir Thomas Black, Ch.
Sir Thomas P. McMahon, R.
Sir John P. Schott, T.
Sir James Ferram, Mar.
Sir James Scott, Sw. B.

MAY 8, 1821, A. O. 703, A. O. E. P. 24.

Sir Bayse Newcomb, E. G. M.
Sir James McAlpin, G.
Sir T. B. Freeman, C. G.
Sir Adam Hatfield, St. B.
Sir Charles Mercier, Her.
Sir Thomas P. McMahon, Chan.
Sir Edward King, R.
Sir Thomas Black, T.
Sir James Ferram, Mar.
Sir James Scott, Sw. B.

MEMBERS.

NAME.	DATE OF KNIGHTING.
Allibone, Thomas, (No. 1), Ch. Mem.,	September 15, 1815.
Anthony, Michael H.,	June 11, 1816.
Barnes, Joseph, (No. 1), Ch. Mem.,	September 15, 1815
Black, Thomas, (No. 1), Ch. Mem.	January 18, 1811.
Budd, C.,	May 14, 1816.
Bedlock, W. J.,	June 13, 1819.
Culin, John,	May 14, 1816.
Carey, Henry C.,	May 14, 1816.

NAME.	DATE OF KNIGHTING.
Cock, Richard F.,	May 14, 1816.
Dillhorn, Nathan'l., (No. 1), Ch. Mem.,	May 21, 1813.
De Silver, Robert, (No. 1), Ch. Mem.,	August 16, 1811.
Durborrow, Sam'l., (No. 1), Ch. Mem.,	December 16, 1814.
Droz, Charles A.,	June 11, 1816.
Dungan, Mahlon,	June 11, 1816.
Ferris, Robert,	May 11, 1819.
Ferram, James,	May 8, 1820.
Freeman, T. B.,	November 7, 1820.
Fernander, J. M.,	November 24, 1820.
Gundelach, C. H., (No. 1), Ch. Mem.,	December 19, 1811.
Goodwin, Thomas,	February 9, 1819.
Graham, John,	May 11, 1819.
Hennessy, Thomas, (No. 1), Ch. Mem.,	October 20, 1815.
Haydock, William,	May 14, 1816.
Hatfield, Adam,	June 13, 1817.
Hannum, Isaac,	September 22, 1818.
Ireland, Alphon. C. (No. 1), Ch. Mem.,	March 19, 1813.
Keating, Lambert,	May 14, 1816.
Kay, Josiah S.,	May 14, 1816.
King, Hermanus,	September 22, 1817.
Keisch, Henry,	February 11, 1818.
King, Edward,	November 13, 1820.
Lewis, J. S.,	November 25, 1820.
Milnor, Robert, (No. 1), Ch. Mem.,	June 17, 1814.
Mercier, Charles,	May 14, 1816.
McMahon, Thomas P.,	February 17, 1817.
McCollin, William,	November 11, 1818.
McAlpin, James,	December 13, 1819.
Newcombe, Bayse,	April 11, 1820.
Porter, John, Jr., (No. 1), Ch. Mem.,	June 21, 1811.
Pierson, T. H.,	June 11, 1816.
Schott, John P. (No. 1), Ch. Mem.,	August 8, 1815.
Seegar, William F.,	May 14, 1816.

10 *

NAME.	DATE OF KNIGHTING.
Stratton, William J.,	May 14, 1816.
Sargeant, Thomas J.,	June 11, 1816.
Scott, John,	February 12, 1819,
Scott, James,	May 13, 1819.
Shaw, Thomas,	December 19, 1819.
Wood, Pierce,	. July 7, 1819.
Webb, Samuel,	June 9, 1819.
Winnemore, P., (No. 4), admitted,	July 19, 1819.

WIVANDA ENCAMPMENT.

Elmira Encampment of the county of Tioga and State of New York, on the 20th of July, 1826, issued a Charter under its seal, and signed by Thomas Maxwell, as *Grand Commander*, Hezekiah W. Atkins, *Generalissimo*, and John H. Knapp, *Captain-General*, authorizing and empowering Sir Knights George H. Bull, as *Grand Commander*, William Kelly, as *Generalissimo* and Thomas Overton, as *Captain-General*, to assemble as a BRANCH of their Encampment, at Towanda, Bradford County, Pennsylvania.   They had authority by the said Charter to elect their successors, and confer the orders of *Knights Templar, Knights of Malta, and of the Mediterranean Pass, and Knights of the Red Cross,* and were required to do all and every act according to ancient usage.

Sir Thomas Maxwell, the Grand Commander of Elmira Encampment, in June, 1860, wrote me, that he received the orders of Knighthood in Jerusalem Encampment, Danby, New York, which was subsequently removed to Ithaca, New York, that this Encampment was chartered by *five Knights* belonging to *five different* Commanderies,

before the establishment of the Grand Encampment of
New York. From Jerusalem Encampment they received
their authority to open Elmira Encampment, of which
he was the first Grand Commander, giving them the same
power to issue Charters. When the Grand Encampment
of New York was established, the Encampments of Ithaca
and Elmira were legalized.

The Books, papers, jewels, etc., etc., (except the Charter) were all destroyed by fire, at the destruction of the
Court House of Towanda, in which place Wivanda Encampment met.

The Charter of Wivanda Encampment was the nucleus
from which sprang NORTHERN COMMANDERY, No. 16.
The original Charter read as follows:

To all to whom these Presents may come, or may concern, Greeting. Know ye, that we the officers of Elmira
Encampment, held at Elmira, in the County of Tioga
and State of New York, to wit: Thomas Maxwell, Grand
Commander, Hezekiah W. Atkins, Generalissimo, and
John H. Knapp, Captain-General, do hereby constitute
and appoint a branch of our said Encampment to be
held at Towanda, in the County of Bradford, in the State
of Pennsylvania, to be managed and governed by the
undernamed Brothers Sir Knights as the first officers of
said Encampment, viz:

Sir George H. Bull, Grand Commander.
Sir William Kelly, Generalissimo.
Sir Thomas Overton, Captain-General,

and such others as they shall choose from time to time,
as their successors when duly assembled, and we will aid
and assist the officers and Brethren of said Encampment,
by giving them such information as shall be in our
power when time and opportunity will permit; hereby
giving to the said Encampment full power and authority
to confer the orders of *Knights Templar*, *Knights of*

Malta, and of the Mediterranean Pass, and Knights of the Red Cross. That the said Branch shall be known and distinguished by the name and title of WIVANDA ENCAMPMENT, and that we will consider ourselves in union with them so long as they proceed agreeable to ancient usage.

Given under our hands and the seal of Elmira Encampment, in regular convocation thereof, this 20th day of July, in the year of our Lord, 1826, of Masonry, 5826, Order of Knights Templar, 708.*

THOS. MAXWELL, *Grand Commander.*

HEZEKIAH W. ATKINS, *Generalissimo.*

JOHN W. KNAPP, *Captain-General.*

Attest, Josiah Dunham, Recorder.

HOLY AND UNDIVIDED TRINITY ENCAMPMENT.

This Encampment was organized at Harrisburg, Dauphin County, Pennsylvania, on the 22d day of November, 1826, by a dispensation issued from the M. E. Sir Dewitt Clinton, General Grand Master of the General Grand Encampment of the United States of America.

The following Sir Knights were the petitioners, viz: Sir Knights Rev. Gregory T. Bedell, John De Pui, Rev. J. Baker Clemson, Rev. Benjamin Allen, Samuel F. Bradford, Rev. Robert Piggot, John Nielson, Rev. William H. Rees, and Theophilus Keckeler.

The *fourth* triennial meeting of the General Grand Encampment not taking place until 1829, and the sudden death of the M. E. Grand Master Dewitt having

---

* Consult Northern Commandery, No. 16, for a continuation of this Encampment.

preceded this meeting, the application for a Charter was consequently mislaid by his death, no Charter was procured, and the State of Pennsylvania was convulsed with the malignant and persecuting spirit of Anti-masonry.

OFFICERS OF HOLY AND UNDIVIDED TRINITY ENCAMPMENT.

DECEMBER 16, 1826, A. O. 708, A. O. E. P. 29.

Rev. Sir Gregory T. Bedell, G. M.
Sir John De Pui, G.
Rev. Sir J. Baker Clemson, C. G.
Rev. Sir Benjamin Allen, St. B.
Sir Samuel F. Bradford, Chan.
Rev. Sir Robert Piggot, Tr.
Sir John Nielson, Rec.
Rev. Sir William Henry Rees, Sw. B.
Sir Theophilus Keckeler, H.

MEMBERS.

NAME.	DATE OF KNIGHTING.
Allen, Rev. Benjamin, (No. 4), Ch. Mem.,	Nov. 22, 1826.
Bedell, Rev. Gregory T., (No. 4), Ch. Mem.,	May 25, 1826.
Bradford, Samuel F., (No. 4), Ch. Mem.,	May 25, 1826.
Clemson, Rev. J. Baker, (No. 4), Ch. Mem.,	Oct. 25, 1826.
Cameron, Simon,	Oct. 25, 1826.
De Pui, John, (No. 4), Ch. Mem.,	Oct. 25, 1826.
De Pui, Rev. James, (No. 4),	Oct. 25, 1826.
Hall, Rev. Richard D.,	Jan. 17, 1827.
Keckeler, Theophilus, (No. 4), Ch. Mem.,	Oct. 25, 1826.
Milnor, Rev. James,	Mar. 16, 1809.
Nielson, John, (Wilm., Del., 1), Ch. Mem.,	June 10, 1825.
Nash, Rev. Norman,	Oct. 25, 1826.
Piggot, Rev. Robert, Ch. Mem.,	Oct. 25, 1826.
Rees, Rev. William Henry, Ch. Mem.,	Oct. 25, 1826.
Scott, William G.,	Feb. 16, 1827.

GRAND ENCAMPMENT OF KNIGHTS TEMPLAR OF
PENNSYLVANIA, UNDER THE AUTHORITY OF
THE RIGHT WORSHIPFUL GRAND LODGE OF
PENNSYLVANIA.

A Convention met in the City of Philadelphia, May
10, 1854, for the purpose of organizing a Grand Encampment for the State of Pennsylvania, under the
authority of the R. W. Grand Lodge of Free and
Accepted Masons. Representatives were in attendance
from St. John's Encampment, No. 4, Philadelphia Encampment, No. 5, Union Encampment, (of Philadelphia),
No. 6, and De Molay Encampment, No. 7, of Reading,
Pennsylvania.

Representatives from No. 4.
Sir Knights Charles Brothers, Jeremiah L. Hutchin-
son, Alfred P. Hesser, William E. Harpur, William
Carr, James Williams, Herman Yerkes, Charles O.
McCord, William O. Fox, James W. Martien, A. de
Leo de Laguina, John Tobin, A. G. Waterman, Jacob
Bennet, Walter A. Watkins, F. Shultz, William H.
Nichols, R. Sterling Wilson, William B. Schneider,
David Jayne, W. P. Hamm, and George F. Sites.

Representatives from No. 5.
Sir Knights William H. Klapp, Anthony E. Stocker,
John L. Goddard, John L. Heylin, and A. B. Camp-
bell.

Representatives from No. 6.
Sir Knights O. A. Norris, Stephen Taylor, and J. C.
Booth.

Representatives from No. 7.
Sir Knights Henry R. Hawman, James Mullin, Henry
Hahn, and David A. Griffiths.

The Convention was organized by calling Sir Wm. H. Klapp to the Chair, and appointing Sir John L. Goddard, Secretary.

The Convention adopted a Constitution in order to form a more perfect union, and to promote peace, harmony, and brotherly love, among the Knights of our ancient and illustrious Order. After the adoption of the Constitution the Convention closed, and the Grand Encampment was duly organized in ample form by regularly opening the same, electing and installing officers, and performing those duties enjoined by the Ritual of the Order.

The mode of application, action of the Grand Lodge, and form of Charter, read as follows:

To all whom it may concern :—

Whereas, at a stated meeting of ——— Lodge No. ——, A. Y. M., held on the — day of ———, A. D. 18—, A. L. 58—, the following communication was presented and read :

To the W. M., Officers and Brethren, of Lodge No. —. We the undersigned, being Knights Templar, and of the Order of St. John, of Jerusalem, are desirous of opening an Encampment of Knights Templar, and the appendant orders under the sanction and warrant of ——— Lodge, No. —, and therefore respectfully pray that you will grant the sanction of the warrant for that purpose, and as in duty bound, will ever pray, etc. (Signed by the petitioners).

This application required the certificate of the Encampment, in which the petitioners received the orders of Knighthood, duly signed by the officers, and attested by the seal of the Encampment.

The application and certificate being in proper form,

the following authority was issued for the use of the Warrant of the Lodge.

Whereas, it has been shown to this Lodge that at a Quarterly Grand Communication of the Grand Lodge of Pennsylvania, held on the 4th day of June, A. D. 1849, it having been announced that Franklin Lodge, No. 134, had granted the sanction of its Warrant to open an Encampment of Knights Templar, the following Resolution was moved and adopted:

Resolved, That the action of Franklin Lodge, No. 134, regarding the granting of the sanction of their Warrant to open an Encampment of Knights Templar, be referred to the Committee of Landmarks: and that at an adjourned Quarterly Meeting and Grand Communication of the Grand Lodge of Pennsylvania, held on the 17th December, A. L. 5849, the following report was received and the resolution thereto adopted.

To the R. W. Grand Master, and Grand Lodge of Pennsylvania.   The undersigned, two of the Committee on Landmarks, to which Committee the action of Franklin Lodge, No. 134, regarding the use of their Warrant to open an Encampment of Knights Templar was referred, respectfully report:

That they have considered the matter referred to them, and that the proceedings of the said Lodge thereon, are according to the usages and customs of Freemasons in the State of Pennsylvania, and therefore offer the following Resolution:

Resolved, That the Grand Lodge approve the action of Franklin Lodge, No. 134, regarding the use of their Warrant to open an Encampment of Knights Templar.

BAYSE NEWCOMBE,   } *Committee on*
SAMUEL H. PERKINS, } *Landmarks.*

On motion duly made and seconded, it was *Resolved,*

That the sanction of the Warrant of ——— Lodge, No.
—, be and the same is hereby granted to Bros. ——— ———
——— ———, etc., etc., Knights of the Temple and of the
Order of St. John of Jerusalem, to open and hold in the
——— of ———, an Encampment of Knights Templar,
and the appendant orders.

Now Know ye, That we the said ——— Lodge, No. —,
by virtue of the power and authority in us vested, by our
Warrant from the Grand Lodge of the State of Pennsylvania, as set forth in the above recited action of the
said Grand Lodge, do hereby authorize and empower the
above named Brethren, ——— ——— ——— ———, to open
and hold in the ——— of ———, an Encampment of
Knights Templar, and the appendant orders, under the
sanction of our said Warrant, to elect their officers, which
officers we hereby authorize and empower to act until
their successors being first duly elected and chosen, to
whom they shall deliver the Warrant, and invest them
with all the powers and dignities to their offices respectively belonging, and such successors shall in like manner, from time to time, install their successors.

And we do hereby further authorize and empower the
above named Brethren and their successors, to admit and
make Knights of the Temple, and the appendant orders,
according to the most ancient and honorable custom of the
Royal Craft in all ages and nations throughout the known
world and not contrariwise.

And we do hereby further empower and appoint the
above Brethren and their successors, to hear and deter-
mine all and singular, matters and things relative to the
Craft within the jurisdiction of the said Encampment,
with the assurance of the members of the said Encampment, provided always, that the said above named Brethren and their successors, pay due respect to the Right
Worshipful Grand Lodge of Pennsylvania, and the or-

dinances thereof, otherwise this Warrant to be of no force or effect.

Given under the hands of our Worshipful Officers and the seal of our Lodge, at ——, this — day of —— in the year of our Lord, 18—, and of Masonry, 58—. (Signed by the Officers of the Lodge).

The Grand Recorder was instructed to inform the R. W. Grand Lodge, that the Pennsylvania Grand Encampment of Knights Templar and the appendant orders, was regularly organized by the adoption of a Constitution, and the election and installation of Grand Officers.

OFFICERS OF THE PENNSYLVANIA GRAND
ENCAMPMENT FROM ITS ORGANIZATION,
MAY 10, 1854, UNTIL ITS REUNION WITH
THE GRAND COMMANDERY OF PENNSYL-
VANIA, FEBRUARY 17, 1857.

MAY 10, 1854, A. O. 736, A. O. E. P. 57.

M. E. Sir Bayse Newcombe, G. M.
M. E. Sir Samuel H. Perkins, G. G.
M. E. Sir Samuel Badger, G. C. G.
M. E. Sir David C. Skerret, G. St. B.
M. E. Sir William H. Klapp, G. Her.
M. E. Sir James Millholland, G. Chan.
M. E. Sir William E. Harpur, G. Mar.
M. E. Sir Jeremiah L. Hutchinson, G. Rec
M. E. Sir David Jayne, G. Tr.
M. E. Sir Ed. H. Butler, G. Sw. B.
M. E. Sir W. B. Schneider, O. G.

JUNE 16, 1854, A. O. 736, A. O. E. P. 57.

M. E. Sir R. Sterling Wilson, G. M.
M. E. Sir Anthony E. Stocker, G. G.
M. E. Sir A. Jordan Swartz, G. C. G.
M. E. Sir David C. Skerret, G. St. B.
M. E. Sir William H. Klapp, G. Her.
M. E. Sir James Millholland, G. Chan.
M. E. Sir W. E. Harpur, G. Mar.
M. E. Sir Jeremiah L. Hutchinson, G. R.
M. E. Sir David Jayne, G. T.

M. E. Sir Ed. H. Butler, G. Sw. B.
M. E. Sir W. B. Schneider, O. G.

JUNE 8, 1855, A. O. 737, A. O. E. P. 58.

M. E. Sir R. Sterling Wilson, G. M.
M. E. Sir Anthony E. Stocker, G. G.
M. E. Sir A. Jordan Swartz, G. C. G.
M. E. Sir David C. Skerret, G. St. B.
M. E. Sir William H. Klapp, G. Her.
M. E. Sir James Millhólland, G. Chan.
M. E. Sir William E. Harpur, G. Mar.
M. E. Sir Jeremiah L. Hutchinson, G. R.
M. E. Sir David Jayne, G. T.
M. E. Sir E. H. Butler, G. Sw. B.
M. E. Sir W. B. Schneider, O. G.

JUNE 13, 1856, A. O. 738, A. O. E. P. 59.

M. E. Sir Anthony E. Stocker, G. M.
M. E. Sir A. Jordan Swartz, G. G.
M. E. Sir David C. Skerret, G. C. G.
M. E. Sir E. H. Butler, G. St. B.
M. E. Sir William H. Klapp, G. Her.
M. E. Sir James Millholland, G. Chan.
M. E. Sir William E. Harpur, G. Mar.
M. E. Sir Jeremiah L. Hutchinson, G. R.
M. E. Sir James Hutchinson, G. T.
M. E. Sir Francis Blackburne, G. Sw. B.
M. E. Sir W. B. Schneider, O. G.

June 13, 1856. A Committee consisting of Sir Knights
Francis Blackburne, A. Jordan Swartz, and William H.
Allen, were appointed to take into consideration the
present condition of Knighthood in this jurisdiction,
(Pennsylvania), and report to a succeeding meeting of

this Grand Encampment, if any means may or can be adopted, to harmonize the present unfortunate claims of parties in opposition to this Grand Encampment,

September 12, 1856. Sir Knights D. C. Skerret, and J. L. Hutchinson, were added to the Committee.

December 12, 1856. The Chairman, Sir F. Blackburne, reported that a Committee had been appointed by the Western body, to meet a similar Committee from this body, with power to settle a Basis of Union of the two Grand bodies, whereupon the Committee with the Grand Officers were clothed with full powers to act.

March 6, 1857. Sir F. Blackburne presented the proceedings of the Convention of February 12, 1854, together with a Basis of Union, which was unanimously approved of, and a copy of the same sent to each subordinate for its approval or rejection.

May 6, 1857. Sir Jeremiah L. Hutchinson reported that Encampments Nos. 4, 5, 6 and 7, had accepted and approved the articles of Union, whereupon a Resolution was adopted, authorizing the M. E. Sir Anthony E. Stocker, Grand Master, to issue his Proclamation, dissolving this Grand Encampment, at such time as he may deem expedient.

June 1, 1857. R. E. Sir William W. Wilson issued a Proclamation that the two Grand Bodies were united in one State Grand Commandery.

June 20, 1857. M. E. William Blackstone Hubbard, G. M., issued a Proclamation, congratulating Knights Templars "on the union of the two Grand Encampments of Pennsylvania," all under the same solemn vows of allegiance and fealty to the same and only Governmental Head, THE GRAND ENCAMPMENT OF THE U. STATES.

It will be proper to state in this connection, that the Articles of Union were also submitted to and approved by the subordinate Commanderies of the Grand Com-

11 *

mandery of Knights Templar of Pennsylvania, acknowledging the authority of the Grand Encampment of the
United States.

The following was the form of Charter issued by the
Pennsylvania Grand Encampment, under the authority
of the R. W. Grand Lodge, at this time.

We, The Most Eminent Sir —— ——, General Grand
Master of the PENNSYLVANIA GRAND ENCAMPMENT OF
KNIGHTS TEMPLAR AND APPENDANT ORDERS.

To all whom it may concern, Greeting:

Know ye, That we, The Most Eminent Sir —— ——,
General Grand Master aforesaid, by virtue of the powers
and authorities in us invested, Do HEREBY CONSTITUTE
AND APPOINT our trusty and well beloved Sir Knight
—— ——, Grand Master, —— ——, Generalissimo, and
—— ——, Captain-General, of an Encampment of
KNIGHTS TEMPLAR, to be held in ———, in the Commonwealth of Pennsylvania, under the jurisdiction of the
said Grand Encampment, and to be called and known
by the name of ——— Encampment, No. —, with full
and adequate powers to confer the orders of KNIGHTS OF
MALTA, and KNIGHTS OF THE RED CROSS, with continuance to their successors in office and members forever; *Provided Nevertheless,* that the said Sir Knights,
—— ——, Grand Master, —— ——, Generalissimo,
—— ——, Captain-General, and the other officers and
their successors and members, pay due respect to our
said Grand Encampment and the regulations thereof,
otherwise this Charter to be of no force or effect.

Given under our hand and the seal of our Grand Encampment, at the City of Philadelphia, in the Commonwealth of Pennsylvania this — day of ———, in the
year of our Lord, 1855, and of our order, 737.

—— ——, *General Grand Master.*

THE GRAND COMMANDERY OF PENNSYL-
VANIA INSTITUTED APRIL 14, 1854, A. O.
736, A. O. E. P. 57.

THE M. E. Sir William Blackstone Hubbard, Grand
Master of the Grand Encampment of Knights Templar
of the United States, issued a Warrant on the 18th day
of February, 1854, authorizing the formation of a Grand
Commandery for the State of Pennsylvania. The three
Commanderies then in existence, viz: Pittsburg, No. 1,
Jacques De Molay, No. 2, of Washington, and St. Omers,
No. 3, of Uniontown, were authorized to meet and form
said Grand Commandery. Three delegates from each of
said Commanderies assembled in Brownsville, Fayette
County, Pennsylvania, on the *12th day of April*, 1854,
and were organized by calling Sir J. B. Musser, of No. 2,
to the Chair, and appointing Sir John Bierer, of No. 3,
Secretary.

Delegates from No. 1, of Pittsburg.—Sir Knights Wm.
W. Wilson, J. H. Fishell, and Alfred Creigh.

Delegates from No. 2, of Washington. — Sir Knights
Joseph B. Musser, George Passmore, and John Gregg.

Delegates from No. 3, of Uniontown.—Sir Knights John
Bierer, Andrew Patrick, and William Thorndell, Jr.

An Encampment was opened in due form, consisting
of the following officers :

R. E. Sir Joseph B. Musser, G. C.
R. E. Sir W. W. Wilson, G. G.
R. E. Sir George Passmore, G. C. G.

M. E. Sir Alfred Creigh, G. S. W.
M. E. Sir Andrew Patrick, G. J. W.
M. E. Sir John Bierer, G. R.
M. E. Sir John H. Fishell, G. St. B.
M. E. Sir John Gregg, G. Sw. B.
M. E. Sir William Thorndell, G. W.

Sir Knights Wilson, Passmore, and Thorndell, were appointed a Committee to draft a Constitution, which was unanimously adopted, and the *Grand Commandery of Pennsylvania,* subordinate to the General Grand Encampment, declared duly organized.

The Charters granted by the General Grand Encampment of the United States, to the three foregoing Encampments, read as follows:

THE GENERAL GRAND ENCAMPMENT OF THE UNITED STATES OF AMERICA.

To whom it may concern, Greeting :—

Whereas, heretofore to wit: on the — day of ——, in the year of our Lord, one thousand eight hundred and —, a Dispensation was granted to certain Sir Knights to open and hold an Encampment of Knights Templar, and the appendant orders, in the —— of —— in the County of ——, and State of ——, by the name of —— Encampment, No. ——. *And Whereas,* application has been made to this *General Grand Encampment,* for a perpetual *Charter* or *Warrant,* to enable them to continue in all the rights and privileges of a regularly constituted Encampment, and a copy of their By-Laws and of the Minutes of their proceedings having been submitted for our inspection and approval, and no cause adverse to the granting the prayer of said applicants to us appearing—

Now know ye, That *we The General Grand Encamp-*

ment of the United States of America, reposing special confidence and trust in the fidelity, zeal, and masonic ability of the officers and members of the said Encampment, and for the purpose of diffusing the benefits of the Order and promoting the happiness of man, by virtue of the power in US vested, Do by *These Presents*, recognize said Encampment, as regularly constituted and established under the jurisdiction of this General Grand Encampment, with full and adequate powers to confer the several degrees of *Knights of the Red Cross, Knights Templar, and Knights of Malta*, upon such person or persons, possessing the requisite qualifications as they may think proper. And we do also recognize the present officers and members of the said Encampment, with continuance of the said powers and privileges to them and their successors forever. *Provided nevertheless*, That the said officers and members and their successors pay due respect to our said General Grand Encampment, and to the Constitution and Edicts thereof, and in no way remove the ancient Landmarks of our Order. Otherwise this Charter and all things therein contained to be void and of no effect.

Given at the City of ———, in the ——— of ——,
this day of ——, in the year of our Lord, one thousand eight hundred and fifty, and of our Order, seven hundred and thirty-two.

By order of the
General Grand Encampment.

To this form of Charter was appended the signatures of the G. G. Master, D. G. G. Master, G. G. Generalissimo, G. G. Captain-General, and G. G. Recorder.

F *

GRAND COMMANDERY OF PENNSYLVANIA.

GRAND OFFICERS OF THE GRAND COMMANDERY OF PENNSYLVANIA SINCE ITS ORGANIZATION, APRIL 12, 1854.

APRIL 12, 1854, A. O. 736, A. O. E. P. 57.

M. E. Sir William W. Wilson, Gr. Com.
E. Sir Joseph B. Musser, D. G. C.
E. Sir John Bierer, G. G.
E. Sir Andrew Patrick, G. C. G.
Rev. E. Sir Noble Gillespie, G. P.
E. Sir J. W. Hailman, G. S. W.
E. Sir John R. Griffith, G. J. W.
E. Sir George Passmore, G. R.
E. Sir William Thorndell, G. T.
E. Sir William Wolf, G. St. B.
E. Sir Thomas Davage, G. Sw. B.
E. Sir D. Zimmerman, G. W.
E. Sir S. B. Cooper, G. S.

JUNE 14, 1854, A. O. 736, A. O. E. P. 57.

M. E. Sir William W. Wilson, G. C.
E. Sir Joseph B. Musser, D. G. C.
E. Sir John Bierer, G. G.
E. Sir Andrew Patrick, G. C. G.
Rev. E. Sir Noble Gillespie, G. P.
E. Sir J. W. Hailman, G. S. W.
E. Sir William Wolf, G. J. W.
E. Sir George Passmore, G. R.
E. Sir William Thorndell, G. T.
E. Sir John R. Griffith, G. Sw. B.
E. Sir Thomas Davage, G. St. B.
E. Sir D. Zimmerman, G. W.
E. Sir S. B. Cooper, G. S.

JUNE 14, 1855, A. O. 737, A. O. E. P. 58.

M. E. Sir Charles E. Blumenthal, G. C.

E. Sir Alfred Creigh, D. G. C.

E. Sir Andrew Patrick, G. G.

E. Sir J. W. Hailman, G. C. G.

Rev. E. Sir William Johnston, G. P.

E. Sir George Z. Bretz, G. S. W.

E. Sir William Noble, G. J. W.

E. Sir George Passmore, G. R.

E. Sir William Thorndell, G. T.

E. Sir Thomas Davage, G. St. B.

E. Sir D. Zimmerman, G. Sw. B.

E. Sir William McKahan, G. W.

E. Sir S. B. Cooper, G. S.

JUNE 12, 1856, A. O. 738, A. O. E. P. 59.

M. E. Sir William W. Wilson, G. C.

E. Sir Benjamin Parke, D. G. C.

E. Sir Andrew H. Tippin, G. G.

E. Sir H. Hopkins Frisbie, G. C. G.

Rev. E. Sir A. B. Clarke, G. P.

E. Sir John Edwards, G. S. W.

E. Sir Chr. S. Kauffman, G. J. W.

E. Sir Alfred Creigh, G. R.

E. Sir Albert Culbertson, G. T.

E. Sir Alexander Wishart, G. St. B.

E. Sir George W. Patton, G. Sw. B.

E. Sir Daniel K. Albright, G. W.

E. Sir Michael Bender, G. S.

February 12, 1857.—The members of the two Committees appointed by the two Grand Encampments claiming jurisdiction in Pennsylvania, assembled in the Masonic Temple in Philadelphia.

DELEGATES from the Grand Encampment of Pennsylvania under the authority of the Grand Encampment
of the United States: Sir Knight W. W. Wilson, of
Pittsburg; Sir Knight Benjamin Parke, of Harrisburg;
Sir Knight A. H. Tippin, of Pottstown; Sir Knight A.
Culbertson, of Pittsburg; Sir Knight John A. Wright,
of Altoona; Sir Knight Solomon A. Stout, of Pottstown.

DELEGATES from the Grand Encampment claiming
authority of the R. W. Grand Lodge of Pennsylvania:
Sir Knights Francis Blackburne and Anthony E. Stocker,
of Philadelphia; Sir Knight A. Jordan Swartz, of Reading; Sir Knights James Hutchinson, D. C. Skerret, W.
H. Allen, J. L. Hutchinson, of Philadelphia.

Sir Knight William W. Wilson was called to the
Chair, and Sir Knight Francis Blackburne, appointed
Secretary.

The Delegates unanimously *resolved*, That the Representatives of the two Grand Encampments of Pennsylvania agree to form a Constitution for a State Grand
Commandery, under the jurisdiction of the General
Grand Encampment of the United States, which, when
adopted, shall unite these bodies and supersede the
present organizations; provided, that the same meet the
approbation of the Grand Lodge of Pennsylvania, so far
as the Encampments formed under her authority are
concerned.

A Committee consisting of Sir Knights Parke, Wright,
Skerret, and Jeremiah L. Hutchinson, were appointed to
draft a Constitution for the United Grand Commandery.
This Committee subsequently reported a Constitution,
which was unanimously adopted, and prefaced with the
following terms and conditions:

1. The Grand Commandery shall consist of all the
Commanderies now in existence in the State, which Commanderies shall rank in number of their Warrants in

accordance with the date of their respective organizations; provided, that the Warrants now held by each Commandery, shall be continued upon being endorsed by the Grand Masters of both Grand Encampments or Commanderies.

2. The officers of the Grand Commandery until the next election (in June) shall be as follows:

R. E. Sir W. W. Wilson, G. C.

V. E. Sir Benjamin Parke, D. G. C.

E. Sir A. H. Tippin, G. G.

E. Sir H. Hopkins Frisbie, G. C. G.

Rev. E. Sir A. B. Clarke, G. P.

E. Sir John Edwards, G. S. W.

E. Sir Chr. S. Kauffman, G. J. W.

E. Sir Albert Culbertson, G. T.

E. Sir Alfred Creigh, G. R.

E. Sir Alexander Wishart, G. Sw. B.

E. Sir James Hutchinson, G. St. B.

E. Sir Francis Blackburne, G. W.

E. Sir William B. Schneider, G. S.

3. The other Present and Past Grand Officers of both bodies shall retain, and be acknowledged by the titles they now hold, and rank as Past Grand Officers—Provided, that the present members in existence in either body, who are not members by service, shall be honorary members of this Grand Commandery now to be formed.

4. The minutes and property of both bodies shall be handed over and become the property of the Grand Commandery now to be formed; and all unfinished business on the records of either Grand Encampment shall be in order for consideration at the first annual Conclave of this Grand Commandery.

June 1, 1857.—The R. E. Sir William W. Wilson

12

issued his Proclamation as Grand Commander, that he had received official notice from the Subordinate Commanderies of their ratification of the proceedings held and the Constitution agreed upon by said Delegates—Whereupon, in accordance with the first term or condition, he numbered the Subordinate Commanderies according to the date of their respective organizations as follows:

No. 1, *St. John's*,* Philadelphia, organized in 1819.
No. 2, Pittsburg, Pittsburg, organized in 1847.
No. 3, *Philadelphia*, Philadelphia, organized in 1849.
No. 4, Jacques De Molay, Washington, organized in 1849.
No. 5, Hubbard, Waynesburg, organized in 1851.
No. 6, *Union*, Philadelphia, organized in 1851.
No. 7, St. Omers, Uniontown, organized in 1853.
No. 8, St. John's, Carlisle, organized in 1854.
No. 9, *De Molay*, Reading, organized in 1854.
No. 10, Blumenthal, Altoona, organized in 1855.
No. 11, Parke, Harrisburg, organized in 1855.
No. 12, Crusade, Bloomsburg, organized in 1856.
No. 13, Columbia, Lancaster, organized in 1856.
No. 14, Palestine, Carbondale, organized in 1856.
No. 15, Jerusalem, Pottstown, organized in 1856.

At the Annual Communication of the Grand Commandery, held June 22, 1857, Nos. 1, 2, 3, and 4 were changed as follows:

No. 1, Pittsburg, organized in 1847.
No. 2, Jacques De Molay, organized in 1849.
No. 3, Philadelphia, organized in 1849.
No. 4, St. John's, organized in 1819.

---

* Those in italics were formerly under the jurisdiction of the Grand Lodge.

Blumenthal Commandery No. 10, was also changed to MOUNTAIN Commandery.

June 22, 1858.—By Resolution, No. 3 became No. 2, and No. 2 was changed to No. 3.

June 20, 1857.—M. E. Sir William Blackstone Hubbard issued his Proclamation, announcing "that no disunion amongst Worthy Templars exists in Pennsylvania, but that all the Subordinate Commanderies, and all the members thereof are in courteous, fraternal and Knightly fellowship with each other, and all in common owing allegiance to the GRAND ENCAMPMENT of the United States of America—that from shore to shore of the Atlantic and Pacific oceans our union is perfect—one and indivisible.

JUNE 22, 1857, A. O. 739, A. O. E. P. 60.

R. E. Sir Benjamin Parke, G. C.
V. E. Sir A. Jordan Swartz, D. G. C.
E. Sir John L. Gore, G. G.
E. Sir Christian Frederick Knapp, G. C. G.
Rev. E. Sir O. H. Tiffany, G. P.
E. Sir William E. Harpur, G. S. W.
E. Sir George W. Patton, G. J. W.
E. Sir Albert Culbertson, G. T.
E. Sir Alfred Creigh, G. R.
E. Sir Francis R. Blackburne, G. St. B.
E. Sir George R. Clarke, G. Sw. B.
E. Sir Alexander Wishart, G. W.
E. Sir W. B. Schneider, G. S.

JUNE 24, 1858, A. O. 740, A. O. E. P. 61.

R. E. Sir A. Jordan Swartz, G. C.
V. E. Sir William H. Allen, D. G. C.
E. Sir Christian Frederick Knapp, G. G.

E. Sir John A. Wright, G. C. G.

Rev. E. Sir Beverly R. Waugh, G. P.

E. Sir Jeremiah L. Hutchinson, G. S. W.

E. Sir Alexander Wishart, G. J. W.

E. Sir Albert Culbertson, G. T.

E. Sir Alfred Creigh, G. R.

E. Sir George R. Clarke, G. St. B.

E. Sir George H. Bull, G. Sw. B.

E. Sir William G. Warden, G. W.

E. Sir H. L. Smith, G. S.

JUNE 23, 1859, A. O. 741, A. O. E. P. 62.

R. E. Sir William Henry Allen, G. C.

V. E. Sir Christian Frederick Knapp, D. G. C.

E. Sir John A. Wright, G. G.

E. Sir Jeremiah L. Hutchinson, G. C. G.

Rev. E. Sir Beverly R. Waugh, G. P.

E. Sir Alexander Wishart, G. S. W.

E. Sir Edmund H. Turner, G. J. W.

E. Sir Albert Culbertson, G. T.

E. Sir Alfred Creigh, G. R.

E. Sir George R. Clarke, G. St. B.

E. Sir George H. Bull, G. Sw. B.

E. Sir William G. Warden, G. W.

E. Sir Stephen Orth, G. S.

JUNE 22, 1860, A. O. 742, A. O. E. P. 63.

R. E. Sir Christian Frederick Knapp, G. C.

V. E. Sir John A. Wright, D. G. C.

E. Sir Jeremiah L. Hutchinson, G. G.

E. Sir Edmund H. Turner, G. C. G.

Rev. E. Sir Milton C. Lightner, G. P.

E. Sir William H. Strickland, G. S. W.

E. Sir George R. Clarke, G. J. W.

E. Sir Albert Culbertson, G. T.
E. Sir Alfred Creigh, G. R.
E. Sir Herbert Thomas, G. St. B.
E. Sir Richard Coulter, G. Sw. B.
E. Sir Henry R. Hawman, G. W.
E. Sir J. M. Scott, G. S.

JUNE 12, 1861, A. O. 743, A. O. E. P. 64.

R. E. Sir John A. Wright, G. C.
V. E. Sir Edmund H. Turner, D. G. C.
E. Sir Henry R. Hawman, G. G.
E. Sir H. D. Lowe, G. C. G.
Rev. E. Sir William H. Locke, G. P.
E. Sir E. C. Smead, G. S. W.
E. Sir George B. Schall, G. J. W.
E. Sir Albert Culbertson, G. T.
E. Sir Alfred Creigh, G. R.
E. Sir Samuel McAllister, G. St. B.
E. Sir Sidney Hayden, G. Sw. B.
E. Sir Samuel B. Cooper, G. W.
E. Sir J. Benedict, G. S.

JUNE 11, 1862, A. O. 744, A. O. E. P. 65.

R. E. Sir Edmund H. Turner, G. C.
V. E. Sir Jeremiah L. Hutchinson, D. G. C.
E. Sir William H. Strickland, G. G.
E. Sir William Chatland, G. C. G. ·
Rev. E. Sir J. Clark Haguey, G. P.
E. Sir H. Stanley Goodwin, G. S. W.
E. Sir Charles A. Bannvart, G. J. W.
E. Sir Isaac Whittier, G. T.
E. Sir Alfred Creigh, G. R.
E. Sir William E. Lilly, G. St. B.
E. Sir George E. Fox, G. Sw. B.

E. Sir William J. Long, G. W.
E. Sir William R. Terry, G. S.

JUNE 10, 1863, A. O. 745, A. O. E. P. 66.

R. E. Sir H. Stanley Goodwin, G. C.
V. E. Sir Isaac Whittier, D. G. C.
E. Sir Robert Pitcairn, G. G.
E. Sir William Chatland, G. C. G.
Rev. E. Sir H. M. Johnson, G. P.
E. Sir Samuel E. Bilger, G. S. W.
E. Sir Joseph Godfrey, G. J. W.
E. Sir John Edwards, G. T.
E. Sir Alfred Creigh, G. R.
E. Sir George E. Fox, G. St. B.
E. Sir Ernest Knapp, G. Sw. B.
E. Sir Z. P. Bierer, G. W.
E. Sir John Hardy, G. S.

JUNE 14, 1864, A. O. 746, A. O. E. P. 67.

R. E. Sir H. Stanley Goodwin, G. C.
V. E. Sir William H. Strickland, D. G. C.
E. Sir Robert Pitcairn, G. G.
E. Sir Charles A. Bannvart, G. C. G.
E. Sir Charles M. Howell, G. P.
E. Sir Ephraim Cornman, G. S. W.
E. Sir John Vallerchamp, G. J. W.
E. Sir Isaac Whittier, G. T.
E. Sir Alfred Creigh, G. R.
E. Sir George E. Fox, G. St. B.
E. Sir Ernest Knapp, G. Sw. B.
E. Sir Z. P. Bierer, G. W.
E. Sir Charles C. Mason, G. S.

JUNE 14, 1865, A. O. 747, A. O. E. P. 68.

R. E. Sir William H. Strickland, G. C.
V. E. Sir Robert Pitcairn, D. G. C.
E. Sir Charles A. Bannvart, G. G.
E. Sir John Vallerchamp, G. C. G.
Rev. E. Sir J. R. Dimm, G. P.
E. Sir James H. Hopkins, G. S. W.
E. Sir H. B. McKean, G. J. W.
E. Sir R. A. O. Kerr, G. T.
E. Sir Alfred Creigh, G. R.
E. Sir Ernest Knapp, G. St. B.
E. Sir Z. P. Bierer, G. Sw. B.
E. Sir Fitz James Evans, G. W.
E. Sir Jacob Westhœffer, G. S.

JUNE 13, 1866, A. O. 748, A. O. E. P. 69.

R. E. Sir Robert Pitcairn, G. C.
V. E. Sir Jeremiah L. Hutchinson, D. G. C.
E. Sir Charles A. Bannvart, G. G.
E. Sir John Vallerchamp, G. C. G.
Rev. E. Sir J. R. Dimm, G. P.
E. Sir James H. Hopkins, G. S. W.
E. Sir H. B. McKean, G. J. W.
E. Sir R. A. O. Kerr, G. T.
E. Sir Alfred Creigh, G. R.
E. Sir Ernest Knapp, G. St. B.
E. Sir Z. P. Bierer, G. Sw. B.
E. Sir Fitz James Evans, G. W.
E. Sir C. F. Porter, G. S.

The Grand Commandery of Pennsylvania adopted the
following form for a Charter for their Subordinates:

THE GRAND COMMANDERY OF THE STATE OF
PENNSYLVANIA, SUBORDINATE TO THE GRAND
ENCAMPMENT OF KNIGHTS TEMPLAR OF THE
UNITED STATES OF AMERICA.

To whom it may concern, Greeting:—

Whereas, heretofore, to wit: On the —— day of ——
in the year of our Lord, one thousand eight hundred and
—— a Dispensation was granted to certain Sir Knights
to open and hold a *Commandery of Knights Templar*, and
the Appendant Orders in the —— of —— in the County
of —— and State of Pennsylvania, by the name of ——
Commandery No. ——.

And whereas, Application has been made to this Grand
Commandery for a perpetual CHARTER or WARRANT to
enable them to continue in all the rights and privileges
of a regularly constituted Commandery, and a copy of
their By Laws and of the Minutes of their Proceedings
having been submitted for our inspection and approval,
and no cause adverse to granting the prayer of said
applicants to Us appearing—

Now know ye, That *We, the Grand Commandery of the
State of Pennsylvania,* United States of America, reposing
special confidence and trust in the fidelity, zeal, and
Masonic ability of the Officers and Members of the said
Commandery, and for the purpose of diffusing the benefit
of the Order and promoting the happiness of man, by
virtue of the power in Us vested, *Do, by these presents,*
recognize said COMMANDERY, as regularly constituted
and established under the jurisdiction of this *Grand
Commandery,* with full powers to confer the several
Orders of *Knights of the Red Cross, Knights Templar,
and Knights of Malta,* upon such person or persons, possessing the requisite qualifications, as they may think
proper, and we do also recognize the present Officers and
Members of the said Commandery with continuance of

the said powers and privileges to them and their successors forever: *Provided, nevertheless,* That the said Officers and Members and their successors pay due respect to our said Grand Commandery, and to the Constitution and Edicts thereof, and in no way remove the ancient landmarks of the Order, otherwise this Charter and all things therein contained, to be void and of no effect.

Given at the —— of —— in the State of Pennsylvania, this —— day of ——, in the year of our Lord, 18—, and of our Order 74.

By order of the

Grand Commandery of the State of Pennsylvania.

NOTE.—All the elected and appointed officers of the Grand Commandery are required to sign the Charter, with the seal thereto attached. The names of the original officers and petitioners are also written upon the Charter.

THE M. E. Sir Wm. B. Hubbard, G. G. Captain-
General of the General Grand Encampment of Knights
Templar for the United States of America in his report
to the General Grand Body at its *tenth* meeting held in
the City of Columbus, Ohio, in September, 1847, says:

On the 13th of May last, I received an application
from Sir Knights Alexander McCammon, William W.
Wilson, James S. Hoon, Samuel McKinley, Charles W.
Ricketson, John Y. C. Bell, John McTiernan, George R.
White, Rev. George S. Holmes, and Francis Bailey, at
Pittsburg, Pennsylvania, praying for authority to establish an Encampment in the City of Pittsburg, subordinate to the General Grand Encampment of the United
States, which application was accompanied by a copy
from the records of Wheeling Encampment, highly ap-
proving of the application, and vouching for the moral
and Masonic qualifications of the several applicants; and
having full confidence in the opinion and judgment of
our illustrious Knights composing the Encampment at
Wheeling, and also confiding in the thus avouched high
character of the Sir Knights at Pittsburg, immediately
on the receipt of the usual fee required by our Constitution, I made out and issued to them my Warrant of
Dispensation authorizing the establishment at Pittsburg
of a COUNCIL OF RED CROSS KNIGHTS and an ENCAMP-
MENT, as prayed for in their petition. From the information I have received, I entertain the belief that this

142

Encampment will be found well worthy of the high honors confided to it.

Sir Knight Gould, from the Committee on Charter and New Encampments, on the 16th of September, 1847, reported favorable, whereupon a charter was issued to PITTSBURG COMMANDERY, No. 1.

OFFICERS OF PITTSBURG COMMANDERY, No. 1, FROM ITS ORGANIZATION TO MARCH, 1866.

MAY 13, 1847, A. O. 729, A. O. E. P. 50.

Sir Alexander McCammon, E. C.
Sir William W. Wilson, G.
Sir James S. Hoon, C. G.
Sir Samuel McKinley, P.
Sir Daniel Zimmerman, S. W.
Sir James Stevens, J. W.
Sir Thomas Sargeant, T.
Sir A. G. Reinhart, R.
Sir Samuel Eakins, St. B.
Sir Thomas W. Wright, Sw. B.
Sir Chas. W. Ricketson, W.
Sir Samuel B. Cooper, S.

DECEMBER 1, 1847, A. O. 729, A. O. E. P. 50.

Sir Alexander McCammon, E. C.
Sir William W. Wilson, G.
Sir James S. Hoon, C. G.
Sir Samuel McKinley, P.
Sir Daniel Zimmerman, S. W.
Sir James Stevens, J. W.
Sir Thomas Sargeant, T.
Sir A. G. Reinhart, R.
Sir Samuel Eakins, St. B.
Sir Thomas W. Wright, Sw. B.

Sir Philip Ross, W.
Sir Samuel B. Cooper, S.

DECEMBER 6, 1848, A. O. 730, A. O. E. P. 51.

Sir Alexander McCammon, E. C.
Sir William W. Wilson, G.
Sir James S. Hoon, C. G.
Sir James W. Hailman, P.
Sir Daniel Zimmerman, S. W.
Sir James Stevens, J. W.
Sir Thompson H. Douglass, T.
Sir Thomas W. Wright, R.
Sir William Scott, St. B.
Sir Samuel McKinley, Sw. B.
Sir H. J. Rogers, W.
Sir Samuel B. Cooper, S.

DECEMBER 5, 1849, A, O. 731, A. O. E. P. 52.

Sir William W. Wilson, E. C.
Sir James S. Hoon, G.
Sir James W. Hailman, C. G.
Sir John Sargeant, P.
Sir Daniel Zimmerman, S. W.
Sir James Stevens, J. W.
Sir Thompson H. Douglass, T.
Sir Samuel McKinley, R.
Sir William Scott, St. B.
Sir R. A. Bausman, Sw. B.
Sir Philip Ross, W.
Sir Samuel B. Cooper, S.

DECEMBER 4, 1850, A. O. 732, A. O. E. P. 53

Sir William W. Wilson, E. C.
Sir James Stevens, G.

Sir Daniel Zimmerman, C. G.
Rev. Sir William Johnston, P.
Sir A. G. Reinhart, S. W.
Sir H. N. Spear, J. W.
Sir Thompson H. Douglass, T.
Sir Samuel McKinley, R.
Sir William Scott, St. B.
Sir James M. Stokeley, Sw. B.
Sir Thomas Davage, W.
Sir Samuel B. Cooper, S.

DECEMBER 3, 1851, A. O. 733, A. O. E. P. 54.

Sir William W. Wilson, E. C.
Sir James S. Hoon, G.
Sir Daniel Zimmerman, C. G.
Rev. Sir William Johnston, P.
Sir H. N. Spear, S. W.
Sir Thomas Davage, J. W.
Sir Alexander Speer, T.
Sir Samuel Eakins, R.
Sir S. B. French, St. B.
Sir William Noble, Sw. B.
Sir Albert Culbertson, W.
Sir Samuel B. Cooper, S.

DECEMBER 14, 1852, A. O. 734, A. O. E. P. 55.

Sir William W. Wilson, E. C.
Sir James S. Hoon, G.
Sir H. N. Speer, C. G.
Rev. Sir William Johnston, P.
Sir Thomas Davage, S. W.
Sir Albert Culbertson, J. W.
Sir Daniel Zimmerman, T.
Sir Samuel McKinley, R.

Sir John M. Scott, St. B.
Sir A. G. Reinhart, Sw. B.
Sir James Rhodes, W.
Sir Samuel B. Cooper, S.

DECEMBER 13, 1853, A. O. 735, A. O. E. P. 56.

Sir William W. Wilson, E. C.
Sir James W. Hailman, G.
Sir Thomas Davage, C. G.
Rev. Sir William Johnston, P.
Sir Albert Culbertson, S. W.
Sir James Rhodes, J. W.
Sir George Armor, T.
Sir J. H. Fishell, R.
Sir J. Stuckrath, St. B.
Sir William P. Thomson, Sw. B.
Sir Daniel Zimmerman, W.
Sir Samuel B. Cooper, S.

DECEMBER 12, 1854, A. O. 736, A. O. E. P. 57.

Sir William W. Wilson, E. C.
Sir James W. Hailman, G.
Sir Thomas Davage, C. G.
Rev. Sir William Johnston, P.
Sir Albert Culbertson, S. W.
Sir James Rhodes, J. W.
Sir George Armor, T.
Sir J. H. Fishell, R.
Sir W. P. Thomson, St. B.
Sir J. Stuckrath, Sw. B.
Sir Daniel Zimmerman, W.
Sir Samuel B. Cooper, S.

APRIL 10, 1855, A. O. 737, A. O. E. P. 58.

Sir William W. Wilson, E. C.
Sir Thomas Davage, G.
Sir William Noble, C. G.
Rev. Sir William Johnston, P.
Sir James Rhodes, S. W.
Sir William P. Thomson, J. W.
Sir Daniel Zimmerman, T.
Sir Thomas W. Wright, R.
Sir J. R. Welden, St. B.
Sir Henry Murphy, Sw. B.
Sir John M. Scott, W.
Sir Samuel B. Cooper, S.

APRIL 8, 1856, A. O. 738, A. O. E. P. 59.

Sir Thomas Davage, E. C.
Sir William Noble, G.
Sir Albert Culbertson, C. G.
Rev. Sir Samuel E. Babcock, P.
Sir William P. Thomson, S. W.
Sir Samuel B. Cooper, J. W.
Sir C. W. Batchelor, T.
Sir James B. Cooper, R.
Sir William Scott, St. B.
Sir Thomas W. Wright, Sw. B.
Sir Daniel Zimmerman, W.
Sir John M. Scott, S.

MAY 13, 1857, A. O. 739, A. O. E. P. 60.

Sir William Noble, E. C.
Sir Albert Culbertson, G.
Sir William P. Thomson, C. G.
Rev. Sir William Johnston, P.
Sir Samuel B. Cooper, S. W.

Sir William G. Warden, J. W.
Sir Isaac Whittier, T.
Sir Thomas W. Wright, R.
Sir George Armor, St. B.
Sir J. R. Welden, Sw. B.
Sir George Neeld, W.
Sir John M. Scott, S.

MAY 12, 1858, A. O. 740, A. O. E. P. 61.

Sir William P. Thomson, E. C.
Sir Samuel B. Cooper, G.
Sir William G. Warden, C. G.
Rev. Sir William Johnston, P.
Sir Isaac Whittier, S. W.
Sir Thomas Davage, J. W.
Sir J. R. Welden, T.
Sir Thomas W. Wright, R.
Sir J. L. Snyder, St. B.
Sir J. Stuckrath, Sw. B.
Sir John M. Scott, W.
Sir F. W. Bates, S.

MARCH 9, 1859, A. O. 741, A. O. E. P. 62.

Sir William P. Thomson, E. C.
Sir Samuel B. Cooper, G.
Sir William G. Warden, C. G.
Sir Thomas Davage, P.
Sir Isaac Whittier, S. W.
Sir John M. Scott, J. W.
Sir J. R. Welden, T.
Sir Thomas W. Wright, R.
Sir John Laughlin, St. B.
Sir J. L. Snyder, Sw. B.
Sir Charles A. Colton, W.
Sir F. W. Bates, S.

MARCH 13, 1860, A. O. 742, A. O. E. P. 63.

Sir Samuel B. Cooper, E. C.
Sir Isaac Whittier, G.
Sir John M. Scott, C. G.
Sir Thomas Davage, P.
Sir Charles A. Colton, S. W.
Sir Thomas Palmer, J. W.
Sir J. R. Welden, T.
Sir Thomas W. Wright, R.
Sir Isaac Sawyer, St. B.
Sir William Scott, Sw. B.
Sir Joseph Graff, W.
Sir F. W. Bates, S.

MARCH 12, 1861, A. O. 743, A. O. E. P. 64.

Sir Isaac Whittier, E. C.
Sir John M. Scott, G.
Sir Charles A. Colton, C. G.
Sir Thomas E. Rose, P.
Sir Thomas Palmer, S. W.
Sir Joseph Graff, J. W.
Sir J. R. Welden, T.
Sir Thomas W. Wright, R.
Sir S. T. Northam, St. B.
Sir B. R. Harbours, Sw. B.
Sir Charles W. Rudyard, W.
Sir F. W. Bates, S.

MARCH 11, 1862, A. O. 744, A. O. E. P. 65.

Sir Isaac Whittier, E. C.
Sir John M. Scott, G.
Sir Thomas Palmer, C. G.
Sir Thomas Davage, P.
Sir Joseph Graff, S. W.

13 *

Sir Charles W. Rudyard, J. W.
Sir Charles A. Colton, T.
Sir Thomas W. Wright, R.
Sir B. R. Harbours, St. B.
Sir John McClean, Sw. B.
Sir Stewart Dickson, W.
Sir Samuel B. Cooper, S.

MARCH 10, 1863, A. O. 745, A. O. E. P. 66.

Sir Joseph Graff, E. C.
Sir Charles W. Rudyard, G.
Sir James H. Hopkins, C. G.
Sir Isaac Whittier, P.
Sir Stewart Dickson, S. W.
Sir Geter C. Shidle, J. W.
Sir Charles A. Colton, T.
Sir Thomas W. Wright, R.
Sir J. P. Henderson, St. B.
Sir R. J. Stoney, Sw. B.
Sir A. V. Scott, W.
Sir J. M. Scott, S.

MARCH 8, 1864, A. O. 746, A. O. E. P. 67.

Sir John M. Scott, E. C.
Sir James H. Hopkins, G.
Sir Stewart Dickson, C. G.
Sir Isaac Whittier, P.
Sir Geter C. Shidle, S. W.
Sir John Evans, J. W.
Sir Charles A. Colton, T.
Sir Thomas W. Wright, R.
Sir D. W. C. Carroll, St. B.
Sir C. F. Porter, Sw. B.
Sir A. V. Scott, W.
Sir Samuel B. Cooper, S.

MARCH 14, 1865, A. O. 747, A. O. E. P. 66.

Sir Thomas Palmer, E. C.
Sir James H. Hopkins, G.
Sir Geter C. Shidle, C. G.
Sir Isaac Whittier, P.
Sir John Evans, S. W.
Sir D. W. C. Carroll, J. W.
Sir Charles A. Colton, T.
Sir Thomas W. Wright, R.
Sir Robert Fairman, St. B.
Sir John Dunwoody, Sw. B.
Sir Charles F. Porter, W.
Sir John M. Scott, S.

MARCH 13, 1866, A. O. 748, A. O. E. P. 69.

Sir James H. Hopkins, E. C.
Sir Geter C. Shidle, G.
Sir John Evans, C. G.
Sir Isaac Whittier, P.
Sir D. W. C. Carroll, S. W.
Sir Joseph L. Lytle, J. W.
Sir Charles A. Colton, T.
Sir Thomas W. Wright, R.
Sir William Little, St. B.
Sir Lewis McIntosh, Sw. B.
Sir Edwin H. Nevin, W.
Sir Charles F. Porter, S.

MEMBERS.

NAME.	DATE OF KNIGHTING.
Armor, George,	December 13, 1847.
Aiken, J. J.,	November 2, 1853.
Anderson, William J.,	June 13, 1859.
Anderson, Alexander,	September 11, 1861.
Agnew, John,	November 18, 1861.
Allston, R. S.,	March 27, 1865.

NAME.	DATE OF KNIGHTING.
Alden, George E.,	September 11, 1866.
Bailey, Francis, (of Phila. No. 1),	
Charter Member,	March 24, 1847.
Babcock, Rev. Samuel E., (No. 2),	
Charter Member,	March 24, 1847.
Bell, John T. C., Ch. Mem.,	March 24, 1847.
Biddle, George W.,	June 22, 1847.
Bausman, R. A.,	August 26, 1847.
Bailey, Thomas J.,	March 21, 1848.
Birminghman, John,	May 10, 1848.
Boyle, Robert,	October 23, 1849.
Boyle, David,	July 12, 1850.
Black, Samuel W.,	March 17, 1851.
Borie, David,	October 1, 1851.
Blackmore, James,	June 14, 1853.
Batchelor, Charles W.,	January 9, 1855.
Brady, Evans R.,	April 24, 1860.
Blinkhorn, George,	July 11, 1862.
Bowman, C.,	August 4, 1864.
Bates, Francis W.,	January 20, 1863.
Blackstock, George M.,	November 13, 1865.
Bradley, J. A.,	February 13, 1866.
Broome, Isaac,	September 11, 1866.
Bown, James,	September 11, 1866.
Cooper, Samuel B.,	June 21, 1847.
Clemner, John,	June 19, 1848.
Creigh, Alfred, (No. 2),	April 2, 1849.
Culbertson, Albert,	April 2, 1851.
Culmer, Stephen,	February 8, 1853.
Campbell, Hugh,	October 18, 1853.
Conner, Cornelius,	December 13, 1854.
Cooper, James B.,	July 11, 1855.
Courtney, D. N.,	November 11, 1855.
Coulter, Richard,	May 11, 1858.

NAME.	DATE OF KNIGHTING.
Colton, Charles C.,	November 22, 1858.
Carroll, D. W. C.,	February 9, 1863.
Cluley, William H.,	September 26, 1864.
Christy, George H.,	October 12, 1864.
Costemagna, Thomas,	March 27, 1865.
Crisswell, William,	April 17, 1865.
Church, Pearson,	October 16, 1865.
Clow, J. B.,	October 16, 1865.
Cullen, Caleb,	September 11, 1866.
Douglass, Thompson H.,	April 19, 1848.
Davage, Thomas,	May 7, 1850.
Douglass, A. A.,	April 2, 1851.
Dain, Thomas,	October 22, 1860.
Dickson, Stewart,	June 7, 1861.
Dunwoody, John,	February 9, 1863.
Dick, Samuel B.,	October 16, 1865.
Dick, Jesse M.,	October 16, 1865.
Dickson, Joseph C.,	July 18, 1866.
Eakens, Samuel, (Keystone),	August 20, 1847.
Evans, John,	September 5, 1859.
Earsman, William A.,	September 26, 1864.
Estep, D. P.,	December 11, 1866.
Eichbaum, Joseph,	October 22, 1864.
Fulton, Andrew,	June 1, 1848.
French, S. B.,	August 20, 1850.
Frazier, J. N.,	April 12, 1853.
Fishell, J. H.,	February 14, 1854.
Florence, W. J.,	June 13, 1854.
Foster, J. Herron,	April 20, 1860.
Fairman, Robert,	January 13, 1863.
Foster, F. H.,	May 31, 1866.
Gummert, Christian P., (No. 2),	May 12, 1848.
Gov. Geary, John W., (No. 18),	October 2, 1848.
Glass, John P.,	January 10, 1851.

G *

NAME.	DATE OF KNIGHTING.
Graff, Joseph,	November 8, 1859.
Gillespie, J. J.,	June 12, 1861.
Glass, George,	March 31, 1863.
Holmes, Rev. George S., (Wheeling, No. 1), Ch. Mem.,	May 16, 1839.
Hoon, James S., (Wheeling, No. 1), Ch. Mem.,	March 24, 1847.
Hailman, James W.,	June 22, 1847.
Heastings, E. H.,	September 23, 1847.
Harrop, Rev. Joseph,	April 24, 1848.
Hazen, Thomas J., (No. 2),	May 4, 1848.
Hill, Isaiah, (No. 2),	May 4, 1849.
Huskins, Richard, (No. 7),	July 16, 1850.
Herd, Charles T.,	May 11, 1852.
Harbours, B. R.,	November 8, 1859.
Hamilton, William,	May 8, 1860.
Hopkins, James H.,	May 2, 1862.
Henderson, John P.,	November 11, 1862.
Humphrey, Henry,	February 10, 1856.
Hellerman, J. H.,	May 24, 1864.
Hamilton, William,	April 17, 1865.
Hoover, C. M.,	February 13, 1866.
Hoover, A. M.,	May 31, 1866.
Hay, M. C.,	May 31, 1866.
Hamilton, C. O.,	December 11, 1866.
Irwin, A.,	November 29, 1851.
Johnston, Rev. Wm.,	April 28, 1848.
Jeffries, J. W., (K. R. C.),	May 7, 1851.
Jackson, Conrad F.,	June 13, 1855.
Jones, F. J.,	April 11, 1860.
Jones, George W.,	June 10, 1862.
Jones, Oliver B.,	October 12, 1864.
Kinzey, Zebulon,	May 24, 1848.
Kerr, James, Jr.,	February 19, 1850.

NAME.	DATE OF KNIGHTING.
Kennedy, Milton,	April 23, 1850.
Kerr, Joseph W.,	May 27, 1852.
Kennedy, D. H.,	November 21, 1855.
Kennedy, Seth T.,	December 18, 1861.
Knox, John D.,	March 12, 1863.
Lafferty, William L., (No. 2),	May 12, 1848.
Logan, Joshua,	September 22, 1851.
Lyon, M. S.,	November 12, 1851.
Loomis, C. O.,	February 21, 1853.
Laughlin, John,	October 13, 1857.
Locke, Rev. W. H., (No. 18),	September 26, 1859.
Lytle, Joseph L.,	May 2, 1862.
Lowry, James, Jr.,	November 10, 1863.
Little, William,	January 9, 1866.
Lang, William F.,	April 18, 1866.
Lashels, Theodore B.,	May 31, 1866.
McCammon, Alexander, Charter Member,	March 24, 1847.
McKinley, Samuel, (Wheeling, No. 1), Ch. Mem.,	March 24, 1847.
McTiernan, John, Ch. Mem.,	March 24, 1847.
McElroy, Rev. Geo. B., (No. 2),	May 23, 1849.
Maple, Robert, (No. 5),	July 4, 1850.
Morrison, James,	July 13, 1852.
Miller, John H.,	May 25, 1853.
Murphy, Henry,	May 12, 1854.
McClean, John,	June 8, 1861.
McIntosh, Lewis,	March 10, 1863.
Marshal, John,	April 17, 1864.
McClelland, Thomas A.,	October 12, 1864.
McGinley, M.,	January 9, 1866.
McClaren, John,	February 13, 1866.
Meredith, J. A.,	April 18, 1866.
Mawhinney, James,	September 11, 1866.

NAME.	DATE OF KNIGHTING.
McClelland, J. Bruce,	December 11, 1866.
Noble, William,	May 10, 1848.
Neeld, George,	January 13, 1857.
Nevin, Edwin H.,	March 31, 1863.
Neeper, Wm. B.,	November 13, 1865.
Northam, Stephen T., (No. 18),	January 5, 1859.
Owens, William,	April 18, 1866.
Parkinson, John A.,	December 1, 1847.
Power, Thos., Jr.,	October 24, 1851.
Palmer, Thomas,	May 10, 1859.
Porter, Charles F.,	February 9, 1863.
Phillips, William,	March 27, 1865.
Pettit, A. J.,	May 8, 1866.
Porter, G. C.,	May 31, 1866.
Power, A. L.,	May 31, 1866.
Petrie, James, Jr.,	July 18, 1866.
Petticord, John,	September 11, 1866.
Ricketson, Charles W., (Wheeling, No. 1), Char. Mem.,	March 24, 1847.
Ross, Philip,	July 14, 1847.
Reinhart, A. G.,	July 19, 1847.
Rogers, H. J.,	August 16, 1847.
Reed, A. L.,	November 7, 1849.
Rossen, James,	April 22, 1850.
Rhodes, James,	March 17, 1851.
Rutter, M. A.,	November 8, 1853.
Reese, Jacob,	April 12, 1859.
Rudyard, Charles W.,	September 11, 1860.
Rose, Thomas E.,	October 1, 1860.
Rupp, Jesse R.,	September 6, 1865.
Rutan, Henry D.,	October 16, 1865.
Rush, John,	March 26, 1866.
Roselle, Dennis E.,	September 11, 1866.
Reymer, J. S.,	December 11, 1866

NAME.	DATE OF KNIGHTING.
Stevens, James,	June 22, 1847.
Stine, William S.,	September 7, 1847.
Sargeant, John,	October 6, 1847.
Stokely, James M., (No. 3),	December 20, 1847.
Scott, William,	March 30, 1848.
Smythers, D. Y.,	January 20, 1849.
Snowden, John,	November 20, 1849.
Sargeant, Thomas,	August 20, 1847.
Stuckrath, Jacob,	February 29, 1849.
Speer, H. N.,	July 3, 1850.
Speer, Alexander,	February 21, 1851.
Scott, Asa,	November 22, 1851.
Snowden, Samuel S.,	May 12, 1852.
Scott, John M.,	May 27, 1852.
Smith, L. W.,	December 11, 1855.
Snyder, J. L.,	December 9, 1857.
Sawyer, Isaac,	December 11, 1858.
Shidle, Geter C.,	May 13, 1862.
Scott, Alexander V.,	May 19, 1862.
Stoney, R. J.,	May 26, 1862.
Shurick, N. M.,	January 20, 1863.
Steele, J. E.,	August 4, 1864.
Shelmadine, W. D.,	September 6, 1865.
Schanlan, J. A.,	March 27, 1865.
Sellars, W. H.,	May 13, 1865.
Speking, W. D.,	May 31, 1866.
Sampson, H.,	February 13, 1866.
Shattuck, Frederick,	May 31, 1866.
Spiking, William D.,	May 31, 1866.
Snowden, George R.,	July 18, 1866.
Torbett, James D.,	September 30, 1847.
Thorndell, William,	February 19, 1850.
Thompson, James,	February 3, 1851.
Thomson, William P.,	September 22, 1851.

14

NAME.	DATE OF KNIGHTING.
Taggart, John J.,	March 12, 1861.
Thomas, S. J.,	May 31, 1866.
Truesdale, N.,	May 31, 1866.
Wilson, Wm. W., (Wheeling, No. 1), Charter Member,	March 24, 1847.
White, George R., Charter Mem.,	March 24, 1847.
Wright, Thomas W.,	November 12, 1847.
Wood, W. D.,	February 7, 1848.
Wolf, C. H., (Keystone),	October 29, 1849.
Welden, J. R.,	August 23, 1850.
Whittier, Isaac,	June 11, 1856.
Warden, William G.,	August 12, 1856.
Wright, Robert M.,	September 24, 1860.
Williams, Rev. A. G.,	June 7, 1861.
Wood, Charles A.,	September 11, 1866.
Walt, David M.,	September 11, 1866.
Zimmerman, Daniel,	June 22, 1847.

THIS Commandery when originally established, was known as No. 5, and with St. John's No. 4, and Union No. 6, of Philadelphia, and De Molay, of Reading, united together to constitute the Grand Encampment of Knights Templar, under the authority of the R. W. Grand Lodge of Pennsylvania. After the union of the two Grand Encampments of this State, it was changed to No. 3, and subsequently by resolution of the present Grand Commandery, it became No. 2. From the records, we learn, that on the 9th day of May, 1849, Sir Knights Anthony E. Stocker, Thomas F. Betton, David C. Skerret, William H. Klapp, George H. Hart, W. W. Downing, Robert P. King, Samuel Badger, H. Weir Workman, Coleman Fisher, Jr., and Samuel B. Ashmead, anxious for the reorganization of the Grand Encampment of Pennsylvania, and believing that the formation of a new Encampment of Knights Templar in Philadelphia would promote that object, resigned their membership in St. John's No. 4.

Franklin Lodge, No. 134, of Philadelphia, granted the sanction of its Warrant to open Encampment No. 5. The Grand Lodge having approved of the action of Franklin Lodge; Union Lodge 121, and Lodge 227, at Reading, created Nos. 6 and 7 in the same way. We extract the following history from the By Laws of No. 2,

*To William H. Klapp, Anthony E. Stocker, Robert
P. King, Thomas F. Betton, William W. Downing, H. Weir Workman, George H. Hart, Samuel
Badger, David C. Skerret, Samuel B. Ashmead,
and Coleman Fisher, Jr.*

At a Special Meeting of FRANKLIN LODGE, No. 134,
held at the Hall, South Third street, on Wednesday,
May 9th, A. D. 1849, A. L. 5849, for the purpose of
receiving the Report of the Committee on the Petition
of certain members of this Lodge and others, praying
the sanction of its Warrant for the purpose of opening
and holding an Encampment of Knights Templar and
the appendant Orders in the City of Philadelphia, the
Report of said Committee was received, and the following resolutions adopted:

1. *Resolved*, That the sanction of the Warrant of FRANKLIN
LODGE, No. 134, be and the same is hereby granted to WILLIAM
H. KLAPP, ANTHONY E. STOCKER, ROBERT P. KING and others,
members of this and other Lodges held in this city, and also
Knights of the Temple and of the Order of St. John of Jerusalem, for opening and holding an Encampment of Knights Templar and the appendant Orders in the City of Philadelphia.

2. *Resolved*, That a copy of the foregoing Resolution be furnished to the Petitioners, signed by the Worshipful Master, and
attested by the Secretary under the Seal of the Lodge.

3. *Resolved*, That the foregoing Report and Resolutions be entered at large upon the Minutes of this Lodge.

Extract from the Minutes.

[L. S.]   E. H. BUTLER, *Worshipful Master.*

Attest: ROBERT MCCULLOCH,
            Secretary of Franklin Lodge, No. 134.

The Grand Lodge of Pennsylvania having, at a Special Communication, February 16, 1857, adopted a resolution by which its jurisdiction over the Templar Orders
has ceased; also, a Joint Committee from the two Grand

Encampments of this State, appointed with full powers to act, having agreed upon Articles of Union, and adopted a Constitution on this, the 17th day of February, A. D. 1857, A. O. 737, we do hereby, agreeably thereto, endorse this as a Charter, under which its members may continue their labors.

[L. S.]   W. W. WILSON,
                    R. E. G. Com. of the G. Com. of Penna.

[L. S.]   ANTHONY E. STOCKER,
          M. E. G. G. M. of Penna. Grand Encampment of Knights Templar, and P. E. G. C. of Grand Commandery of Penna.

PHILADELPHIA, February 17, 1857.

We, the Most Eminent Sir R. STIRLING WILSON, General Grand Master of Pennsylvania Grand Encampment of Knights Templar, and Appendant Orders—

To all whom it may concern, Greeting:—

Know ye, That we, the said Most Eminent Sir R. Stirling Wilson, General Grand Master aforesaid, by virtue of the powers and authorities in us vested, Do hereby constitute and appoint our trusty and well-beloved Sir Knights John L. Goddard, Grand Master, John F. Hutchinson, Generalissimo, and H. Weir Workman, Captain-General of an Encampment of Knights Templar, to be held in Philadelphia, in the Commonwealth of Pennsylvania, under the jurisdiction of our said Grand Encampment, and to be called and known by the name of PHILADELPHIA ENCAMPMENT No. 5, with full and adequate powers to confer the Orders of Knights of Malta and Knights of the Red Cross, with continuance to their successors in office and Members forever. Provided, nevertheless, That the said Sir Knights John L. Goddard, Grand Master, John F. Hutchinson, Generalissimo, and

14 *

H. Weir Workman, Captain-General, and the other officers and their successors and members, pay due respect to our said Grand Encampment, and the Regulations thereof, otherwise this Charter to be of no force or effect.

Given under our hand, and the Seal of our Grand Encampment, at the City of Philadelphia, in the Commonwealth of Pennsylvania, this Tenth day of May, in the year of our Lord one thousand eight hundred and fifty-five, and of our Order seven hundred and thirty-seven.

[L. S.].   R. STERLING WILSON,
                                          General Grand Master.
J. L. HUTCHINSON,
        Grand Recorder.

In accordance with the provision in the Proceedings preparatory to the union of the Knights Templar of Pennsylvania, page 7, Resolution 1st, adopted February 17th, 1857, A. O. 739, we do hereby endorse this Charter.

[L. S.]   W. W. WILSON,
                                          R. E. Grand Commander.

[L. S.]   ANTHONY E. STOCKER,
                                          M. E. Gen. Grand Master.

MAY 9, 1849, A. O. 731, A. O. E P. 52.

Sir David C. Skerret, E. C.
Sir Anthony E. Stocker, G.
Sir George H. Hart, C. G.
Sir William H. Klapp, P.
Sir Robert P. King, S. W.
Sir W. W. Downing, J. W.
Sir Samuel Badger, T.
Sir Samuel B. Ashmead, R.

Sir Thomas F. Betton, St. B.
Sir H. Weir Workman, Sw. B.
Sir Coleman Fisher, Jr., W.
Sir W. B. Schneider, S.

JUNE 1, 1850, A. O. 732, A. O. E. P. 53.

Sir Anthony E. Stocker, E. C.
Sir George H. Hart, G.
Sir William H. Klapp, C. G.
Sir Robert P. King, P.
Sir W. W. Downing, S. W.
Sir Samuel B. Ashmead, J. W.
Sir Samuel Badger, T.
Sir David C. Skerret, R.
Sir Thomas F. Betton, St. B.
Sir Coleman Fisher, Jr., Sw. B.
Sir H. Weir Workman, W.
Sir W. B. Schneider, S.

JUNE 1, 1851, A. O. 733, A. O. E. P. 54.

Sir George H. Hart, E. C.
Sir William H. Klapp, G.
Sir E. H. Butler, C. G.
Sir Samuel B. Ashmead, P.
Sir Robert P. King, S. W.
Sir H. Weir Workman, J. W.
Sir Anthony E. Stocker, T.
Sir David C. Skerret, R.
Sir Emanuel Eyre, St. B.
Sir Thomas F. Betton, Sw. B.
Sir Coleman Fisher, Jr., W.
Sir W. B. Schneider, S.

JUNE 1, 1852, A. O. 734, A. O. E. P. 55

Sir William H. Klapp, E. C.
Sir John L. Goddard, G.
Sir John F. Hutchinson, C. G.
Sir Octavius A. Norris, P.
Sir James C. Booth, S. W.
Sir Samuel B. Ashmead, J. W.
Sir Robert P. King, T.
Sir Anthony E. Stocker, R.
Sir Thomas F. Betton, St. B.
Sir Coleman Fisher, Jr., Sw. B.
Sir Emanuel Eyre, W.
Sir W. B. Schneider, S.

JUNE 1, 1853, A. O. 735, A. O. E. P. 56.

Sir John L. Goddard, E. C.
Sir John F. Hutchinson, G.
Sir H. Weir Workman, C. G.
Sir Archibald B. Campbell, P.
Sir Samuel B. Ashmead, S. W.
Sir Charles Neff, J. W.
Sir Robert P. King, T.
Sir Anthony E. Stocker, R.
Sir Thomas F. Betton, St. B.
Sir Emanuel Eyre, Sw. B.
Sir Coleman Fisher, Jr., W.
Sir W. B. Schneider, S.

JUNE 1, 1854, A. O. 736, A. O. E. P. 57

Sir A. B. Campbell, E. C.
Sir John Notman, G.
Sir William H. Allen, C. G.
Sir Charles Neff, P.
Sir John L. Heylin, S. W.

Sir Samuel B. Ashmead, J. W.
Sir Robert P. King, T.
Sir A. E. Stocker, R.
Sir John L. Goddard, St. B.
Sir Thomas F. Betton, Sw. B.
Sir Spencer Bonsall, W.
Sir W. B. Schneider, S.

JUNE 1, 1855, A. O. 737, A. O. E. P. 58.

Sir A. B. Campbell, E. C.
Sir John Notman, G.
Sir William H. Allen, C. G.
Sir Edwin A. Lewis, P.
Sir Thomas F. Betton, S. W.
Sir Edmund Claxton, J. W.
Sir Robert P. King, T.
Sir Anthony E. Stocker, R.
Sir Spencer Bonsall, St. B.
Sir John L. Goddard, Sw. B.
Sir Samuel B. Ashmead, W.
Sir W. B. Schneider, S.

JUNE 1, 1856, A. O. 738, A. O. E. P. 59.

Sir William H. Allen, E. C.
Sir Edwin A. Lewis, G.
Sir Spencer Bonsall, C. G.
Sir Charles C. Hafflefinger, P.
Sir E. Freeman Prentiss, S. W.
Sir John L. Goddard, J. W.
Sir Robert P. King, T.
Sir Anthony E. Stocker, R.
Sir Charles M. Jackson, St. B.
Sir A. B. Campbell, Sw. B.
Sir John Notman, W.
Sir W. B. Schneider, S.

JUNE 1, 1857, A. O. 739, A. O. E. P. 60.

Sir Edwin A. Lewis, E. C.
Sir Charles Neff, G.
Sir Edmund Claxton, C. G.
Sir William H. Allen, P.
Sir Spencer Bonsall, S. W.
Sir John L. Goddard, J. W.
Sir Robert P. King, T.
Sir Anthony E. Stocker, R.
Sir A. B. Campbell, St. B.
Sir William H. Klapp, Sw. B.
Sir Thomas F. Betton, W.
Sir W. B. Schneider, S.

JUNE 1, 1858, A. O. 740, A. O. E. P. 61.

Sir Charles Neff, E. C.
Sir Edmund Claxton, G.
Sir M. Richards Muckle, C. G.
Sir Kingston Goddard, P.
Sir Spencer Bonsall, S. W.
Sir George S. Bethell, J. W.
Sir Wm. H. Allen, LL.D., T.
Sir Anthony E. Stocker, R.
Sir M. Richards Muckle, St. B.
Sir Richard Vaux, Sw. B.
Sir Charles M. Jackson, W.
Sir W. B. Schneider, S.

JUNE 24, 1859, A. O. 741, A. O. E. P. 62.

Sir Edmund Claxton, E. C.
Sir M. Richards Muckle, G.
Sir George S. Bethell, C. G.
Rev. Sir W. H. Odenheimer, D. D., P.
Sir Charles C. Hafflefinger, S. W.

Sir Samuel C. Collins, J. W.
Sir William H. Allen, LL. D., T.
Sir Edwin A. Lewis, R.
Sir Edwin Henderson, St. B.
Sir Richard Vaux, Sw. B.
Sir Owen Evans, W.
Sir W. B. Schneider, S.

MARCH 12, 1860, A. O. 742, A. O. E. P. 63.

Sir M. Richards Muckle, E. C.
Sir George S. Bethell, G.
Sir T. Ellwood Zell, C. G.
Rev. Sir W. H. Odenheimer, D. D., P.
Sir Alexander Muckle, S. W.
Sir Samuel C. Collins, J. W.
Sir W. H. Allen, LL. D., T.
Sir Albert S. Goodall, R.
Sir W. P. Westervelt, St. B.
Sir George L. Harrison, Jr., Sw. B.
Sir A. B. Campbell, W.
Sir W. B. Schneider, S.

MARCH 13, 1861, A. O. 743, A. O. E. P. 64.

Sir George S. Bethell, E. C.
Sir T. Ellwood Zell, G.
Sir Charles C. Hafflefinger, C. G.
Rev. Sir W. H. Odenheimer, D. D., P.
Sir Albert G. Goodall, S. W.
Sir Samuel C. Collins, J. W.
Sir William H. Allen, LL. D., T.
Sir M. Richards Muckle, R.
Sir W. P. Westervelt, St. B.
Sir George L. Harrison, Jr., Sw. B.
Sir J. G. Barnwell, W.
Sir W. B. Schneider, S.

MARCH 14, 1862, A. O. 744, A. O. E. P. 65.

Sir T. Elwood Zell, E. C.
Sir Charles C. Hafflefinger, G.
Sir Albert G. Goodall, C. G.
Rev. Sir W. H. Odenheimer, D. D., P.
Sir Samuel C. Collins, S. W.
Sir W. P. Westervelt, J. W.
Sir William H. Allen, LL. D., T.
Sir M. Richards Muckle, R.
Sir George L. Harrison, Jr., St. B.
Sir J. G. Barnwell, Sw. B.
Sir Strickland Kneass, W.
Sir W. B. Schneider, S.

MARCH 15, 1863, A. O. 745, A. O. E. P. 66.

Sir Charles C. Hafflefinger, E. C.
Sir Albert G. Goodall, G.
Sir Samuel C. Collins, C. G.
Rev. Sir W. H. Odenheimer, D. D., P.
Sir W. P. Westervelt, S. W.
Sir George L. Harrison, Jr., J. W.
Sir William H. Allen, LL. D., T.
Sir M. Richards Muckle, R.
Sir J. G. Barnwell, St. B.
Sir Strickland Kneass, Sw. B.
Sir Alexander Muckle, W.
Sir W. B. Schneider, S.

November 7, 1863.—Philadelphia Commandery, No. 2,
gave notice to the Grand Commandery, that by resolution it had disbanded. But action having been taken
thereon, at the Grand Annual Conclaves of 1864-5, it
was reopened on "the 11th of April, 1866, application
having been made by nine Sir Knights, former members

of Philadelphia Commandery, No. 2, and others, desiring the R. E. Sir William H. Strickland to reopen the same," which he accordingly did, upon the recommendation of St. John's Commandery, No. 4.

MARCH 13, 1866, A. O. 748, A. O. E. P. 69.

Rev. Sir R. H. Pattison, E. C.
Sir John R. Seibert, G.
Sir John Krickbaum, C. G.
Sir M. Richards Muckle, P.
Sir George Henderson, Jr., S. W.
Sir A. H. Peterson, J. W.
Sir E. S. Hall, T.
Sir J. Henry Hays, R.
Sir Peter Leetin, St. B.
Sir W. P. Walters, Sw. B.
Sir W. A. Mass, W.

LIST OF MEMBERS FROM THE ORGANIZATION OF PHILADELPHIA ENCAMPMENT, No. 2, TO THE PRESENT TIME.

NAME.	DATE OF KNIGHTING.
Ashmead, Sam'l. B., (No. 4), Ch. Mem.	February 23, 1849.
Allen, William H., LL. D.,	March 18, 1853.
Betton, Thos. F., (No. 4), Ch. Mem.,	January 26, 1849.
Badger, Samuel,	June 14, 1849.
Butler, E. H.,	April 12, 1850.
Booth, James C.,	December 13, 1850.
Balch, Thomas,	April 11, 1851.
Beck, Charles F.,	November 14, 1851.
Bonsall, Spencer,	March 17, 1854.
Brown, T. Horace,	October 19, 1855.
Bethell, George S.,	April 18, 1856.
Bowen, James K.,	February 20, 1857.

15   H

NAME.	DATE OF KNIGHTING.
Barnwell, James G.,	May 14, 1858.
Blakely, John,	June 5, 1866.
Bardsley, J. W.,	Septemb'r 10, 1866.
Campbell, Archibald B.,	April 9, 1852.
Claxton, Edmund,	April 20, 1855.
Collins, Samuel C.,	April 18, 1856.
Collier, D. C.,	May 8, 1866.
Colburn, Arthur,	November 13, 1866.
Downing, W. W., (No. 4), Ch. Mem.,	November 24, 1848.
De Silver, R. Wilson,	December 21, 1849.
Ely, Rev. Ezra Stiles, D. D.,	February 14, 1850.
Eyre, Emanuel,	October 15, 1850.
Evans, Owen,	March 21, 1856.
Emerick, Albert G.,	October 17, 1856.
Fisher, Coleman, Jr., (No. 4), C. Mem.,	March 23, 1849.
Goddard, Rev. Kingston,	April 12, 1850.
Goddard, John L.,	December 12, 1851.
Goodall, Albert G.,	December 19, 1856.
Gibson, Charles H.,	May 8, 1866.
Hart, Geo. H., (No. 4), Ch. Mem.,	November 24, 1848.
Hutchinson, John F.,	May 9, 1851.
Hewston, John, Jr.,	November 14, 1851.
Heylin, John L.,	January 21, 1853.
Hanson, Hugh Cooper,	April 20, 1855.
Hafflefinger, Charles C.,	April 20, 1855.
Henderson, Edwin,	May 16, 1856.
Harrison, George L. Jr.,	May 13, 1859.
Hall, E. S.,	April 10, 1866.
Hayes, J. Henry,	April 10, 1866.
Henderson, George, Jr.,	May 8, 1866.
Jackson, Charles M.,	October 19, 1855.
Johnson, Theo. F.,	November 16, 1855.
Klapp, W. H., (No. 4), Ch. Mem.,	November 4, 1848.
King, Robert P., (No. 4), Ch. Mem.,	April 27, 1849

NAME.	DATE OF KNIGHTING.
Kneass, Strickland,	January 18, 1856.
Krickbaum, John,	April 10, 1866.
Lewis, Edwin A.,	March 16, 1855.
Leetin, Peter,	April 10, 1816.
Muckle, M. Richards,	March 21, 1856.
Muckle, Alexander,	March 21, 1856.
Marache, H. D.,	March 20, 1857.
Maas, William A.,	April 10, 1866.
McGowan, James,	Septemb'r 10, 1866.
Norris, Octavius A.,	June 13, 1851.
Neff, Charles,	June 11, 1852.
Notman, John,	January 21, 1853.
Nixon, William H.,	June 5, 1866.
Odenheimer, Rev. W. H., D. D.,	May 14, 1858.
Prentiss, E. Freeman,	May 18, 1855.
Pattison, Rev. Robert H.,	April 10, 1866.
Peterson, A. H.,	April 10, 1866.
Stocker, A. E., (No. 4), Ch. Mem.,	July 28, 1848.
Skerret, David C., (No. 4), Ch. Mem.,	May 26, 1848.
Seibert, John R.,	March 31, 1865.
Stillman, Thomas,	April 10, 1866.
Snowden, John C.,	November 13, 1866.
Taylor, Absalom,	June 5, 1866.
Taylor, John,	November 13, 1866.
Vaux, Richard,	November 16, 1855.
Workman, H. W., (No. 4), Ch. Mem.,	December 22, 1848.
Westervelt, W. P.,	June 20, 1856.
Woodside, W.,	June 20, 1856.
Walters, Wm. Penn,	April 20, 1866.
Walton, Loyd H.,	April 20, 1866.
Zell, T. Ellwood,	April 10, 1866.

JACQUES DE MOLAY COMMANDERY, No. 3.

APPLICATION was made to the M. E. William B. Hubbard, G. G. Master of the G. G. Encampment of Knights Templar of the United States, for an Encampment to be located at Washington, Washington County, Pennsylvania. The Dispensation was issued September 12, 1849, and the Encampment was named and numbered *Jacques De Molay Encampment, No.* 2; but after the union of the two Grand Encampments of this State, it was changed to No. 3, on the 23d of June, 1857.

The Petitioners for the Dispensation were: Sir Alfred Creigh, Rev. Sir George B. McElroy, Sir Isaiah Hill, Rev. Sir Samuel E. Babcock, Sir Christian P. Gummert, Sir Thomas Hazen, Sir William L. Lafferty, and Sir James M. Stokely, of Pittsburg, No. 1, and Rev. Wesley Kenney, of Wheeling, Va., No. 1.

The Charter was subsequently granted by the General Grand Encampment of Knights Templar of the United States, on the 24th of October, 1850, at its triennial meeting held in Lexington, Kentucky.

OFFICERS OF JACQUES DE MOLAY COMMANDERY FROM ITS ORGANIZATION TO THE PRESENT TIME.

NOVEMBER 1, 1849, A. O. 731, A. O. E. P. 52.

Sir Alfred Creigh, E. C.
Rev. Sir George B. McElroy, G.

Sir Isaiah Hill, C. G.
Rev. Sir Wesley Kenney, P.
Sir William L. Lafferty, S. W.
Rev. Sir Samuel E. Babcock, J. W.
Sir John Best, T.
Sir Christian P. Gummert, R.
Sir Thomas Hazen, St. B.
Sir James M. Stokely, Sw. B.
Sir Peter Kennedy, W.
Sir Samuel Potter, S.

DECEMBER 7, 1849, A. O. 731, A. O. E. P. 52.

Sir Alfred Creigh, E. C.
Sir William Wolf, G.
Sir Isaiah Hill, C. G.
Rev. Sir George B. McElroy, P.
Sir Peter Kennedy, S. W.
Sir William McClelland, J. W.
Sir John Best, T.
Sir Christian P. Gummert, R.
Sir James M. Byers, St. B.
Sir William L. Lafferty, Sw. B.
Sir Thomas Hazen, W.
Sir Samuel Potter, S.

JANUARY 3, 1851, A. O. 733, A. O. E. P. 54

Sir Alfred Creigh, E. C.
Sir William Wolf, G.
Sir James M. Byers, C. G.
Sir William Smith, P.·
Sir Joseph B. Musser, S. W.
Sir James T. Dagg, J. W.
Sir Andrew Hopkins, T.
Sir Peter Kennedy, R.
Sir George Passmore, St. B.

15 *

Sir William Gaston, Sw. B.
Sir William Nicholls, W.
Sir Samuel Potter, S.

DECEMBER 5, 1851, A. O. 733, A. O. E. P. 54.

Sir Joseph B. Musser, E. C.
Sir William Smith, G.
Sir William Nicholls, C. G.
Sir James T. Dagg, P.
Sir Peter Kennedy, S. W.
Sir William Wolf, J. W.
Sir James S. Bushfield, T.
Sir William Nicholls, R.
Sir James Mathews, St. B.
Sir Andrew Hopkins, Sw. B.
Sir George Passmore, W.
Sir Samuel Potter, S. .

DECEMBER 3, 1852, A. O. 734, A. O. E. P. 55.

Sir Joseph B. Musser, E. C.
Sir George Passmore, G.
Sir James S. Bushfield, C. G.
Sir James T. Dagg, P.
Sir Peter Kennedy, S. W.
Sir William Wolf, J. W.
Sir William Smith, T.
Sir William Nicholls, R.
Sir Andrew Hopkins, St. B.
Sir John Best, Sw. B.
Sir William Gaston, W.
Sir Samuel Potter, S.

DECEMBER 2, 1853, A. O. 735, A. O. E. P. 56.

Sir Joseph B. Musser, E. C.
Sir George Passmore, G.

Sir John R. Griffith, C. G.
Sir William Boardman, P.
Sir Peter Kennedy, S. W.
Sir William Wolf, J. W.
Sir Hezekiah Hopkins Frisbie, T.
Sir William Nicholls, R.
Sir William L. Robb, St. B.
Sir William Gaston, Sw. B.
Sir Andrew Hopkins, W.
Sir Samuel Potter, S.

APRIL 12, 1855, A. O. 737, A. O. E. P. 58.

Sir Joseph B. Musser, E. C.
Sir William McKahan, G.
Sir H. H. Frisbie, C. G.
Sir William Smith, P.
Sir William R. Terry, S. W.
Sir William Wolf, J. W.
Sir John R. Griffith, T.
Sir Alfred Creigh, R.
Sir James Smith, St. B.
Sir Joseph Weirich, Sw. B.
Sir James M. Byers, W.
Sir William Boardman, S.

APRIL 4, 1856, A. O. 738, A. O. E. P 59.

Sir William Wolf, E. C.
Sir Alexander Wishart, G.
Sir Daniel Keim Albright, C. G.
Sir William Smith, P.
Sir H. H. Frisbie, S. W.
Sir William McKahan, J. W.
Sir John R. Griffith, T.

Sir Alfred Creigh, R.
Sir James S. Bushfield, St. B.
Sir Casper S. Wyland, Sw. B.
Sir William B. Rose, W.
Sir Samuel Potter, S.

APRIL 3, 1857, A. O. 739, A. O. E. P. 60.

Sir William Wolf, E. C.
Sir William H. Stoy, G.
Sir John Murphy, Jr., C. G.
Sir William Smith, P.
Sir William McKahan, S. W.
Sir Alexander Wishart, J. W.
Sir John R. Griffith, T.
Sir Alfred Creigh, R.
Sir William Chatland, St. B.
Sir John Whiting, Sw. B.
Sir H. H. Frisbie, W.
Sir Peter Kennedy, S.

MAY 5, 1858, A. O. 740, A. O. E. P. 61.

Sir Alexander Wishart, E. C.
Sir William Hart, G.
Sir James M. Byers, C. G.
Sir William Smith, P.
Sir James R. Patton, S. W.
Sir William Wolf, J. W.
Sir John Whiting, T.
Sir Alfred Creigh, R.
Sir E. L. Christman, St. B.
Sir George Passmore, Sw. B.
Sir H. H. Frisbie, W.
Sir Peter Kennedy, S.

MARCH 4, 1859, A. O. 741, A. O. E. P. 62.

Sir Alfred Creigh, E. C.
Sir William Hart, G.
Sir James M. Byers, C. G.
Sir William Smith, P.
Sir Casper S. Wyland, S. W.
Sir William Wolf, J. W.
Sir John Whiting, T.
Sir Alexander Wishart, R.
Sir John R. Griffith, St. B.
Sir John Hall, Sw. B.
Sir John W. Acheson, W.
Sir Peter Kennedy, S.

MARCH 1, 1860, A. O. 742, A. O. E. P. 63.

Sir Alfred Creigh, E. C.
Sir James E. Smiley, G.
Sir William Hart, C. G.
Sir William Smith, P.
Sir William Wolf, S. W.
Sir John W. Acheson, J. W.
Sir John Whiting, T.
Sir Alexander Wishart, R.
Sir John R. Griffith, St. B.
Sir James S. Bushfield, Sw. B.
Sir John G. Ruple, W.
Sir Peter Kennedy, S.

MARCH 9, 1861, A. O. 743, A. O. E. P. 64

Sir Alfred Creigh, E. C.
Sir James E. Smiley, G.
Sir James M. Byers, C. G.
Sir William Smith, P.
Sir William Wolf, S. W.

Sir John W. Acheson, J. W.
Sir John Whiting, T.
Sir James S. Bushfield, R.
Sir John R. Griffith, St. B.
Sir John Hall, Sw. B.
Sir Alexander Wishart, W.
Sir John G. Ruple, S.

MARCH 7, 1862, A. O. 744, A. O. E. P. 65.

Sir Alexander Wishart, E. C.
Sir James E. Smiley, G.
Sir William Hart, C. G.
Sir William Smith, P.
Sir William Wolf, S. W.
Sir James M. Byers, J. W.
Sir John R. Griffith, T.
Sir Alfred Creigh, R.
Sir John Whiting, St. B.
Sir James S. Bushfield, Sw. B.
Sir Peter Kennedy, W.
Sir John G. Ruple, S.

MARCH 6, 1863, A. O. 745, A. O. E. P. 66

Sir Alexander Wishart, E. C.
Sir James M. Byers, G.
Sir James E. Smiley, C. G.
Sir William Smith, P.
Sir William Wolf, S. W.
Sir John G. Ruple, J. W.
Sir John R. Griffith, T.
Sir Alfred Creigh, R.
Sir James S. Bushfield, St. B.
Sir William Hart, Sw. B.
Sir John Whiting, W.
Sir Peter Kennedy, S.

MARCH 5, 1864, A. O. 746, A. O. E. P. 67.

Sir Alexander Wishart, E. C.
Sir James E. Smiley, G.
Sir William Hart, C. G.
Sir William Smith, P.
Sir William Wolf, S. W.
Sir John G. Ruple, J. W.
Sir John R. Griffith, T.
Sir Alfred Creigh, R.
Sir James S. Bushfield, St. B.
Sir James M. Byers, Sw. B.
Sir John Whiting, W.
Sir Peter Kennedy, S.

MARCH 5, 1865, A. O. 747, A. O. E. P. 68.

Sir Alexander Wishart, E. C.
Sir James E. Smiley, G.
Sir William Hart, C. G.
Sir William Smith, P.
Sir William Wolf, S. W.
Sir John G. Ruple, J. W.
Sir John R. Griffith, T.
Sir Alfred Creigh, R.
Sir James S. Bushfield, St. B.
Sir James M. Byers, Sw. B.
Sir John Whiting, W.
Sir Peter Kennedy, S.

MARCH 12, 1866, A. O. 748, A. O. E. P. 69.

Sir James M. Byers, E. C.
Sir John W. Acheson, G.
Sir James S. Bushfield, C. G.
Sir William Smith, P.
Sir William Wolf, S. W.

Sir Alexander Wishart, J. W.
Sir John R. Griffith, T.
Sir Alfred Creigh, R.
Sir John Whiting, St. B.
Sir James M. House, Sw. B.
Sir John G. Ruple, W.
Sir Peter Kennedy, S.

MEMBERS.

NAME.	DATE OF KNIGHTING.
Adams, Elijah, Jr., (No. 5),	May 23, 1850.
Albright, Daniel Keim,	April 4, 1856.
Acheson, John W.,	May 6, 1859.
Babcock, Rev. S. E., (No. 1), Ch. M.	November 1, 1849.
Best, John,	November 1, 1849.
Byers, James M.,	March 1, 1850.
Bushfield, James S.,	January 2, 1851.
Buchanan, J. A. J., (No. 5),	October 16, 1851.
Boardman, William,	March 5, 1853.
Bierer, John, (No. 7),	June 16, 1853.
Blumenthal, Charles E.,	July 20, 1853.
Bentley, Shazbazar,	November 21, 1854.
Burchinell, Rev. W. J.,	January 4, 1856.
Brackny, Benjamin,	August 28, 1866.
Creigh, Alfred, (No. 1), Ch. Mem.,	November 1, 1849.
Craft, Israel L., (No. 5),	March 16, 1850.
Cross, Anderson G., (No. 5),	October 16, 1851.
Clarke, Rev. John,	September 17, 1853.
Chatland, William,	February 3, 1854.
Christman, Enos L.,	September 4, 1857.
Dagg, James T.,	January 17, 1851.
Dorsey, Rev. S. J.,	May 4, 1855.
Frisbie, Hezekiah Hopkins,	February 4, 1853.
Gummert, Christian P., (No. 1), C. M.,	November 1, 1849.
Gaston, William,	June 14, 1850.

NAME.	DATE OF KNIGHTING.
Gregg, John,	June 1, 1852.
Griffith, John R.,	September 19, 1853.
Gow, John L.,	January 4, 1855.
Hill, Isaiah, (of No. 1), Ch. Mem.,	November 1, 1849.
Hazen, Thomas, (of No. 1), Ch. M.,	November 1, 1849.
Hopkins, Andrew,	April 22, 1850.
Hughes, Rev. D. D.,	September 17, 1853.
Hickman, Rev. S. M.,	July 4, 1855.
Harrison, J. B.,	March 14, 1857.
Hart, William,	March 24, 1857.
Hall, John,	May 6, 1859.
Harbison, Adam, Jr.,	August 28, 1866.
House, James M.,	August 28, 1866.
Harter, George H.,	August 28, 1866.
Kenney, Rev. Wesley, (of Wheeling, No. 1), Charter Member,	November 1, 1849.
Kennedy, Peter,	November 22, 1849.
Lafferty, William L., (of No. 1), C. M.,	November 1, 1849.
Lynch, John W., (No. 5),	April 5, 1851.
Laishley, Rev. Peter T.,	June 28, 1851.
Ludington, H. Z.,	June 15, 1853.
Long, Rev. Albert G.,	July 17, 1853.
McElroy, Rev. Geo. B., (of No.1), C.M.,	November 1, 1849.
McClelland, William, (No. 5),	November 22, 1849.
Musser, Joseph B.,	January 17, 1851.
Mathews, James, •	October 4, 1851.
Mickle, Reuben D., (No, 5),	October 16, 1851.
McMillen, William B., (No. 7),	June 16, 1853.
McKahan, William,	March 3, 1854.
McGlaughlin, Andrew, (K. R. C.),	April 7, 1855.
Murphy, John, Jr.,	December 7, 1855.
Miller, Hugh, (admitted),	March 26, 1857.
Minesinger, Henry M.,	January 14, 1859.
Nicholls, William,	May 13, 1851.

16

NAME.	DATE OF KNIGHTING.
Potter, Samuel, (admitted),	November 1, 1849.
Passmore, George,	April 23, 1850.
Patton, James R.,	January 1, 1858.
Piper, James, (No. 7),	February 24, 1853.
Patrick, Andrew, (No. 7),	June 16, 1853.
Pauley, W. T. H., (No. 5),	July 21, 1853.
Robb, William L.,	June 23, 1851.
Reeves, Jesse,	August 30, 1854.
Rose, William B.,	August 28, 1855.
Ruple, John G.,	November 26, 1860.
Stokely, James M., (of No. 1), C. M.,	November 1, 1849.
Smith, William,	April 27, 1850.
Smith, James,	February 5, 1853.
Sliffe, Philip,	March 15, 1853.
Simington, Rev. R. T.,	September 17, 1853.
Stouch, George C.,	February 17, 1854.
Stillians, Rev. John,	March 23, 1854.
Stillians, William,	July 14, 1854.
Stoy, H. W.,	January 4, 1855.
Stoy, William H.,	January 19, 1855.
Shutterly, John J.,	May 4, 1855.
Stephens, Israel,	May 24, 1856.
Smiley, James E.,	June 11, 1860.
Terry, William R., (No. 18),	September 30, 1854.
Tracy, George P., (No. 16),	September 13, 1855.
Thompson, R. N.,	March 14, 1856.
Taylor, Robert Finney,	April 12, 1858.
Thompson, John H.,	March 4, 1859.
Wolf, William,	November 22, 1849.
Wishart, David,	December 2, 1853.
Whiting, John,	December 26, 1854.
Werich, Joseph,	January 5, 1855.
Wyland, Casper S.,	June 9, 1855.
Wishart, Alexander,	September 20, 1855.

ST. JOHN'S COMMANDERY, No. 4, OF PHIL-ADELPHIA.

On the 8th day of June, 1819, Sir Knights Stephen P. Barbier, John W. Kelly, John D. Ferguson, Philip Winnemore, Frederick Nice, Ylair F. Deluy, George Russel, John Thomas, Benjamin Haverland, Charles F. Lott, Benjamin Mollineaux, and John H. Starr, hailing from different Commanderies, made application to the M. E. Sir William McCorkle, General Grand Master for a Charter for St. John's Commandery, No. 4, to be located in the City of Philadelphia. In their application they state that they had been members of regular Commanderies, and regularly withdrawn; but having the prosperity of the Order at heart, they promised to exert their best endeavors to promote and diffuse the genuine principles of the Christian religion, and discharge the duties of the Order in a regular and constitutional manner.

The Charter was granted on the 8th day of June, 1819, and was constituted June 15, 1819.

OFFICERS OF ST. JOHN'S COMMANDERY, No. 4, FROM ITS ORGANIZATION TO MARCH, 1866.

JUNE 8, 1819, A. O. 701, A. O. E. P. 22.

Sir Stephen P. Barbier, E. G. M.
Sir John W. Kelly, G.
Sir John D. Ferguson, C. G.

Sir Philip Winnemore, Chan.
Sir Frederick Nice, R.
Sir Ylair F. Deluy, T.
Sir George Russel, St. B.
Sir John Thomas, Mar.
Sir Benjamin Haverland, Her.
Sir Charles F. Lott, Sw. B.
Sir Benjamin Mollineaux, S.

MAY 17, 1820, A. O. 702, A. O. E. P. 23

Sir Stephen P. Barbier, E. G. M.
Sir John W. Kelly, G.
Sir John D. Ferguson, C. G.
Sir Ylair F. Deluy, Chan.
Sir Frederick Nice, R.
Sir Philip Winnemore, T.
Sir John Thomas, St. B.
Sir John H. Starr, Mar.
Sir Benjamin Haverland, Her.
Sir Charles F. Lott, Sw. B.
Sir Benjamin Mollineaux, S.

MAY 16, 1821, A. O. 703, A. O. E. P. 24.

Sir George Russel, E. G. M.
Sir John Horton, G.
Sir John Kenworthy, C. G.
Sir Richard Perry, Chan.
Sir William H. Vail, R.
Sir Philip Winnemore, T.
Sir Simeon Gleason, St. B.
Sir James Clarke, Mar.
Sir Adna Wood, Her.
Sir George Gloninger, Sw. B.
Sir Benjamin Mollineaux, S.

MAY 15, 1822, A. O. 704, A. O. E. P. 25.

Sir George Russel, E. G. M.
Sir John Horton, G.
Sir John Kenworthy, C. G.
Sir Richard Perry, Chan.
Sir William H. Vail, R.
Sir Philip Winnemore, T.
Sir Simeon Gleason, St. B.
Sir James Clarke, Mar.
Sir Adna Wood, Her.
Sir George Gloninger, Sw. B.
Sir Benjamin Mollineaux, S.

MAY 14, 1823, A. O. 705, A. O. E. P. 26.

Sir George Russel, E. G. M.
Sir John Kenworthy, G.
Sir John Horton, C. G.
Sir Philip Winnemore, Chan.
Sir Richard Perry, R.
Sir William H. Vail, T.
Sir Simeon Gleason, St. B.
Sir James Clarke, Mar.
Sir George Gloninger, Her.
Sir Adna Wood, Sw. B.
Sir Benjamin Mollineaux, S.

MAY 13, 1824, A. O. 706, A. O. E. P. 27.

Sir John Horton, E. G. M.
Sir Nathaniel Fowle, G.
Sir John Kenworthy, C. G.
Sir Richard Perry, Chan.
Sir William H. Vail, R.
Sir T. H. Craig, T.
Sir Simeon Gleason, St. B.

Sir James Clarke, Mar.
Sir Adna Wood, Her.
Sir George Gloninger, Sw. B.
Sir Benjamin Mollineaux, S.

MAY 27, 1825, A. O. 707, A. O. E. P. 28.

Sir Nathaniel Fowle, E. G. M.
Sir Philip Winnemore, G.
Sir Charles Felt, C. G.
Sir Thomas S. Manning, Chan.
Sir John Horton, R.
Sir T. H. Craig, T.
Sir Anthony Fannen, St. B.
Sir John Kenworthy, Mar.
Sir William Van Metre, Her.
Sir Alexander Caldwell, Sw. B.
Sir Charles Schneider, S.

MAY 26, 1826, A. O. 708, A. O. E. P. 29.

Sir Anthony Fannen, E. G. M.
Sir Charles Felt, G.
Sir Thomas S. Manning, C. G.
Sir Richard Perry, Chan.
Sir John Horton, R.
Sir T. H. Craig, T.
Sir Anthony Fannen, St. B.
Sir William Van Metre, Mar.
Sir John Kenworthy, Her.
Sir Alexander Caldwell, Sw. B.
Sir Charles Schneider, S.

MAY 25, 1827, A. O. 709, A. O. E. P. 30.

Rev. Sir Gregory T. Bedell, E. G. M.
Sir Samuel F. Bradford, G.

Sir Samuel Badger, C. G.
Sir Thomas S. Manning, Chan.
Sir John Horton, R.
Sir Nathaniel Fowle, T.
Sir Anthony Fannen, St. B.
Sir John Kenworthy, Mar.
Sir Alexander Caldwell, Her.
Sir William Van Metre, Sw. B.
Sir Charles Schneider, S.

MAY 23, 1828, A, O. 710, A. O. E. P. 31.

Sir Samuel Badger, E. G. M.
Sir Samuel H. Perkins, G.
Sir Samuel Huggins, C. G.
Sir Anthony Fannen, Chan.
Sir John Horton, R.
Sir Nathaniel Fowle, T.
Sir John Kenworthy, St. B.
Sir Alexander Caldwell, Mar.
Sir Richard Perry, Her.
Sir William Van Metre, Sw. B.
Sir Charles Schneider, S.

MAY 22, 1829, A. O. 711, A. O. E. P. 32.

Sir Samuel H. Perkins, E. G. M.
Sir Samuel Huggins, G.
Sir John Y. Black, C. G.
Sir John Kenworthy, Chan.
Sir John Horton, R.
Sir Nathaniel Fowle, T.
Sir Alexander Caldwell, St. B.
Sir Richard Perry, Mar.
Sir Benjamin Mollineaux, Her.
Sir John H. Starr, Sw. B.
Sir Charles Schneider, S.

MAY 28, 1830, A. O. 712, A. O. E. P. 33.

Sir John Y. Black, E. G. M.
Sir Enos S. Gandy, G.
Sir Charles Mercier, C. G.
Sir Anthony Fannen, Chan.
Sir Samuel H. Perkins, R.
Sir Nathaniel Fowle, T.
Sir Benjamin Mollineaux, St. B.
Sir John H. Starr, Mar.
Sir Samuel Huggins, Her.
Sir Richard Perry, Sw. B.
Sir Charles Schneider, S.

MAY 27, 1831, A. O. 713, A. O. E. P. 34.

Sir John Y. Black, E. G. M.
Sir Charles Mercier, G.
Sir Enos S. Gandy, C. G.
Sir Anthony Fannen, Chan.
Sir Samuel H. Perkins, R.
Sir Nathaniel Fowle, T.
Sir Benjamin Mollineaux, Sw. B.
Sir John H. Starr, Mar.
Sir Richard Perry, Her.
Sir Alexander Caldwell, St. B.
Sir Charles Schneider, S.

MAY 26, 1832, A. O. 714, A. O. E. P. 35.

Sir Charles Mercier, E. G. M.
Sir John Y. Black, G.
Sir Enos S. Gandy, C. G.
Sir Samuel H. Perkins, Chan.
Sir Anthony Fannen, R.
Sir Nathaniel Fowle, T.
Sir Alexander Caldwell, Sw. B.

Sir Richard Perry, Mar.
Sir William Van Meter, Her.
Sir John H. Starr, St. B.
Sir Charles Schneider, S.

MAY 25, 1833, A. O. 715, A. O. E. P. 36.

Sir Enos S. Gandy, E. G. M.
Sir Benjamin Mollineaux, G.
Sir Alexander Caldwell, C. G.
Sir Anthony Fannen, Chan.
Sir Nathaniel Fowle, R.
Sir Samuel H. Perkins, T.
Sir Thomas S. Manning, Sw. B.
Sir Richard Perry, Mar.
Sir John H. Starr, Her.
Sir William Van Meter, St. B.
Sir Charles Schneider, S.

MAY 24, 1834, A. O. 716, A. O. E. P. 37.

Sir John Y. Black, E. G. M.
Sir Charles Mercier, G.
Sir Enos S. Gandy, C. G.
Sir Anthony Fannen, Chan.
Sir Samuel H. Perkins, R.
Sir Nathaniel Fowle, T.
Sir Benjamin Mollineaux, Sw. B.
Sir John H. Starr, Mar.
Sir Alexander Caldwell, Her.
Sir Richard Perry, St. B.
Sir Charles Schneider, S.

St. John's Commandery, No. 4, continued to work
until January 23, A. D. 1835, when it adjourned to meet
at the call of the Eminent Grand Master, the Constitu-

tion having previously been amended in 1823, which
provided that officers elected should continue in office
until their successors are duly elected. Under this provision of the Constitution, a meeting was held April 28,
1848, A. O. 730.

APRIL 28, 1848, A. O. 730, A. O. E. P. 51.

Sir R. Sterling Wilson, E. G. M.
Sir Alexander Diamond, G.
Sir David C. Skerret, C. G.
Sir William H. Klapp, Chan.
Sir Anthony E. Stocker, R.
Sir John Thomas, T.
Sir William W. Downing, Sw. B.
Sir G. Parker Cummings, Mar.
Sir Charles B. Headley, Her.
Sir John Reynolds, St. B.
Sir William B. Schneider, S.

APRIL 27, 1849, A. O. 731, A. O. E. P. 52.

Sir Alexander Diamond, E. G. M.
Sir John Reynolds, G.
Sir Charles B. Headley, C. G.
Sir Jesse Williamson, Jr., Chan.
Sir William H. Adams, R.
Sir John Thomas, T.
Sir James B. Wood, Sw. B.
Sir G. Parker Cummings, Mar.
Sir Henry C. Oliver, Her.
Sir Charles Gilpin, St. B.
Sir William B. Schneider, S.

APRIL 26, 1850, A. O. 732, A. O. E. P. 53.

Sir John Reynolds, E. G. M.
Sir G. Parker Cummings, G.

Sir William E. Harpur, C. G.
Sir Charles E. Wentz, Chan.
Sir William H. Adams, R.
Sir Thomas E. Baxter, T.
Sir John W. Whetham, Sw. B.
Sir Charles Brothers, Mar.
Sir Charles Gilpin, Her.
Sir Herman Yerkes, St. B.
Sir William B. Schneider, S.

APRIL 25, 1851, A. O. 733, A. O. E. P. 54.

Sir G. Parker Cummings, E. G. M.
Sir William E. Harpur, G.
Sir Charles Brothers, C. G.
Sir Joseph Y. Long, Chan.
Sir William H. Adams, R.
Sir Thomas E. Baxter, T.
Sir John W. Whetham, Sw. B.
Sir John L. Heylin, Mar.
Sir Herman Yerkes, Her.
Sir Charles E. Wentz, St. B.
Sir William B. Schneider, S.

APRIL 24, 1852, A. O. 734, A. O. E. P. 55.

Sir William E. Harpur, E. G. M.
Sir Charles Brothers, G.
Sir Charles E. Wentz, C. G.
Sir Samuel Miller, Chan.
Sir R. Sterling Wilson, R.
Sir Thomas E. Baxter, T.
Sir Thomas Bell, Sw. B.
Sir Henry Wilson, Mar.
Sir Joseph Y. Long, Her.
Sir Alfred P. Hesser, St. B.
Sir William B. Schneider, S.

APRIL 23, 1853, A. O. 735, A. O. E. P. 56.

Sir Charles Brothers, E. G. M.
Sir Alfred P. Hesser, G.
Sir Jeremiah L. Hutchinson, C. G.
Sir Samuel A. Patton, Chan.
Sir R. Sterling Wilson, R.
Sir Thomas E. Baxter, T.
Sir Thomas Bell, Sw. B.
Sir William C. Henszey, Mar.
Sir Joseph Y. Long, Her.
Sir Frederick Lennig, St. B.
Sir William B. Schneider, S.

APRIL 22, 1854, A. O. 736, A. O. E. P. 57.

Sir Alfred P. Hesser, E. G. M.
Sir Jeremiah L. Hutchinson, G.
Sir Herman Yerkes, C. G.
Sir Murray Whallon, Chan.
Sir R. Sterling Wilson, R.
Sir William E. Harpur, T.
Sir John E. Marshall, Sw. B.
Sir Thomas Snowden, Mar.
Sir David W. Cameron, Her.
Sir George F. Sites, St. B.
Sir William B. Schneider, S.

MAY 10, 1855, A. O. 737, A. O. E. P. 58.

Sir Jeremiah L. Hutchinson, E. G. M.
Sir Herman Yerkes, G.
Sir George F. Sites, C. G.
Sir Nathaniel B. Mosley, Chan.
Sir R. Sterling Wilson, R.
Sir William E. Harpur, T.
Sir James Williams, Sw. B.

Sir George W. Hall, Mar.
Sir George F. Sites, Her.
Sir William Carr, St. B.
Sir William B. Schneider, S.

MAY 9, 1856, A. O. 738, A. O. E. P. 59.

Sir Herman Yerkes, E. G. M.
Sir George F. Sites, G.
Sir John E. Marshall, C. G.
Sir George H. Dodge, Chan.
Sir R. Sterling Wilson, R.
Sir William E. Harpur, T.
Sir Charles P. Anderson, Sw. B.
Sir William A. Fox, Mar.
Sir George W. Hall, Her.
Sir James W. Martien, St. B.
Sir William B. Schneider, S.

APRIL 24, 1857, A. O. 739, A. O. E. P. 60.

Sir John E. Marshall, E. C.
Sir George F. Sites, G.
Sir Thomas D. Wattson, C. G.
Rev. Sir R. Broadhead Westbrooke, P.
Sir J. B. Whitaker, S. W.
Sir H. D. Lawrence, J. W.
Sir William E. Harpur, T.
Sir R. Sterling Wilson, R.
Sir Joseph Hutchinson, St. B.
Sir Frank S. Johnson, Sw. B.
Sir William A. Fox, W.
Sir William B. Schneider, S.

1858, A. O. 740, A. O. E. P. 61.

Sir George F. Sites, E. C.
Sir Thomas D. Wattson, G.

17   I

Sir John B. Whitaker, C. G.
Sir Jeremiah L. Hutchinson, P.
Sir John Hanold, S. W.
Sir William S. Stokely, J. W.
Sir William E. Harpur, T.
Sir R. Sterling Wilson, R.
Sir Samuel McIlree, St. B.
Sir Frank S. Johnson, Sw. B.
Sir Francis Funk, W.
Sir William B. Schneider, S.

1859, A. O. 741, A. O. E. P. 62.

Sir John B. Whitaker, E. C.
Sir John Hanold, G.
Sir George W. Hufty, C. G.
Rev. Sir R. Broadhead Westbrooke, P
Sir George W. Edleman, Jr., S. W.
Sir William C. Murphy, J. W.
Sir William E. Harpur, T.
Sir Timothy P. Russel, R.
Sir James W. Martien, St. B.
Sir George S. Painter, Sw. B.
Sir Francis Funk, W.
Sir William B. Schneider, S.

MARCH 23, 1860, A. O. 742, A. O. E. P. 63.

Sir John Hanold, E. C.
Sir George W. Hufty, G.
Sir George W. Edleman, Jr., C. G.
Sir R. Broadhead Westbrooke, P.
Sir C. C. Burns, S. W.
Sir John L. Young, J. W.
Sir Thomas J. Jefferies, T.
Sir Timothy P. Russel, R.

Sir Francis Funk, St. B.
Sir J. M. Whitby, Sw. B.
Sir William M. Ireland, W.
Sir William B. Schneider, S.

MARCH 22, 1861, A. O. 743, A. O. E. P. 64.

Sir George W. Hufty, E. C.
Sir George W. Edleman, Jr., G.
Sir John L. Young, C. G.
Sir Jeremiah L. Hutchinson, P.
Sir George Alkins, S. W.
Sir Alfred R. Potter, J. W.
Sir Thomas J. Jeffries, T.
Sir William M. Ireland, R.
Sir Edward Strickland, St. B.
Sir Francis Funk, Sw. B.
Sir Wolcott R. Harrison, W.
Sir W. B. Schneider, S.

MARCH 28, 1862, A. O. 744, A. O. E. P. 65

Sir George W. Edleman, Jr., E. C.
Sir John L. Young, G.
Sir George Alkins, C. G.
Sir William M. Ireland, P.
Sir J. Madison Whitby, S. W.
Sir Wolcott R. Harrison, J. W.
Sir Thomas J. Jeffries, T.
Sir Alfred R. Potter, R.
Sir Francis Funk, St. B.
Sir Thomas Stillman, Sw. B.
Sir Morris Hansell, W.
Sir William B. Schneider, S.

MARCH 27, 1863, A. O. 745, A. O. E. P. 66.

Sir George Alkins, E. C.
Sir William M. Ireland, G.
Sir J. Madison Whitby, C. G.
Sir Israel R. Deacon, P.
Sir Thomas R. Patton, S. W.
Sir Thomas Stillman, J. W.
Sir John Hanold, T.
Sir Morris Hansell, R.
Sir Edward Strickland, St. B.
Sir Nathan Smith, Sw. B.
Sir Charles E. Meyer, W.
Sir William B. Schneider, S.

MARCH 25, 1864, A. O. 746, A. O. E. P. 67.

Sir William Morton Ireland, E. C.
Sir J. Madison Whitby, G.
Sir Nathan Smith, C. G.
Sir J. Andrew Harris, P.
Sir Andrew Robeno, Jr., S. W.
Sir A. K. Smith, J. W.
Sir John Hanold, T.
Sir J. Atlee White, R.
Sir Edward Strickland, St. B.
Sir Thomas Brown, Sw. B.
Sir Charles L. Hale, W.
Sir William B. Schneider, S.

MARCH 24, 1865, A, O. 747, A. O. E. P. 68.

Sir J. Madison Whitby, E. C.
Sir Nathan Smith, G.
Sir Charles E. Meyer, C. G.
Rev. Sir Robert H. Pattison, P.
Sir Andrew Robeno, Jr., S. W.

Sir Charles L. Hale, J. W.
Sir John Hanold, T.
Sir J. Atlee White, R.
Sir John Smith, St. B.
Sir S. Grant Smith, Sw. B.
Sir H. C. Yarrow, W.
Sir W. B. Schneider, S.

MARCH 23, 1866, A. O. 748, A. O. E. P. 69.

Sir Nathan Smith, E. C.
Sir Charles E. Meyer, G.
Sir Andrew Robeno, Jr., C. G.
Rev. Sir J. Andrew Harris, P.
Sir Charles L. Hale, S. W.
Sir Edward Strickland, J. W.
Sir John Hanold, T.
Sir William M. Ireland, R.
Sir John Smith, St. B.
Sir William Baldwin, Sw. B.
Sir Molledore Spiegle, W.
Sir Wm. B. Schneider, S.

MEMBERS.

NAME.	DATE OF KNIGHTING.
Adams, William,	May 27, 1825.
Allen, Rev. Benjamin, (Trinity Enc't, Harrisburg),	November 22, 1826.
Ashmead, Samuel B., (No. 2),	November 2, 1831.
Adams, William H.,	September 22, 1848.
Ancona, S. C., (No. 9),	January 26, 1849.
Anderson, Charles P.,	February 4, 1854.
Ashton, George H.,	April 11, 1855.
Alkins, George,	November 23, 1855.
Apple, T. M.,	May 27, 1859.
Allen, William Henry, LL. D.,	January 27, 1860.

17 *

NAME.	DATE OF KNIGHTING.
Ashford, Henry, (Admitted),	March 24, 1864.
Barbier, Stephen P., (No. 1), Ch.	
Mem.,	August 16, 1816.
Badger, Samuel,(No. 2), Admit'd,	May 17, 1816.
Bedell, Rev. Gregory T., (Trinity	
Enc't, Harrisburg),	May 25, 1827.
Bradford, Samuel F., (Trinity	
Enc't, Harrisburg),	May 25, 1827.
Black, J. Y.,	November 23, 1827.
Byrne, H. C.,	June 10, 1821.
Buchan, E.,	November 16, 1823.
Burke, R. M.,	September 8, 1831.
Barclay, George C.,	October 27, 1848.
Bertolett, Mahlon,	October 27, 1848.
Betton, Thomas F., (No. 2),	January 26, 1849.
Baxter, Thomas E.,	March 23, 1849.
Beard, Herman,	April 27, 1849.
Brothers, Charles,	April 26, 1850.
Bell, Thomas,	July 25, 1851.
Benners, William J.,	March 25, 1852.
Bennet, Jacob,	September 24, 1852.
Blackburne, Francis,	November 25, 1853.
Brown, William R.,	February 25, 1855.
Balderston, Jonathan,	April 11, 1855.
Bradley, John,	April 27, 1855.
Barnes, George H.,	April 27, 1855.
Beckett, Thomas J.,	December 28, 1855.
Brault, Prosper,	June 27, 1856.
Benezet, John F.,	September 26, 1856.
Brown, Samuel, Jr.,	December 26, 1856.
Bladen, Washington L.,	January 22, 1858.
Benezet, Samuel,	June 18, 1858.
Barnes, Isaac N.,	October 28, 1859.
Burns, Charles C.,	November 25, 1859.

NAME.	DATE OF KNIGHTING.
Brault, Alphonso,	February 24, 1860.
Boley, F. W., (Admitted)	December 23, 1860.
Brown, Thomas,	September 25, 1863.
Burkhardt, William H.,	May 27, 1864.
Birnie, Robert W.,	September 23, 1864.
Bazley, J. E.,	November 25, 1864.
Brearly, Preston,	February 24, 1865.
Brooks, Richard W.,	March 31, 1865.
Baldwin, William,	March 31, 1865.
Brooks, Lambert B.,	March 31, 1865.
Bruce, John R.,	April 28, 1865.
Brannon, Paul M., (K. R. C.),	May 26, 1865.
Baker, William H., ·	June 6, 1865.
Clarke, James,	May 4, 1821.
Craig, T. H.,	May 27, 1825.
Caldwell, Alexander,	May 27, 1825.
Cameron, Simon, (Trinity Encampment, Harrisburg),	October 25, 1826.
Clemson, Rev. J. Baker, (Trinity Enc't, Harrisburg),	October 25, 1826.
Costa, John P., (Admitted),	May 3, 1827.
Chandler, Joseph R.,	November 23, 1827.
Clinton, William,	May 28, 1830.
Cummings, G. Parker,	June 23, 1848.
Childs, George K.,	November 24, 1848.
Campbell, John P.,	February 23, 1850.
Crossby, John,	August 27, 1852.
Clark, Robert,	January 23, 1853.
Cooper, Alfred,	February 25, 1853.
Carr, William,	September 23, 1853.
Cameron, David W.,	January 27, 1854.
Cowan, Joseph W.,	March 16, 1855.
Cooper, Ralph V. M.,	June 13, 1855.
Connell, George,	November 23, 1855.

NAME.	DATE OF KNIGHTING.
Coleman, John M.,	January 25, 1856.
Cline, William F.,	February 22, 1856.
Collins, James H.,	March 28, 1856.
Carrick, John,	April 25, 1856.
Campbell, Charles B.,	September 26, 1856.
Craig, Joseph B.,	January 23, 1857.
Chandler, James B.,	February 27, 1857.
Carlton, James Henry,	June 26, 1857.
Cole, Isaiah, (No. 19),	April 11, 1860.
Conrad, Thomas K.,	January 24, 1862.
Collins, Samuel C., (Admitted),	March 24, 1864.
Campbell, Archibald B.,	March 24, 1864.
Claxton, Edmund,	March 24, 1864.
Cahoon, James W.,	November 25, 1864.
Cresswell, Samuel, Jr.,	December 23, 1864.
Chambers, Rev. John,	November 26, 1866.
Deluy, Ylair F., Ch. Mem.,	June 8, 1819.
De Pui, John, (Trinity Encampment, Harrisburg),	November 3, 1819.
Dickinson, L.,	March 15, 1820.
Dolherts, John,	June 16, 1822.
De Pui, Rev. James,	October 25, 1826.
Decklyne, Theodore,	February 29, 1828.
Downing, W. W., (No. 2),	November 4, 1848.
Davis, Justinian F.,	March 13, 1823.
Ducachet, Rev. Henry W.,	January 26, 1849.
Dawson, Jonathan S.,	March 22, 1850.
Deacon, Israel R.,	June 25, 1852.
Dodge, George H., (Admitted),	September 22, 1854.
Darling, John A.,	April 23, 1858.
Depuy, Watson,	November 25, 1864.
Day, Conrad B.,	May 26, 1865.
Ellis, Thomas,	January 27, 1854.
Evans, Joseph,	November 24, 1854.

NAME.	DATE OF KNIGHTING.
English, William,	April 27, 1855.
Eberhardt, Jonas,	November 23, 1855.
Edelman, George W., Jr.,	October 22, 1858.
Erskine, Rufus M.,	June 15, 1859.
Evans, Joseph S.,	September 25, 1863.
Evans, George G.,	January 22, 1864.
Eldridge, Charles H.,	December 23, 1864.
Ferguson, John D., Ch. Mem.,	June 8, 1819.
Fowle, Nathaniel, (Admitted),	February 25, 1823.
Felt, Charles,	May 27, 1825.
Fannen, Anthony, (No. 1, N. Y.),	May 21, 1813.
Fisher, Coleman, Jr., (No. 2),	January 26, 1849.
Fox, William A.,	January 28, 1853.
Field, Thomas Y.,	April 28, 1854.
Fry, John W.,	February 25, 1855.
Fidler, James B.,	March 16, 1855.
Ferguson, James,	June 22, 1855.
Fuguet, Stephen,	January 25, 1856.
Funk, Francis,	October 2, 1857.
Freeman, Samuel, (No. 19),	April 11, 1860.
Fellows, A. W.,	April 27, 1860.
Franklin, B. D.,	September 23, 1864.
Foster, W. D.,	November 25, 1864.
Fetters, B. W.,	March 31, 1865.
Gleason, Simeon,	June 15, 1819.
Gloninger, George,	November 15, 1820.
Gandy, Enos,	February 23, 1827.
Gilman, Charles,	May 25, 1827.
Gilpin, Charles,	December 15, 1848.
Goodwin, W. W.,	April 25, 1856.
Gries, W. Richards,	June 27, 1856.
Gaskill, Edward,	October 31, 1856.
Gesemyer, George,	February 27, 1857.
Gaunt, Franklin,	April 23, 1858.

I *

NAME.	DATE OF KNIGHTING.
Green, John, (No. 19),	March 23, 1860.
Geyer, Henry E.,	October 23, 1863.
Goddard, John L.,	March 24, 1864.
Gayley, A. T.,	January 27, 1865.
Griscom, George,	March 31, 1865.
Greyhill, Jerome B.,	November 28, 1865.
Haviland, Benjamin, Ch. Mem.,	June 8, 1819.
Horton, John,	June 15, 1819.
Hart, L. F.,	February 23, 1822.
Huggins, Samuel,	February 29, 1828.
Haywood, John,	April 8, 1824.
Headley, Charles B.,	May 26, 1848.
Hart, George H., (No. 2),	November 24, 1848.
Heister, F. A. M.,	November 24, 1848.
Harpur, William E.,	January 26, 1850.
Hodge, William R.,	February 23, 1850.
Heylin, John L.,	September 27, 1850.
Hesser, Alfred P.,	October 24, 1851.
Hutchinson, Jeremiah L.,	March 25, 1852.
Hoxie, Solomon K.,	June 25, 1852.
Harvey, Joseph A.,	January 28, 1853.
Hamm, William P.,	February 25, 1853.
Hutchinson, James,	March 25, 1853.
Henszey, William C.,	April 22, 1853.
Horner, John W.,	June 24, 1853.
Hand, John K.,	July 5, 1853.
Hutchinson, Joseph,	January 26, 1855.
Hughs, John C.,	January 26, 1855.
Hall, George W.,	March 23, 1855.
Harrington, William,	May 25, 1855.
Healey, John,	October 26, 1855.
Hanold, John,	December 28, 1855
Harper, T. Esmonde,	October 24, 1856.
Harley, J. W.,	January 22, 1858.

NAME.	DATE OF KNIGHTING.
Hufty, George W.,	October 22, 1858.
Hayhurst, E. Hicks,	February 25, 1859.
Harrison, Wolcott R.,	February 24, 1860.
Heaton, C. F.,	December 4, 1860.
Hansell, Morris,	June 26, 1861.
Harris, J. Andrews,	November 27, 1863.
Howell, George W.,	January 22, 1864.
Hallock, Samuel A.,	February 26, 1864.
Hafflefinger, C. C., (Admitted),	March 24, 1864.
Harrison, G. L., Jr., (Admitted),	March 24, 1864.
Hale, Charles L.,	December 23, 1864.
Hubbert, Christian,	January 27, 1865.
Heins, John,	March 31, 1865.
Hays, J. Henry,	March 31, 1865.
Hall, E. L.,	April 28, 1865.
Ireland, William Morton,	April 11, 1860.
Ide, Charles K.,	January 23, 1864.
Ireland, Alphonso C.,	June 6, 1865.
Jones, Samuel,	February 29, 1829.
Jackson, Rev. William,	January 26, 1850.
Jayne, David,	June 24, 1853.
Jackson, B. Franklin,	July 5, 1853.
Johnson, Frank S.,	September 26, 1856.
Jeffries, Thomas J.,	October 22, 1858.
Jeffries, Mortimer T.,	October 28, 1864.
Jackson, John W.,	June 6, 1865.
Kelly, John W., Ch. Mem.,	June 8, 1819.
Kneeland, Rev. Abner,	July 19, 1819.
Kenworthy, John,	July 19, 1819.
Keyser, Jacob,	May 31, 1826.
Kelly, Daniel R.,	May 31, 1826.
Keckeler, Theophilus, (Trinity Encampment, Harrisburg),	October 25, 1826.
King, Robert P., (No. 2),	September 22, 1848.

NAME.	DATE OF KNIGHTING.
Klapp, William H., (No. 2),	October 27, 1848.
Keim, J. H.,	February 4, 1854.
Kelley, James,	December 15, 1854.
Killgore, John, K. R. C.,	April 27, 1855.
Kline, John,	March 28, 1856.
Klett, C. Oakford,	July 27, 1864.
Krickbaum, John,	April 28, 1865.
Kelley, Michael,	June 6, 1865.
Lott, Charles F., Ch. Mem.,	June 8, 1819.
Long, Reading S.,	December 6, 1827.
Lafferty, Edward,	February 29, 1828.
Le Fevre, John B.,	December 28, 1849.
Long, Joseph Y.,	May 28, 1851.
Le Brun, L.,	November 28, 1851.
Lennig, Frederick,	May 28, 1852.
Leppien, John,	June 25, 1852.
Laguna, A. de Leo de,	June 10, 1853.
Lawrence, H. D.,	October 27, 1854.
Lambert, W. M.,	April 25, 1856.
Levering, Francis L.,	April 24, 1857.
Logan, John W.,	June 15, 1859.
Lombart, Herman J., (Admitted),	March 22, 1861.
Lowrey, Casper F.,	March 31, 1865.
Leetin, Peter,	April 28, 1865.
Livingston, Joseph H.,	April 24, 1866.
Mollineux, Benjamin, Ch. Mem.,	June 8, 1819.
Manning, Thomas L.,	July 19, 1819.
Mercier, Charles H.,	February 29, 1829.
McDonough, Thomas, (K. R. C.),	December 28, 1849.
McCullough, Thomas,	February 23, 1850.
Maxwell, W. W.,	March 22, 1850.
Miller, Samuel,	September 27, 1850.
Mangham, George,	September 24, 1852.
McCreary, J. B., (No. 20),	March 25, 1853.

NAME.	DATE OF KNIGHTING.
McCord, Charles O.,	March 25, 1853.
Martien, J. W.,	October 28, 1853.
Masser, Peter B.,	January 27, 1854.
Millholland, James, (No. 9),	February 4, 1854.
McDonnell, Samuel, (No. 9),	February 4, 1854.
McCauley, J. B.,	March 24, 1854.
Marshall, John E.,	October 27, 1854.
McIlree, Samuel,	November 24, 1854.
Milnes, John,	November 24, 1854.
Mosely, Nathaniel B.,	January 26, 1855.
Mann, Charles H.,	February 25, 1855.
Murphy, Alexander,	March 16, 1855.
McClure, W. M.,	April 27, 1855.
Matthews, Seleck H.,	May 25, 1855.
Murphy, William C.,	April 25, 1856.
Mackay, John E. P.,	October 31, 1856.
Milnor, Charles G.,	April 23, 1858.
Matthews, Thomas,	June 18, 1858.
Miller, Abraham, (C), (No. 19),	March 23, 1860.
Mustin, George S.,	May 23, 1862.
Meyer, Charles E.,	January 2, 1863.
Muckle, M. Richards, (Admitted),	March 24, 1864.
Moore, Edwin F.,	December 23, 1864.
Muff, Isaac,	June 27, 1865.
McClintock, Daniel,	June 27, 1865.
Maas, William A.,	May 26, 1865.
Moon, Samuel L.,	June 23, 1865.
McLanan, James,	November 28, 1865.
Matthews, Hanold S.,	January 23, 1866.
Nice, Frederick, Charter Mem.,	June 8, 1819.
Neal, Benjamin T.,	May 31, 1826.
Nash, Rev. Norman,	May 31, 1826.
Newlin, Robert,	March 28, 1851.
Nichols, Wm. Hayward,	July 5, 1853.

18

NAME.	DATE OF KNIGHTING.
Oat, Charles J.,	November 26, 1830.
Oliver, Henry C.,	November 4, 1848.
Ogilby, James,	February 22, 1850.
Osterhaut, P. M.,	October 22, 1853.
O'Farrel, W. J.,	December 28, 1855.
Osborne, Joseph,	February 24, 1865.
Perroteau, B.,	August 18, 1819.
Perry, Richard,	June 17, 1820.
Piggot, Rev. Robert, (Trinity Encampment, Harrisburg),	October 25, 1826.
Perkins, Samuel H.,	November 23, 1827.
Penoza, Charles S.,	December 16, 1828.
Patton, Samuel A.,	June 25, 1852.
Pedrick, Samuel P.,	December 15, 1854.
Pepper, Lawrence S.,	March 28, 1856.
Philips, William J.,	March 28, 1856.
Painter, George,	October 24, 1856.
Potter, Alfred R.,	January 23, 1857.
Powell, John B.,	June 26, 1857.
Pennel, William,	October 2, 1857.
Purdy, John H.,	November 25, 1859.
Porter, James M., Jr., (No. 19),	March 23, 1860.
Petit, Abraham,	March 23, 1860.
Pomp, C., (No. 19),	April 11, 1860.
Patton, Thomas R.,	October 24, 1862.
Pattison, Rev. Robert H.,	December 23, 1864.
Peterson, A. H.,	June 23, 1865.
Russel, George, Ch. Mem.,	June 8, 1819.
Rees, Rev. William Henry, (Trinity Enc'pt., Harrisburg),	October 25, 1826.
Reynolds, John,	May 26, 1848.
Reiff, Josiah,	October 27, 1848.
Ritter, Joel,	November 24, 1848.
Rubicam, Charles A.,	December 15, 1854.

NAME.	DATE OF KNIGHTING.
Randal, J. M., (K. R. C.),	April 27, 1855.
Richmond, E. Bowen,	April 27, 1855.
Roney, John,	November 23, 1855.
Read, Charles T.,	October 24, 1856.
Russel, Timothy P.,	June 26, 1857.
Robeno, Andrew, Jr.,	January 22, 1864.
Roberts, W. H. H.,	February 24, 1865.
Riley, Michael,	November 28, 1865.
Starr, John H., Ch. Mem.,	June 8, 1819.
Schneider, Charles,	April 16, 1813.
Stout, Charles,	July 21, 1819.
Schwartz, John E.,	June 20, 1824.
Scott, James B.,	November 23, 1827.
Skerret, David C., (No. 2),	May 26, 1848.
Schneider, William B.,	June 23, 1848.
Stocker, Anthony E., (No. 2),	July 28, 1848.
Steiner, Jacob, (K. R. C.),	January 26, 1849.
Smith, Rev. J. Brinton,	September 27, 1850.
Smith, John V.,	October 31, 1850.
Sartori, Edmund,	May 28, 1852.
Snowden, Thomas S.,	November 26, 1852.
Swaim, W. M.,	June 24, 1853.
Sites, George F.,	September 23, 1853.
Smith, George,	November 25, 1853.
Sloan, Samuel,	November 25, 1853.
Schultze, Frederick,	January 27, 1854.
Swartz, A. Jordan, (No. 9),	February 4, 1854.
Strickland, William H., (No. 9),	February 4, 1854.
Stout, David E.,	February 4, 1854.
Smith, Marshall B.,	November 24, 1854.
Stevenson, William G.,	March 23, 1855.
Sweatman, V. C.,	April 25, 1856.
Stokely, William S.,	February 27, 1857.
Stewart, William S.,	April 24, 1857.

NAME.	DATE OF KNIGHTING.
Shugard, William N.,	June 26, 1857.
Smith, William R.,	April 23, 1858.
Seltzer, J. H.,	October 28, 1859.
Strickland, Edward,	November 25, 1859.
Semple, W. B., (No. 19),	March 23, 1860.
Stout, Lewis H., (No. 19),	March 23, 1860.
Stillman, Thomas,	April 26, 1861.
Smith, Nathan,	June 27, 1862.
Smith, John,	April 24, 1863.
Smith, Andrew K.,	January 22, 1864.
Smith, S. Grant,	September 23, 1864.
Simpson, J. Alexander,	October 28, 1864.
Sears, William T.,	November 25, 1864.
Shindler, James S.,	March 31, 1865.
Scibert, John R.,	March 31, 1865.
Smith, Wilbur F.,	April 28, 1865.
Spiegle, Molledore,	May 26, 1865.
Sciberling, John,	November 28, 1865.
Thomas, John, Charter Member,	June 8, 1819.
Taylor, Luther,	May 16, 1821.
Thomson, W. L.,	November 14, 1822.
Tobin, John,	January 28, 1853.
Thornley, John,	April 28, 1854.
Thompson, Daniel,	April 27, 1855.
Turley, Albert,	April 9, 1856.
Thomas, Herbert, (No. 19),	April 11, 1860.
Toy, William M.,	January 25, 1861.
Turner, James L.,	January 23, 1866.
Uhler, William M.,	June 26, 1857.
Vail, William H.,	June 15, 1819.
Van Meter, Marmaduke,	June 27, 1825.
Van Houten, Isaac W.,	January 22, 1858.
Van Osten, James B.,	October 23, 1863.
Winnemore, Philip, Ch. Member,	June 8, 1819.

NAME.	DATE OF KNIGHTING.
Wood, Adna,	July 3, 1819.
Wiske, John,	September 23, 1825.
Wilson, William S.,	May 3, 1827.
Wetherill, S. P.,	June 10, 1827.
Weaver, William,	November 18, 1828.
Wilson, R. Sterling,	May 26, 1848.
Wood, James B.,	August 25, 1848.
Williamson, Jesse,	October 27, 1848.
Workman, H. Weir, (No. 2),	December 22, 1848.
Whitaker, Samuel A.,	September 28, 1849.
Whetham, John W.,	April 26, 1850.
Wentz, Charles E.,	August 26, 1850.
Wilson, Henry,	April 23, 1852.
Watkins, Walter A.,	September 24, 1852.
Waterman, Alfred G.,	March 11, 1853.
Waas, Samuel C.,	March 25, 1853.
Wetherill, John Price,	May 27, 1853.
Wright, Charles W.,	June 24, 1853.
Whallon, Murray,	October 28, 1853.
Williams, James,	January 27, 1854.
Warden, W. W.,	April 28, 1854.
Wortinger, Henry,	November 24, 1854.
Wright, Peter T.,	May 9, 1855.
Wilhelm, Charles,	May 25, 1855.
Wattson, Thomas D.,	November 23, 1855.
Wilson, James G.,	December 28, 1855.
Wilson, Charles R., (K. R. C.),	December 28, 1855.
Westbrooke, Rev. R. B.,	December 28, 1855.
Wood, Joseph, Jr.,	March 28, 1856.
Whitaker, John C.,	April 25, 1856.
Whartnaby, John,	January 23, 1857.
Wolfersberger, William A.,	January 22, 1858.
Watson, Charles,	October 22, 1858.
Whitby, J. Madison,	November 25, 1859.

18 *

NAME.	DATE OF KNIGHTING.
Warner, Albert,	January 2, 1863.
White, J. Atlee,	November 27, 1863.
Wallace, Henry,	March 24, 1864.
Walker, Rev. Jarvis E.,	July 27, 1864.
Walton, Loyd B.,	February 24, 1865.
Wertz, Samuel A.,	March 31, 1865.
Walters, William Penn.,	June 6, 1865.
Yerkes, Herman,	February 22, 1850.
Youmans, William M.,	November 24, 1854.
Young, John L.,	November 25, 1859.
Young, H. C.,	November 25, 1859.
Young, Richard,	November 27, 1863.
Yarrow, H. C.,	December 23, 1864.
Zimmerman, Lemuel C.,	January 23, 1857.
Zell, T. Ellwood,	March 24, 1864.

HONORARY DEGREES CONFERRED IN ST. JOHN'S COMMANDERY, NO. 4.

Among the Archives of this ancient Commandery, was a list of Sir Knights upon whom the degrees of *Knight of the Holy Sepulchre, Knight of the Mediterranean Pass, Knight of the Roman Eagle, Knight of Jericho, Royal Master, and Select Master*, were conferred, at various times, from November 17, 1819, to April 11, 1855. To perpetuate so important a fact, which may be useful for future reference, I add the names of those who received these degrees.

KNIGHTS OF THE HOLY SEPULCHRE.

NAME.	DATE OF KNIGHTING.
Simeon Gleason,	November 17, 1819.
John Horton,	November 17, 1819.
Frederick Nice,	November 17, 1819

NAME.	DATE OF KNIGHTING.
Charles Stout,	November 17, 1819.
Benjamin Perroteau,	November 17, 1819.
William H. Vail,	November 17, 1819.
John Kenworthy,	November 17, 1819.
Philip Winnemore,	November 17, 1819.
H. C. Byrne,	November 17, 1819.
S. D. Ferguson,	January 19, 1820.
Rev. Abner Kneeland,	January 19, 1820.
Alphonso C. Ireland,	January 19, 1820.
B. Mollineaux,	January 19, 1820.
L. Dickenson,	January 19, 1820.
Adna Wood,	April 26, 1820.
W. L. Thomson,	April 26, 1820.
R. Perry,	April 26, 1820.
Robert Ferris,	April 26, 1820.
S. P. Wetherill,	April 26, 1820.
John De Pui,	April 26, 1820.
Anthony Fannen,	October 18, 1820.
Luther Taylor,	April 18, 1821.
J. M. Fernander,	April 18, 1821.
J. Dolbert,	April 18, 1821.
G. Gloninger,	April 18, 1821.
Alexander Caldwell,	May 6, 1823.
M. Van Meter,	May 6, 1823.
C. Felt,	May 6, 1823.
N. Fowle,	June 15, 1824.
E. Buchan,	June 15, 1824.
William Adams,	June 15, 1824.

KNIGHTS OF THE MEDITERRANEAN PASS.

NAME.	DATE OF KNIGHTING.
John Thomas,	November 30, 1820.
Adna Wood,	November 30, 1820.

NAME.	DATE OF KNIGHTING.
Luther Taylor,	November 30, 1820.
J. M. Fernander,	November 30, 1820.
J. Dolbert,	November 30, 1820.
B. Mollineaux,	November 30, 1820.
S. P. Wetherill,	November 30, 1820.
G. Gloninger,	November 30, 1820.
M. Van Meter,	May 6, 1823.
W. Weaver,	May 6, 1823.
Alexander Caldwell,	May 6, 1823.
William Adams,	June 15, 1824.
E. Buchan,	June 15, 1824.
N. Fowle,	June 15, 1824.
Jacob Keyser,	February 29, 1828.
Samuel H. Perkins,	February 29, 1828.
James B. Scott,	February 29, 1828.
Samuel Huggins,	February 29, 1828.
Edward Lafferty,	February 29, 1828.
Theodore Decklyne,	February 29, 1828.
E. S. Gandy,	February 29, 1828.
J. T. Black,	February 29, 1828.
Reading S. Long,	February 29, 1828.
S. Jones,	February 29, 1828.
Charles Mercier,	February 29, 1828.
John Wiske,	June 26, 1828.

KNIGHTS OF THE ROMAN EAGLE.

NAME.	DATE OF KNIGHTING.
John Thomas,	November 30, 1820.
Adna Wood,	November 30, 1820.
Luther Taylor,	November 30, 1820
J. M. Fernander,	November 30, 1820.
B. Mollineaux,	November 30, 1820.
J. Dolbert,	November 30, 1820

NAME.	DATE OF KNIGHTING.
G. Gloninger,	November 30, 1820.
W. Weaver,	May 6, 1823.
M. Van Meter,	May 6, 1823.
N. Fowle,	June 15, 1824.
William Adams,	June 15, 1824.
E. Buchan,	June 15, 1824.
Jacob Keyser,	March 19, 1830.
Samuel H. Perkins,	March 19, 1830.
E. S. Gandy,	March 19, 1830.
Charles Mercier,	March 19, 1830.
R. Sterling Wilson,	February 21, 1849.
W. B. Schneider,	February 21, 1849.
William H. Adams,	February 21, 1849.
Alexander Diamond,	February 23, 1849.
William H. Klapp,	February 23, 1849.
W. W. Downing,	February 23, 1849.
H. Weir Workman,	February 23, 1849.
S. B. Ashmead,	February 23, 1849.
David C. Skerret,	May 23, 1849.
Charles A. Headly,	November 23, 1849.
Anthony E. Stocker,	November 23, 1849.
George H. Hart,	November 23, 1849.
G. Parker Cummings,	November 23, 1849.

KNIGHTS OF JERICHO.

NAME.	DATE OF KNIGHTING.
Frederick Nice,	November 30, 1820.
John Thomas,	November 30, 1820.
Simeon Gleason,	November 30, 1820.
Charles Stout,	November 30, 1820.
Adna Wood,	November 30, 1820.
J. Dolbert,	November 30, 1820.
G. Gloninger,	November 30, 1820.

NAME.	DATE OF KNIGHTING
Philip Winnemore,	November 30, 1820.
B. Mollineaux,	November 30, 1820.
John Horton,	November 30, 1820.
John Kenworthy,	November 30, 1820.
S. P. Wetherill,	November 30, 1820.
Luther Taylor,	November 30, 1820.
J. M. Fernander,	November 30, 1820.
W. Weaver,	May 6, 1823.
M. Van Meter,	May 6, 1823.
Jacob Keyser,	March 19, 1830.
Samuel H. Perkins,	March 19, 1830.
E. S. Gandy,	March 19, 1830.
Charles Mercier,	March 19, 1830.

ROYAL AND SELECT MASTER.

NAME.	DATE OF KNIGHTING.
E. S. Gandy,	March 29, 1833.
Samuel Ashmead,	March 29, 1833.
Richard M. Burke,	March 29, 1833.
G. Parker Cummings,	June 23, 1848.
D. C. Skerret,	June 30, 1848.
Alexander Diamond,	June 30, 1848.
John Reynolds,	July 30, 1848.
A. E. Stocker,	November 4, 1848.
William H. Klapp,	November 4, 1848.
James B. Wood,	January 18, 1849.
George H. Hart,	January 18, 1849.
H. C. Oliver,	January 18, 1849.
Charles A. Headley,	July 27, 1849.
Marshall B. Smith,	April 11, 1854.
George W. Hall,	April 11, 1854.
Daniel Thompson,	May 9, 1854.
Robert Clarke,	March 9, 1855.

NAME.	DATE OF KNIGHTING.
W. E. Harpur,	April 11, 1855.
Herman Yerkes,	April 11, 1855.
Samuel A. Ritters,	April 11, 1855.
W. Hayward Nicholls,	April 11, 1855.
William Carr,	May 9, 1855.
George F. Sites,	May 9, 1855.

The following letter was addressed to St. John's Encampment, No. 4, dated

PHILADELPHIA, *March* 21, 1821.

Officers and Gentlemen Sir Knights comprising St. John's Encampment, No. 4, held in Philadelphia:

Holding your honorable institution in high estimation, I take the liberty through one of your members of presenting you with a Holy Bible. This Sacred Volume placed in such hands, will, I have no doubt, be of general use to your fellow-man.

I pray you, therefore, accept the same from your well-wisher, ANN B. WINNEMORE.

June 8, 1821.

The Committee appointed on the last stated meeting to present the thanks of this Encampment to Mrs. Ann B. Winnemore, for her handsome present of a Bible, have attended to the duty assigned them.

GEORGE RUSSELL, ⎫
JOHN KENWORTHY, ⎬ *Committee.*
JOHN HORTON, ⎭

June 8, 1821.—The Committee appointed to furnish a suitable *Apron* report, That in their opinion, a *Black Apron with a white border* with suitable devices, and shaped as a triangle, would be the one proper to be adopted. The report was accepted, and the Grand Encampment passed the following resolution:

Resolved, That the Members of the Grand Encampment be requested to procure suitable Aprons previous to the next annual meeting of the Grand Encampment.

Resolved, That no visitor shall be admitted in the Grand Encampment without a suitable Apron.

ADDITIONAL MEMBERS.

NAME.	DATE OF KNIGHTING.
Bolton, Clifton,	June 26, 1866.
Bell, Thomas H.,	December 28, 1866.
Castle, William H.,	May 31, 1866.
Colton, Franklin B.,	September 25, 1866.
Campbell, James H.,	November 23, 1866.
Ewing, William C.,	November 23, 1866.
Godfrey, William,	October 26, 1866.
Gutekunst, F.,	October 26, 1866.
Goldsmith, T. O.,	December 28, 1866.
Haines, George W.,	May 22, 1866.
Hamilton, William C.,	May 22, 1866.
Hansill, William A.,	May 31, 1866.
Joins, William,	January 25, 1867.
Knipe, Frank C.,	May 31, 1866.
Keeler, E. S.,	September 25, 1866.
Masson, Edward,	May 31, 1866.
Roats, George A.,	November 23, 1866.
Sommerville, Maxwell,	May 22, 1866.
Taylor, D. B.,	May 31, 1866.
Vanneman, T. H.,	December 28, 1866.
Watt, Frank H.,	October 26, 1866.

216½

HUBBARD COMMANDERY, No. 5.

APPLICATION was made to the M. E. Sir William Blackstone Hubbard, Grand Master of the Grand Encampment of Knights Templar of the United States, and a Dispensation issued by him on the 10th day of November, 1851, to the following petitioners, viz.: Sir Knights William McClelland, John W. Lynch, Elijah Adams, Jr., J. A. J. Buchanan, Reuben D. Mickle, Anderson G. Cross, W. T. H. Pauley, Israel L. Craft, and Robert Maple.

The Commandery was opened by the M. E. Morgan Nelson, G. G., assisted by other Sir Knights, on December 10, 1851.

Hubbard Commandery continued its connection with the General Grand Encampment of the United States until March 26, 1857, when, by resolution, it became attached to the Grand Commandery of Pennsylvania.

The Charter was granted September 12, 1856, by the General Grand Encampment of the United States.

OFFICERS OF HUBBARD COMMANDERY SINCE ITS ORGANIZATION.

DECEMBER 11, 1851, A. O. 733, A. O. E. P. 54.

Sir William McClelland, G. C.
Sir Anderson G. Cross, G.
Sir Reuben D. Mickle,

Sir Elijah Adams, Jr., T.
Sir J. A. J. Buchanan, R.
Sir J. W. Lynch, P.
Sir W. T. H. Pauley, W.
Sir William A. Porter, St. B.
Sir Joshua C. Phillips, S.

SEPTEMBER 21, 1853, A. O. 735, A. O. E. P. 56.

Sir J. A. J. Buchanan, E. C.
Sir Lewis Roberts, G.
Sir Anderson G. Cross, C. G.
Sir William A. Porter, P.
Sir James Lindsey, S. W.
Sir William McClelland, J. W.
Sir F. B. Wilson, T.
Sir Benjamin F. Campbell, R.
Sir Simon Rinehart, St. B.
Sir John Lindsey, Sw. B.
Sir W. T. H. Pauley, W.
Sir J. C. Phillips, S.

SEPTEMBER 12, 1856, A. O. 738, A. O. E. P. 59.

Sir J. A. J. Buchanan, E. C.
Sir Anderson G. Cross, G.
Sir Lewis Roberts, C. G.
Sir William A. Porter, P.
Sir James Lindsey, S. W.
Sir William McClelland, J. W.
Sir F. B. Wilson, T.
Sir B. F. Campbell, R.
Sir John Lindsey, St. B.
Sir Arthur Inghram, Sw. B.
Sir W. T. H. Pauley, W.
Sir Joshua C. Phillips, S.

MARCH 27, 1857, A. O. 739, A. O. E. P. 60.

Sir William McClelland, E. C.
Sir Arthur Inghram, G.
Sir Samuel McCallister, C. G.
Sir Anderson G. Cross, P.
Sir James Lindsey, S. W.
Sir W. T. H. Pauley, J. W.
Sir J. A. J. Buchanan, T.
Sir William Linn Creigh, R.
Sir Simon Rinehart, St. B.
Sir William A. Porter, Sw. B.
Sir John Lindsey, W.
Sir Joshua C. Phillips, S.

MARCH 26, 1858, A. O. 740, A. O. E. P. 61.

Sir William McClelland, E. C.
Sir Arthur Inghram, G.
Sir Samuel McCallister, C. G.
Sir Anderson G. Cross, P.
Sir W. T. H. Pauley, S. W.
Sir James Lindsey, J. W.
Sir J. A. J. Buchanan, T.
Sir William Linn Creigh, R.
Sir William A. Porter, St. B.
Sir Simon Rinehart, Sw. B.
Sir James S. Jennings, W.
Sir Joshua C. Phillips, S.

MARCH 25, 859, A. O. 741, A. O. E. P 62.

Sir William McClelland, E. C.
Sir Arthur Inghram, G.
Sir Samuel McCallister, C. G.
Sir Anderson G. Cross, P.
Sir James Lindsey, S. W.

Sir James Lindsey, J. W.
Sir D. W. Braden, T.
Sir William Linn Creigh, R.
Sir J. A. J. Buchanan, St. B.
Sir Justus F. Temple, Sw. B.
Sir Remack Clarke, W.
Sir Joshua C. Phillips, S.

MARCH 12, 1865, A. O. 747, A. O. E. P. 68.

Sir William McClelland, E. C.
Sir Samuel McCallister, G.
Sir D. W. Braden, C. G.
Sir Anderson G. Cross, P.
Sir J. A. J. Buchanan, S. W.
Sir Absalom Hedge, J. W.
Sir D. W. Braden, T.
Sir Justus F. Temple, R.
Sir Joseph Sedgwick, St. B.
Sir Jacob Lemley, Sw. B.
Sir Samuel Sedgwick, W.
Sir Joshua C. Phillips, S.

MARCH 11, 1866, A. O. 748, A. O. E. P. 69.

Sir William McClelland, E. C.
Sir Samuel McCallister, G.
Sir D. W. Braden, C. G.
Sir Anderson G. Cross, P.
Sir J. A. J. Buchanan, S. W.
Sir Absalom Hedge, J. W.
Sir William Cotterel, T.
Sir Justus F. Temple, R.
Sir Joseph Sedgwick, St. B.
Sir Jacob Lemley, Sw. B.
Sir Samuel Sedgwick, W.
Sir Joshua C. Phillips, S.

MEMBERS.

NAME.	DATE OF KNIGHTING.
Adams, Elijah, Jr., (No. 3), Ch. Mem.;	May 23, 1850.
Allison, William,	November 5, 1864.
Buchanan, J. A. J. (No. 3), Ch. Mem.,	October 16, 1851.
Braden, D. W.,	June 9, 1858.
Barnes, H. L.,	June 12, 1858.
Brock, John A.,	August 23, 1865.
Craft, Israel L., (No. 3), Ch. Mem.,	March 16, 1850.
Cross, Anderson G., (No. 3), Ch. M.,	October 16, 1851.
Campbell, B. Franklin,	April 15, 1852.
Creigh, Alfred, (Admitted),	May 15, 1854.
Creigh, William Linn,	May 13, 1858.
Clarke, Remack,	July 11, 1858.
Clarke, Nathaniel,	December 16, 1864.
Cotterel, William,	August 23, 1866.
Dorsey, Rev. J. F.,	May 20, 1852.
Henderson, Rev. E. P.,	June 20, 1854.
Huss, J. K.,	May 13, 1858.
Hedge, Absalom,	July 21, 1858.
Hartzell, Samuel,	August 6, 1862.
Inghram, Arthur,	June 19, 1854.
Jennings, James S.,	April 26, 1865.
Kroner, H.,	July 6, 1858.
Lynch, J. W., (No. 3), Ch. Mem.,	April 5, 1851.
Lindsey, Hon. James,	February 23, 1852.
Lindsey, John,	April 21, 1852.
Loar, A.,	June 9, 1858.
Lemley, Jacob,	June 5, 1860.
Maple, Robert, (No. 1), Ch. Mem.,	July 4, 1850.
McClelland, W., (No. 3), Ch. Mem.,	November 22, 1849.
Mickle, Reuben D., (No. 3), Ch. Mem.,	October 16, 1851.
Mahanna, Bradley, (K. R. C.),	September 21, 1853.
McCallister, Samuel,	May 13, 1858.
Moss, G. W.,	July 19, 1858.

NAME.	DATE OF KNIGHTING.
Milliken, J. M.,	June 2, 1859.
Mix, Eli,	October 7, 1864.
Pauley, W. T. H., (No. 3), Ch. Mem.,	July 21, 1851.
Phillips, Joshua C.,	April 14, 1852.
Porter, William A.,	April 16, 1852.
Porter, James,	July 29, 1858.
Pierce, Frank,	November 27, 1864.
Pugh, M. B.,	December 2, 1864.
Rinehart, Simon,	April 22, 1852.
Robert, Lewis,	February 11, 1853.
Randlett, Nathan H.,	October 27, 1864.
Scott, James,	June 19, 1858.
Sedgwick, Joseph,	June 2, 1859.
Sedgwick, Samuel,	July 30, 1862.
Temple, Justus F.,	June 18, 1858.
Taylor, Joseph,	October 20, 1858.
Wilson, F. B.,	February 11, 1853.
Zimmers, Henry,	May 13, 1858.

IMMEDIATELY after the organization of the Pennsylvania Grand Encampment in 1855, the R. E. Sir William W. Wilson, Grand Commander, deemed it advisable for the interests of Templarism, that a Commandery be instituted in the City of Philadelphia. Accordingly the Grand Commander published the following notice:

An Encampment of Knights Templar, under the jurisdiction of the Grand Encampment of Pennsylvania, subordinate to the General Grand Encampment of the United States, will be legally constituted in the City of Philadelphia, on THIS (Monday) EVENING, April 23, 1855, at 7½ o'clock, P. M. It is expected that the Officers of the State Grand Encampment, and also of New York and Maryland, will be present. Resident and visiting Sir Knights in this city, who may be under the jurisdiction of the General Grand Encampment of the United States of America, are invited to be present. The reception room will be the parlors of the United States Hotel, Chestnut street.

W. W. WILSON, *R. E. G. C.*

On the 23d of April, 1855, Keystone Commandery was instituted by issuing a Dispensation to the following Sir Knights:

Sir James L. Bugh, E. C., No. 7.
Sir C. A. Wolfe, G., No. 1.
Sir Samuel Eakin, C. G., No. 1.

K   225

The organization of this Commandery was never perfected.   The union of the two bodies being accomplished,
the R. E. Grand Commandery circumscribed Templarism in Philadelphia to Commanderies Nos. 2 and 4, which
were in a highly prosperous condition.

A CHARTER was granted to this Encampment by the Pennsylvania Grand Encampment, dated May 10, 1855, during the Grand Mastership of the M. E. Sir R. Sterling Wilson. At the union of the two Grand Encampments it was subsequently endorsed by R. E. Sir William W. Wilson, Grand Commander, and M. E. Sir Anthony E. Stocker, February 17, 1857.

Union Lodge, No. 121, granted the sanction of its Warrant to open Union Encampment, No. 6.

LIST OF OFFICERS.

MAY 10, 1855, A. O. 737, A. O. E. P. 59.

Sir Thomas Balch, G. M.
Sir Charles F. Beck, G.
Sir William Camac, C. G.

All the minutes and papers appertaining to this Commandery, we learn, are in the hands of Sir A. E. Stocker, and regret our inability to procure them; his absence from the city on important business preventing it. However, after the union of the two Grand Commanderies, it returned its Charter to the Grand Commandery. We have given the officers and members as far as they could be obtained.

227

MEMBERS.

NAME.	DATE OF KNIGHTING.
Balch, Thomas, (No. 2), Ch. Mem.,	April 15, 1851.
Béck, C. F., (No. 2), Ch. Mem.,	November 14, 1851.
Booth, J. C., (No. 2), Ch. Mem.,	January 10, 1851.
Butler, E. H.,	June 14, 1850.
Camac, William,	June 9, 1851.
Norris, O. A.,	November 24, 1851.
Skerret, D. C.,	May 26, 1848.
Taylor, Stephen,	December 16, 1851.

ST. OMERS COMMANDERY, No. 7, is located in Brownsville, (but formerly in Uniontown), Fayette County,
Pennsylvania.

On the first day of September, 1853, application was
made for a Charter to the M. E. William Blackstone
Hubbard, Grand Master of the Grand Encampment of
Knights Templar of the United States, by Sir Knights
Rev. Noble Gillespie, John Bierer, Andrew Patrick,
James Piper, Rev. George B. McElroy, Richard Hus-
kin, William Thorndell, Jr., William B. McMillan,
and Robert Boyle, which application was recommended
by Jacques De Molay Commandery of Washington,
Pennsylvania.

In reference to the application for this Charter, Grand
Master Hubbard, in his annual address at the triennial
meeting of the Grand Encampment of Knights Templar,
held at Lexington, Kentucky, in 1853, said it was the design of the petitioners, in unison with the other chartered
Commanderies in Pennsylvania, that although but a
brief time would elapse, the Dispensation should issue so
as to entitle them to obtain a Charter at your present
session, (for the purpose of organizing a Grand Encampment). As the time was too limited for that purpose, I
deemed it best to refer the same to you for your appropriate action in the premises. The question was referred
to the Committee on the Doings of the Grand Officers,
whereupon Sir Philip C. Tucker, Chairman of the Com-

mittee, on the 19th of September, 1853, recommended that a Charter should be granted at the present session for the establishment of an Encampment at Uniontown, Pennsylvania. The recommendation was adopted, and *St. Omers Commandery* was organized December 14, 1853.

OFFICERS OF ST. OMERS COMMANDERY, No. 7.

DECEMBER 14, 1853, A. O. 735, A. O. E. P. 56.

Sir John Bierer, E. C.
Sir Andrew Patrick, G.
Sir William Thorndell, Jr., C. G.
Sir Rev. Noble Gillespie, P.
Sir William B. McMillan, Sw. B.
Sir Moses Sheehan, J. W.
Sir William Thorndell, Jr., T.
Sir Richard Huskin, R.
Sir Rev. N. Gillespie, St. B.
Sir Robert Boyle, S. B.
Sir Z. Ludington, W.
Sir G. H. Thorndell, S.

DECEMBER 13, 1854, A. O. 736, A. O. E. P. 57.

Sir John Bierer, E. C.
Sir Andrew Patrick, G.
Sir William Thorndell, Jr., C. G.
Rev. Sir George Brown, P.
Sir James Piper, S. W.
Sir William B. McMillan, J. W.
Sir William Thorndell, Jr., T.
Sir Richard Huskin, R.
Sir Moses Sheehan, St. B.
Sir Robert Boyle, Sw. B.
Sir Z. Ludington, W.
Sir George H. Thorndell, S.

DECEMBER 12, 1855, A. O. 737, A. O. E. P. 58.

Rev. Sir Noble Gillespie, E. C.
Sir Andrew Patrick, G.
Sir William Thorndell, Jr., C. G.
Rev. Sir George B. McElroy, P.
Sir William B. McMillan, S. W.
Sir Richard Huskin, J. W.
Sir Moses Sheehan, T.
Sir James Piper, R.
Sir Robert Boyle, St. B.
Sir Z. Ludington, Sw. B.
Sir W. B. McMillan, W.
Sir George H. Thorndell, S.

MARCH 11, 1856, A. O. 738, A. O. E P. 59.

Sir John Bierer, E. C.
Sir Andrew Patrick, G.
Sir William Thorndell, Jr., C. G.
Rev. Sir George B. McElroy, P.
Sir William B. McMillan, S. W.
Sir Charles S. Seaton, J. W.
Sir Moses Sheehan, T.
Sir Richard Huskin, R.
Sir Robert Boyle, St. B.
Sir Z. Ludington, Sw. B.
Sir James Piper, W.
Sir George H. Thorndell, S.

MARCH 10, 1857, A. O. 739, A. O. E. P. 60.

Sir John Bierer, E. C.
Sir Andrew Patrick, G.
Sir William Thorndell, C. G.
Rev. Sir George B. McElroy, P.
Sir William B. McMillan, S. W.

Sir Charles S. Seaton, J. W.
Sir Moses Sheehan, T.
Sir Richard Huskin, R.
Sir Robert Boyle, St. B.
Sir Z. Ludington, Sw. B.
Sir James Piper, W.
Sir George H. Thorndell, S.

At the meeting of the Grand Commandery, held in 1858, it was *resolved*, That St. Omers Commandery have permission to remove to Brownsville, as a majority of the members resided in that neighborhood.

In 1860, R. E. Sir William H. Allen, Grand Commander, says: Having been informed that *St. Omers Commandery, No.* 7, stationed at Uniontown, Fayette County, had not reported to the Grand Commandery for the two years past, from the fact that Officers had removed and left the Commandery destitute of members expert in the work, and that the Sir Knights of said Commandery desired to be congregated, to hold an election of officers and to be instructed in the work and drill, I issued a Warrant to Sir Alfred Creigh to reopen said Commandery, hold an election, install the officers, and exemplify the work of the Orders.

In 1862, R. E. Sir John A. Wright, G. C., in his annual address, says: St. Omers Commandery, No. 7, having paid their dues, I issued a Dispensation to E. Sir Alfred Creigh to place this Commandery and her membership in their true position as Courteous Knights, by the election of officers which has been accomplished, and at their own request, and by a former resolution of this Grand Commandery, I gave authority for its removal to Brownsville, in said county, at which place exists a Lodge, Chapter, and Council, in a prosperous condition.

OCTOBER 23, 1862, A. O. 744, A. O. E. P. 65.

Sir William Chatland, E. C.
Sir William Thorndell, Jr., G.
Sir Charles T. Herd, C. G.
Sir William L. Lafferty, P.
Sir Edward Toynbee, S. W.
Sir William Snowden, J. W.
Sir Thomas Duncan, T.
Sir Samuel S. Snowden, R.
Sir Charles Seaton, St. B.
Sir Redding Bunting, Sw. B.
Sir George H. Thorndell, W.
Sir John S. Marsh, S.

These officers were re-elected in March 1863, A. O. 745, A. O. E. P. 66.

MARCH 9, 1864, A. O. 746, A. O. E. P. 67.

Sir William Chatland, E. C.
Sir William Thorndell, Jr., G.
Sir Charles T. Herd, C. G.
Sir William L. Lafferty, P.
Sir Edward Toynbee, S. W.
Sir William Snowden, J. W.
Sir Thomas Duncan, T.
Sir Samuel S. Snowden, R.
Sir George H. Thorndell, St. B.
Sir J. Clark Breading, Sw. B.
Sir Z. Ludington, W.
Sir John S. Marsh, S.

MARCH 10, 1865, A. O. 747, A. O. E. P. 68.

Sir William Chatland, E. C.
Sir William L. Lafferty, G. *

20 *

Sir D. D. Williams, C. G.
Sir Charles T. Herd, P.
Sir James A. Hill, S. W.
Sir William Snowden, J. W.
Sir Thomas Duncan, T.
Sir Samuel S. Snowden, R.
Sir William Thorndell, Jr., St. B.
Sir Alfred N. Vanhorn, Sw. B.
Sir Z. Ludington, W.
Sir John S. Marsh, S.

MARCH 11, 1866, A. O. 748, A. O. E. P. 69.

Sir William Chatland, E. C.
Sir Charles T. Herd, G.
Sir D. D. Williams, C. G.
Sir John S. Marsh, P.
Sir Edward Toynbee, S. W.
Sir William Snowden, J. W.
Sir Thomas Duncan, T.
Sir Samuel S. Snowden, R.
Sir John Moyer, St. B.
Sir James A. Hill, Sw. B.
Sir Alfred N. Vanhorn, W.
Sir David Anderson, S.

MEMBERS.

NAME.	DATE OF KNIGHTING.
Anderson, David,	March 9, 1866.
Acklin, John,	July 19, 1866.
Ailes, Nixon A.	July 19, 1866.
Bierer, John, (No. 3), Ch. Mem.,	June 16, 1853.
Boyle, Robert, (No. 1), Ch. Mem.,	October 23, 1849.
Brown, Rev. George,	December 15, 1853

NAME.	DATE OF KNIGHTING.
Bugh, James L., (Keystone, No. 5),	January 29, 1854.
Bunting, Redding,	March 16, 1854.
Breading, J. Clarke,	March 17, 1854.
Beall, Hunter Samuel,	July 19, 1866.
Chatland, William, (No. 3),	February 3, 1854.
Duncan, Thomas,	June 12, 1854.
Devore, Abraham A.,	July 19, 1866.
Gillespie, Rev. Noble, Ch. Mem.,	June 12, 1852.
Hague, A. G., (K. R. C.),	January 17, 1856.
Huskin, Richard, (No. 3), Ch. Mem.,	June 16, 1853.
Herd, Charles T., (No. 1), '	May 11, 1852.
Hill, James A.,	November 12, 1864.
Johnston, William H.,	June 12, 1854.
Jacobs, Adam,	March 9, 1866.
Jones, Ahira,	July 19, 1866.
Ludington, Zalmon,	December 16, 1853.
Lafferty, William L.,	May 12, 1848.
McMillan, W. B., (No. 3), Ch. Mem.,	June 16, 1853.
McElroy, Rev. G. B., (No. 1), Ch. M.,	May 23, 1849.
Murphy, John H.,	July 17, 1855.
Marsh, John S.,	January 8, 1863.
Morrison, George,	May 8, 1863.
Mason, Isaac M.,	June 18, 1863.
Moyer, John,	March 9, 1866.
Patrick, Andrew, (No. 3), Ch. Mem.,	June 16, 1853.
Piper, James, (No. 3), Ch. Mem.,	February 24, 1853.
Post, Jacob,	June 20, 1854.
Sheehan, Moses,	December 15, 1853.
Springer, James H.,	June 12, 1854.
Seaton, Charles S.,	June 20, 1854.
Shellenberger, George A.,	June 20, 1854.
Snowden, William,	October 22, 1862.
Snowden, Samuel S., (No. 1), Ch. M.,	May 12, 1852.
Smith, Charles W.,	July 15, 1863.

NAME.	DATE OF KNIGHTING.
Streebe, W. W.,	July 15, 1863.
Thorndell, W., Jr., (No. 1), Ch. Mem.,	February 19, 1850.
Thorndell, George H.,	December 16, 1853.
Toynbee, Edward,	October 16, 1862.
Van Horn, Alfred N.,	June 19, 1863.
Williams, Dunham D.,	June 12, 1863.

St. John's Commandery, No. 8, is located in Carlisle, Cumberland County, Pennsylvania.

The following Sir Knights, viz., Charles E. Blumenthal, George Z. Bretz, John Palmer, Rev. J. N. McJilton, H. W. Heath, D. A. Woodward, D. Martin, Rev. Robert Piggot, and James Webb, presented a petition to the Grand Commandery of this State for a Charter to enable them to organize a Commandery of Knights Templar. The petition was recommended by St. Omers Commandery of Uniontown, Pennsylvania.

The prayer of the Petitioners was granted June 14, 1854, and St. John's Commandery, (then No. 4), was organized August 31, 1854, by Rev. Sir J. N. McJilton, of Baltimore, Maryland, who acted as the proxy of the R. E. Sir W. W. Wilson, G. C.

OFFICERS OF ST. JOHN'S COMMANDERY.

AUGUST 31, 1854, A. O. 736, A. O. E. P. 57.

Sir Charles E. Blumenthal, E. C.
Sir George Z. Bretz, G.
Sir John Palmer, C. G.
Rev. Sir O. H. Tiffany, P.
Sir James H. Weise, S. W.
Sir John Gutshall, J. W.
Sir John Delancey Gorgas, T.

Sir James M. Allen, R.
Sir Christian Eberley, St. B.
Sir Jacob Squier, Sw. B.
Sir John G. McFarlane, W.
Sir N. R. Sturdivant, S.

MARCH 25, 1855, A. O. 737, A. O. E. P. 58.

Rev. Sir A. A. Reese, E. C.
Sir John Palmer, G.
Rev. Sir O. H. Tiffany, C. G.
Rev. Sir Thomas Daugherty, P.
Sir Ephraim Cornman, S. W.
Sir John Gutshall, J. W.
Sir John Delancey Gorgas, T.
Sir James M. Allen, R.
Sir Jacob Squier, St. B.
Sir John G. McFarlane, Sw. B.
Sir N. R. Sturdivant, W.
Sir John F. Yeingst, S.

MARCH 26, 1856, A. O. 738, A. O. E. P. 59.

Sir John Palmer, E. C.
Sir John Hyer, G.
Rev. Sir H. M. Johnson, C. G.
Rev. Sir Thomas Daugherty, P.
Sir Ephraim Cornman, S. W.
Sir John Gutshall, J. W.
Sir John Delancey Gorgas, T.
Sir James M. Allen, R.
Sir William B. Mullen, St. B.
Sir H. C. Metcalf, Sw. B.
Sir Jacob Squier, W.
Sir John Harder, S.

MARCH 25, 1857, A. O. 739, A. O. E. P. 60.

Rev. Sir Thomas Daugherty, E. C.
Sir John Gutshall, G.
Sir George Weise, Jr., C. G.
Rev. Sir A. G. Marlatt, P.
Sir Ephraim Cornman, S. W.
Sir Peter Monyer, J. W.
Sir John Delancey Gorgas, T.
Sir James M. Allen, R.
Sir George Z. Bretz, St. B.
Rev. Sir H. M. Johnson, Sw. B.
Sir Jacob Squier, W.
Sir John Harder, S.

MARCH 24, 1858, A. O. 740, A. O. E. P. 61.

Sir John Gutshall, E. C.
Sir George Weise, Jr., G.
Sir John A. Humerick, C. G.
Rev. Sir John A. Gere, P.
Sir E. Powell, S. W.
Sir John Campbell, J. W. ˙
Sir John Delancey Gorgas, T.
Sir James M. Allen, R.
Sir William W. Dale, St. B.
Sir W. H. Haller, Sw. B.
Sir Ephraim Cornman, W.
Sir John Harder, S.

MARCH 23, 1859, A. O. 741, A. O. E. P. 62

Sir John Gutshall, E. C.
Sir George Weise, Jr., G.
Sir John A. Humerick, C. G.
Sir John Hyer, P.
Sir Peter Monyer, S. W.

Sir Joshua P. Bixler, J. W.
Sir John Campbell, T.
Sir James M. Allen, R.
Sir William D. A. Naugle, St. B.
Sir John Harder, Sw. B.
Sir Jacob Squier, W.
Sir John F. Yeingst, S.

MARCH 22, 1860, A. O. 742, A. O. E. P. 63.

Sir George Z. Bretz, E. C.
Rev. Sir H. M. Johnson, G.
Sir John A. Humerick, C. G.
Sir John Hyer, P.
Sir William W. Dale, S. W.
Sir John Gutshall, J. W.
Sir John Campbell, T.
Sir James M. Allen, R.
Sir W. D. A. Naugle, St. B.
Sir John Harder, Sw. B.
Sir John Delancey Gorgas, W.
Sir J. F. Yeingst, S.

MARCH 21, 1861, A. O. 743, A. O. E. P. 64.

Sir George Z. Bretz, E. C.
Rev. Sir H. M. Johnson, G.
Sir John A. Humerick, C. G.
Sir John Hyer, P.
Sir William W. Dale, S. W.
Sir John Gutshall, J. W.
Sir John Campbell, T.
Sir James M. Allen, R.
Sir W. D. A. Naugle, St. B.
Sir John Harder, Sw. B.

Sir John Delancey Gorgas, W.
Sir J. F. Yeingst, S.

MARCH 20, 1862, A. O. 744, A. O. E. P. 65.

Rev. Sir H. M. Johnson, E. C.
Sir William W. Dale, G.
Sir Joshua P. Bixler, C. G.
Sir John Hyer, P.
Sir John A. Humerick, S. W.
Sir William Vance, J. W.
Sir John Campbell, T.
Sir Ephraim Cornman, R.
Sir John Delancey Gorgas, St. B.
Sir Jacob Squier, Sw. B.
Sir W. D. A. Naugle, W.
Sir John Harder, S.

MARCH 14, 1863, A. O. 745, A. O. E. P. 66.

Rev. Sir H. M. Johnson, E. C.
Sir William W. Dale, G.
Rev. Sir J. Clarke Haguey, C. G.
Sir John Heyer, P.
Sir John A. Humerick, S. W.
Sir William Vance, J. W.
Sir John Delancey Gorgas, T.
Sir Ephraim Cornman, R.
Sir John Campbell, St. B.
Sir Jacob Squier, Sw. B.
Sir W. D. A. Naugle, W.·
Sir John Harder, S.

MARCH 13, 1864, A. O. 746, A. O. E. P. 67.

Rev. Sir H. M. Johnson, E. C.
Sir William W. Dale, G.

Rev. Sir J. Clarke Haguey, C. G.
Sir John Hyer, P.
Sir William B. Mullen, S. W.
Sir John Campbell, J. W.
Sir John D. Gorgas, T.
Sir Ephraim Cornman, R.
Sir Jacob Squier, St. B.
Sir William Vance, Sw. B.
Sir W. D. A. Naugle, W.
Sir John Harder, S.

MARCH 12, 1865, A. O. 747, A. O. E. P. 68.

Sir John Palmer, E. C.
Sir John Gutshall, G.
Sir Henry Porter, C. G.
Sir John Hyer, P.
Sir William Vance, S. W.
Sir Joseph W. Patton, J. W.
Sir John Delancey Gorgas, T.
Sir Ephraim Cornman, R.
Sir Alfred J. Herman, St. B.
Sir Henry S. Ferris, Sw. B.
Sir James M. Allen, W.
Sir John Harder, S.

MARCH 11, 1866, A. O. 748, A. O. E. P. 69

Sir John Palmer, E. C.
Sir John Gutshall, G.
Sir John Hyer, C. G.
Rev. Sir Thomas Daugherty, P.
Sir R. H. Thomas, S. W.
Sir T. J. Kerr, J. W.
Sir John Delancey Gorgas, T.
Sir Ephraim Cornman, R.

Sir C. E. McGlaughlin, St. B.
Sir William Vance, Sw. B.
Sir Edgar Lee, W.
Sir John Harder, S.

MEMBERS.

NAME.	DATE OF KNIGHTING.
Allen, James M.,	August 31, 1854.
Ale, Lemuel, (No. 8),	August 13, 1855.
Adams, William,	November 24, 1859.
Ahl, David,	April 28, 1864.
Blumenthal, Chas. E., (No. 3), C. M.,	July 20, 1853.
Bretz, Geo. Z., (Maryland Commandery, No. 1), Charter Mem.,	September 16, 1853.
Baker, Rev. Henry R., (No. 10),	August 13, 1855.
Brooks, Horace,	January 9, 1856.
Bixler, Joshua P.,	April 28, 1859.
Baker, J. C.,	June 4, 1860.
Burkholder, Henry L.,	February 22, 1866.
Bowman, H. A.,	February 22, 1866.
Bowman, John D.,	May 24, 1866.
Consor, S. M. L.,	May 31, 1855.
Clarke, Rev. A. B., (No. 10),	August 13, 1855.
Cornman, Ephraim,	October 18, 1855.
Cooke, W. H.,	January 9, 1856.
Campbell, John,	November 26, 1857.
Chambers, Rev. R. D.,	December 23, 1858.
Chenoworth, G. D.,	May 25, 1865.
Daugherty, Rev. Thomas,	July 13, 1855.
Diehl, J. S.,	August 13, 1856.
Dale, William W.,	August 27, 1857.
De Pew, Ezra,	June 15, 1864.
Eberley, Christian,	August 31, 1854.
Edwards, John, (No. 11),	November 8, 1855.
Emminger, J.,	December 24, 1857.

NAME.	DATE OF KNIGHTING.
Fetterly, John,	July 13, 1855.
Ferris, H. S.,	December 26, 1861
Gutshall, John,	August 31, 1854.
Gorgas, John Delancey,	December 11, 1854.
Gere, Rev. J. A.,	July 13, 1855.
Haller, William L.,	September 6, 1854.
Harder, John,	November 22, 1854.
Hogan, Andrew,	February 23, 1855.
Hardy, Charles,	October 18, 1855.
Hamaker, H. R.,	January 24, 1856.
Hyer, John,	October 30, 1856.
Humerick, John A.,	April 22, 1858.
Heath, H. W., (Maryland Encampment, (No. 1), Charter Mem.,	October 16, 1853.
Herman, Alfred J.,	November 24, 1859.
Haguey, Rev. J. Clarke,	December 6, 1861.
Heiser, Henry D.,	February 22, 1866.
Herbst, Augustus,	February 22, 1866.
Heck, George B.,	May 24, 1866.
Johnson, Rev. H. M.,	September 6, 1854.
Kerr, Thomas J.,	September 28, 1865.
Kauffman, Levi,	October 26, 1865.
Lloyd, A. M., (No. 10),	July 13, 1855.
Lee, Edgar,	September 28, 1865.
Martin, D., Charter Member,	December 16, 1852.
McJilton, Rev. J. N., Charter Mem.,	January 12, 1850.
McFarlane, J. G.,	August 31, 1854.
Monyer, Peter,	March 28, 1855.
Mullen, William B.,	July 13, 1855.
Metcalf, Hiram C.,	October 18, 1855.
McCalla, G. W.,	November 22, 1855.
Marlett, Rev. A. G.,	May 22, 1857.
McLaughlin, N. B.,	May 27, 1858.
McKesson, Samuel,	November 24, 1859.

NAME.	DATE OF KNIGHTING.
McLaughlin, Charles T.,	September 28, 1865.
Maglaughlin, Charles E.,	September 28, 1865.
Mooney, George K.,	October 26, 1865.
Naugle, W. D. A.,	April 29, 1858.
Piggot, Rev. R., (No. 4), Ch. Mem.,	October 25, 1826.
Palmer, John, (Maryland Encampment, No. 1), Charter Mem.,	September 16, 1853.
Parke, Benjamin, (No. 11),	July 13, 1855.
Patton, G. W., (No. 10),	August 13, 1855.
Powell, Edward,	March 3, 1858.
Phelps, C. C.,	March 3, 1858.
Peters, H. C.,	June 26, 1860.
Porter, Henry,	November 5, 1863.
Patton, Joseph W.,	June 15, 1864.
Reese, Rev. A. A.,	November 1, 1854.
Riley, J. M.,	July 13, 1855.
Reifsnyder, J. L.,	August 13, 1858.
Rheem, A. K.,	May 25, 1865.
Squier, Jacob,	August 31, 1854.
Sturdivant, N. R.,	September 6, 1854.
Sellars, H. A., (No. 10),	August 13, 1855.
Stewart, A. R., (No. 10),	August 13, 1855.
Scheffer, Theodore F., (No. 11),	November 22, 1855.
Snively, Rev. W. A.,	January 31, 1856.
Schriner, J. W., (No. 12),	February 28, 1856.
Stoner, H. L.,	April 23, 1857.
Schaffert, A. F.,	April 23, 1857.
Shoemaker, W. B.,	February 22, 1866.
Tiffany, Rev. O. H.,	September 6, 1854.
Tonner, John,	July 13, 1855.
Thomas, Charles F.,	October 26, 1865.
Vance, William,	January 26, 1860.
Woodward, D. A., (Maryland Encampment, No. 1), Ch. Mem.,	March 16, 1852.

21 *

NAME.	DATE OF KNIGHTING.
Webb, James, Charter Member,	July 20, 1851.
Weise, James H.,	August 31, 1854.
Wright, John A., (No. 10),	August 13, 1855.
Wallower, John, (No. 11),	November 8, 1855.
Wilson, John T., (No. 11),	November 22, 1855.
Weise, George,	January 9, 1856.
Weseman, G. P.,	May 25, 1865.
Yeingst, J. F.,	February 23, 1855.
Zug, Ephraim,	April 26, 1855.

DE MOLAY COMMANDERY, No. 9.

DE MOLAY COMMANDERY, No. 9, of Reading, Berks County, Pennsylvania.

This Commandery was originally No. 6, under the authority of the Grand Encampment of Pennsylvania, which derived its authority from the R. W. Grand Lodge of Pennsylvania, which permitted Chandler Lodge, No. 227, of Reading, to use their Charter for conferring the Orders of Knighthood. The Charter was granted February 7, 1854.

OFFICERS OF DE MOLAY COMMANDERY, No. 9, SINCE ITS ORGANIZATION.

MARCH 16, 1854, A. O. 736, A. O. E. P. 57.

Sir S. E. Ancona, E. C.
Sir James Millholland, G.
Sir A. Jordan Swartz, C. G.
Sir Samuel McDonald, P.
Sir William H. Strickland, R.
Sir John H. Keim, T.
Sir David E. Stout, S. W.
Sir Henry R. Hawman, J. W.
Sir William Lilly, W.
Sir Stephen Orth, Sw. B.

MARCH 15, 1855, A. O. 737, A. O. E. P. 58.

Sir James Millholland, E. C.
Sir A. Jordan Swartz, G.

Sir David E. Stout, C. G.
Sir S. E. Ancona, P.
Sir Samuel McDonald, S. W.
Sir Franklin Beidler, J. W.
Sir John H. Keim, T.
Sir William H. Strickland, R.
Sir William Lilly, St. B.
Sir Henry R. Hawman, Sw. B.

MARCH 25, 1856, A. O. 738, A. O. E. P. 59.

Sir A. Jordan Swartz, E. C.
Sir John F. Bellemere, G.
Rev. Sir Milton C. Lightner, C. G.
Sir S. E. Ancona, P.
Sir Henry C. L. Crecelius, S. W.
Sir David A. Griffith, J. W.
Sir J. Millholland, T.
Sir George Knopp, R.
Sir Frederick Lauer, St. B.
Sir William H. Keim, Sw. B.
Sir O. H. Wiley, W.
Sir Stephen Orth, S.

MARCH 24, 1857, A. O. 739, A. O. E. P. 60.

Sir John F. Bellemere, E. C.
Sir William H. Strickland, G.
Sir Henry D. Lowe, C. G.
Rev. Sir Milton C. Lightner, P.
Sir Henry R. Hawman, S. W.
Sir Frederick Lauer, J. W.
Sir J. Millholland, T.
Sir George L. Knopp, R.
Sir David A. Griffith, St. B.
Sir William H. Keim, Sw. B.

Sir O. P. Wiley, W.
Sir Stephen Orth, S.

MARCH 23, 1858, A. O. 740, A. O. E. P. 61.

Sir William H. Strickland, E. C.
Sir H. D. Lowe, G.
Sir Henry R. Hawman, C. G.
Rev. Sir Milton C. Lightner, P.
Sir Henry C. L. Creccelius, S. W.
Sir D. A. Griffith, J. W.
Sir J. Millholland, T.
Sir George L. Knopp, R.
Sir J. V. H. Stevenson, St. B.
Sir Henry Hahn, Sw. B.
Sir A. C. Henry, W.
Sir Stephen Orth, S.

MARCH 22, 1859, A. O. 741, A. O. E. P. 62.

Sir H. D. Lowe, E. C.
Sir Henry R. Hawman, G.
Sir D. A. Griffith, C. G.
Rev. Sir Milton C. Lightner, P.
Sir H. C. L. Crecelius, S. W.
Sir Lewis Heilman, J. W.
Sir William H. Strickland, T.
Sir A. C. Henry, R.
Sir J. V. H. Stevenson, St. B.
Sir Henry Hahn, Sw. B.
Sir George L. Knopp, W.
Sir Stephen Orth, S.

MARCH 12, 1860, A. O. 742, A. O. E. P. 63.

Sir Henry R. Hawman, E. C.
Sir David A. Griffith, G.

L *

Sir Frederick S. Hunter, C. G.
Rev. Sir Milton C. Lightner, P.
Sir Lewis Heilman, S. W.
Sir William H. Gernant, J. W.
Sir William H. Strickland, T.
Sir Albert C. Henry, R.
Sir Job H. Cole, St. B.
Sir Adam H. Gernant, Sw. B.
Sir Henry C. L. Crecelius, W.
Sir Stephen Orth, S.

MARCH 13, 1861, A. O. 743, A. O. E. P. 64.

Sir David A. Griffith, E. C.
- Rev. Sir Milton C. Lightner, G.
Sir Samuel McDonnell, C. G.
Sir Thomas T. Jaeger, P.
Sir Washington L. Reifsnyder, S. W.
Sir S. H. Garrigues, J. W.
Sir William H. Strickland, T.
Sir Henry C. L. Crecelius, R.
Sir Adam H. Gernant, St. B.
Sir William H. Keim, Sw. B.
Sir Lewis Heilman, W.
Sir Stephen Orth, S.

MARCH 14, 1862, A. O. 744, A. O. E. P. 65.

Sir Samuel McDonnell, E. C.
Sir Seymour H. Garrigues, G.
Sir Christian Stoltz, C. G.
Sir Thomas T. Jaeger, P.
Sir Lewis Heilman, S. W.
Sir John Phillipson, J. W.
Sir John S. Schroeder, T.
Sir Henry C. L. Crecelius, R.
Sir Adam H. Gernant, St. B.

Sir Albert C. Henry, Sw. B.
Sir William Milnes, Jr., W.
Sir Stephen Orth, S.

MARCH 15, 1863, A. O. 745, A. O. E. P. 66.

Sir S. H. Garrigues, E. C.
Sir Christian Stoltz, G.
Sir Lewis Heilman, C. G.
Sir Thomas T. Jaeger, P.
Sir William H. Gernant, S. W.
Sir William Milnes, Jr., J. W.
Sir John S. Schroeder, T.
Sir Henry C. L. Crecelius, R.
Sir Levi G. Coleman, St. B.
Sir Adam H. Gernant, Sw. B.
Sir John Phillipson, W.
Sir Stephen Orth, S.

MARCH 16, 1864, A. O. 746, A. O. E. P. 67.

Sir Christian Stoltz, E. C.
Sir William Milnes, Jr., G.
Sir John Keppleman, C. G.
Sir William H. Strickland, P.
Sir Frederick W. Lauer, S. W.
Sir John Ulrich, J. W.
Sir John S. Schroeder, T.
Sir Henry C. L. Crecelius, R.
Sir Thomas T. Jaeger, St. B.
Sir Henry R. Hawman, Sw. B.
Sir Lewis Heilman, W.
Sir Stephen Orth, S.

MARCH 17, 1865, A. O. 747, A. O. E. P. 68.

Sir William Milnes, Jr., E. C.
Sir Henry C. L. Crecelius G.

Sir John C. A. Hoffeditz, C. G.
Sir William H. Strickland, P.
Sir Frederick W. Lauer, S. W.
Sir Ephraim Moser, J. W.
Sir John S. Schroeder, T.
Sir John Keppleman, R.
Sir William Briner, St. B.
Sir Jacob R. Harwick, Sw. B.
Sir Louis Heilman, W.
Sir Stephen Orth, S.

MARCH 18, 1866, A. O. 748, A. O. E. P. 69.

Sir Henry C. L. Crecelius, E. C.
Sir John C. A Hoffeditz, G.
Sir Ephraim Moser, C. G.
Sir Charles W. L. Hoffeditz, P.
Sir Frederick W. Lauer, S. W.
Sir Charles A. Saylor, J. W.
Sir John S. Schroeder, T.
Sir John Keppleman, R.
Sir Bartolett Grant, St. B.
Sir John Chason, Sw. B.
Sir Calvin B. Rhoads, W.
Sir Stephen Orth, S.

MEMBERS.

NAME.	DATE OF KNIGHTING.
Ancona, S. E., (No. 4), Ch. Mem.,	February 4, 1854.
Auman, William,	January 11, 1860.
Allebach, William S.,	February 13, 1866.
Anthony, John C.,	April 28, 1866.
Bellemere, J. F.,	June 14, 1854.
Beidler, Franklin,	September 23, 1854.
Borrel, John F., (K. R. C.),	April 28, 1857.

NAME.	DATE OF KNIGHTING.
Bechtel, J. Y., (No. 20),	February 28, 1860.
Briner, William,	June 21, 1860.
Bancroft, Thomas B.,	April 11, 1865.
Brown, John M.,	July 25, 1865.
Brooks, William,	March 13, 1866.
Bricker, L. C.,	February 13, 1866.
Burkholder, Edward,	July 10, 1866.
Bowman, William G.,	April 28, 1866.
Cole, Job H.,	November 9, 1854.
Crecelius, Henry C. L.,	July 28, 1857.
Chapman, L. F., (No. 20),	February 28, 1860.
Coleman, Levi G.,	December 8, 1860.
Chason, John,	July 25, 1865.
Clewell, William,	July 25, 1865.
Donges, John A.,	April 22, 1865.
Derr, Benneville,	February 13, 1866.
Fernley, T. A.,	November 27, 1855.
Fry, Emanuel G.,	March 13, 1866.
Griffith, David A.,	March 31, 1854.
Garrigues, Seymour H.,	November 28, 1854.
Guilden, W. C.,	January 30, 1855.
Gernant, A. H.,	November 27, 1855.
Graeff, Herman B.,	February 26, 1856.
Gockley, L. D.,	April 27, 1858.
Gernant, W. H.,	January 24, 1860.
Griesemer, Solomon, (No. 20),	February 28, 1860.
Grant, Bartolett,	August 22, 1865.
Griesemer, E. E.,	July 10, 1866.
Hawman, Henry R.	March 25, 1854.
Hahn, Henry,	June 25, 1854.
Hunter, F. S.,	November 9, 1854.
Hunter, Cyrus,	April 24, 1855.
Henry, Albert C.,	July 28, 1857.
Heilman, Louis,	July 28, 1857.

22

NAME.	DATE OF KNIGHTING.
Hunter, Charles H.,	April 24, 1855.
Houston, James, (No. 20),	February 28, 1860.
Hain, Frank H.,	March 15, 1860.
Hollenback, Samuel U.,	December 8, 1860.
Heller, Frederic P.,	December 8, 1860.
Hopkins, William H.,	July 28, 1863.
Harwick, Jacob R.,	June 28, 1864.
Hoffeditz, John C. A.,	February 13, 1865.
Hoffmaster, Zeno,	February 14, 1865.
Hoffeditz, Charles W. L.,	July 25, 1865.
Hertzler, John C.,	August 22, 1865.
Hesser, Franklin H.,	March 13, 1866.
Hunter, William D.,	April 28, 1866.
Hunter, Henry A.,	May 18, 1866.
Hagy, Benjamin F.,	May 18, 1866.
Horning, Michael B.,	July 10, 1866.
Jeffry, William,	March 25, 1854.
Jaeger, Thomas T.,	July 28, 1857.
Jacobs, Jacob Howard,	April 28, 1866.
Keim, William H.,	March 25, 1854.
Knopp, George L.,	September 23, 1854.
Keim, John H., (No. 4), Ch. Mem.,	February 4, 1854.
Kain, F. R.,	March 15, 1860.
Keim, George M.,	June 21, 1860.
Keppleman, John,	March 12, 1863.
Koch, Henry,	February 14, 1865.
Lilly, William, (No. 20),	March 25, 1854.
Lauer, Frederick,	March 25, 1854.
Lowe, Henry D.,	September 23, 1854.
Lightner, Rev. Milton C.,	February 26, 1856.
Lechner, G. W.,	April 27, 1858.
Lauer, Frederick W.,	February 14, 1865.
Luks, Emil C.,	April 11, 1866.
McDonnell, S., (No. 4), Ch. Mem.,	February 4, 1854.

NAME.	DATE OF KNIGHTING.
Millholland, Jas., (No. 4), Ch. Mem.,	February 4, 1854.
Mullin, James,	March 25, 1854.
Moore, William,	February 2, 1856.
Mengle, Jeremiah,	March 25, 1856.
Manberbeck, Martin,	April 27, 1858.
Mosser, David O., (No. 20),	May 25, 1858.
Milnes, William, Jr.,	June 18, 1860.
Moser, Ephraim,	February 13, 1865.
McManus, Redmond,	February 14, 1865.
Myers, Franklin,	August 22, 1865.
Maxton, John B.,	October 24, 1865.
Mellert, Arnold,	February 13, 1866.
Martz, Jacob H.,	February 13, 1866.
Moll, John,	March 13, 1866.
Murray, William W.,	April 28, 1866.
Orth, Stephen	April 28, 1857.
Oberly, J. H.,	April 27, 1858.
Otis, William R., (No. 20),	February 28, 1860.
Ordway, Joseph C. P.,	August 25, 1863
Phillips, Charles,	April 27, 1858.
Price, Samuel H., (No. 20),	April 16, 1860.
Phillipson, John,	February 25, 1862.
Reifsnyder, Washington L.,	March 9, 1858.
Ruth, Henry,	February 25, 1862.
Reichenbach, E. Charles,	June 2, 1865.
Reichard, Jacob,	February 13, 1866.
Rhoads, Calvin B.,	December 12, 1865.
Ritter, William S.,	December 12, 1865.
Rightmeyer, Albert F.,	March 13, 1866.
Reider, Emanuel,	May 18, 1866.
Ritter, Ferdinand S.,	February 13, 1865.
Swartz, A. Jordan, (No. 4), Ch. Mem.,	February 4, 1854.
Stout, David E., (No. 4.), Ch. Mem.,	February 4, 1854.
Strickland, William H., (No. 4), C. M.,	February 4, 1854.

NAME.	DATE OF KNIGHTING.
Stephen, John,	February 2, 1856.
Schonower, J. B.,	February 2, 1856.
Stevenson, J. V. H.,	July 28, 1857.
Smith, E. Penn.,	April 27, 1858.
Schall, George B., (No. 20),	February 28, 1860.
Smith, Levi J.,	June 12, 1860.
Schroeder, John S.,	June 21, 1860.
Stoltz, Christian,	December 8, 1860.
Seltzer, George L.,	November 26, 1863.
Streng, Martin,	February 13, 1865.
Stamm, Cornelius S.,	August 22, 1865.
Saylor, Charles A.,	October 24, 1865.
Sellars, Mahlon A.,	February 13, 1866.
Sowers, Frederick,	March 13, 1866.
Tea, Samuel H.,	October 24, 1865.
Trichler, Jacob F.,	March 13, 1866.
Ulrich, John,	December 15, 1863.
Wells, W. A.,	April 7, 1854.
Wiley, O. Penrose,	November 9, 1854.
Washburn, Daniel,	June 18, 1860.
Witman, Henry S.,	March 12, 1863.
Weidman, W. Murray,	March 13, 1866.
Witman, William C.,	March 13, 1866.
Weidman, Grant,	April 28, 1866.
Weimer, Lucius E.,	April 28, 1866.
Weidle, Jacob,	May 16, 1866.

MOUNTAIN COMMANDERY, No. 10, was organized at Altoona, Blair County, Pennsylvania, on the 20th day of September, 1855. When organized it was named and numbered *Blumenthal Commandery, No. 6*, on account of the services rendered to Templarism in the State by the R. E. Sir Charles E. Blumenthal, Grand Commander.

The Petitioners for the Dispensation were Sir Knights, Rev. A. B. Clarke, H. A. Sellars, George W. Patton, A. R. Stewart, Lemuel Ale, John A. Wright, J. L. Reif-snyder, Rev. Henry R. Baker, A. M. Lloyd.

The Charter was granted June 11, 1856.

OFFICERS OF MOUNTAIN COMMANDERY, No. 10, FROM ITS ORGANIZATION.

SEPTEMBER 20, 1855, A. O. 737, A. O. E. P. 58.

Rev. Sir A. B. Clarke, E. C.
Sir H. A. Sellars, G.
Sir George W. Patton, C. G.
Rev. Sir Henry R. Baker, P.
Sir A. R. Stewart, S. W.
Sir Lemuel Ale, J. W.
Sir John A. Wright, T.
Sir A. F. McKinney, R.
Sir G. B. Cramer, St. B.
Sir Jesse R. Crawford, Sw. B.

22 *

Sir C. W. O'Donnell, W.
Sir J. L. Reifsnyder, S.

MARCH 20, 1856, A O. 738, A. O. E. P. 59.

Rev. Sir A. B. Clarke, E. C.
Sir H. A. Sellars, G.
Sir George W. Patton, C. G.
Rev. Sir Henry R. Baker, P.
Sir A. R. Stewart, S. W.   .
Sir Lemuel Ale, J. W.
Sir John A. Wright, T.
Sir A. F. McKinney, R.
Sir G. B. Cramer, St. B.
Sir John M. Gilmore, Sw. B.
Sir C. W. O'Donnell, W.
Sir H. L. Smith, S.

MARCH 21, 1857, A. O. 739, A. O. E. P. 60

Sir John A. Wright, E. C.
Rev. Sir Henry R. Baker, G.
Sir George B. Cramer, C. G.
Rev. Sir C. M. Clink, P.
Sir J. M. Gilmore, S. W.
Sir C. F. Sargent, J. W.
Sir F. A. Denning, T.
Rev. Sir A. B. Clarke, R.
Sir J. L. Reifsnyder, St. B.
Sir Henry E. Grey, Sw. B.
Sir J. P. Levan, W.
Sir G. B. Cramer, S.

MARCH 22, 1858, A. O. 740, A. O. E. P. 61

Sir C. F. Sargent, E. C.
Sir George B. Cramer, G.

Sir John McConnel, C. G.
Sir John Shoemaker, P.
Sir A. R. Stewart, S. W.
Sir John P. Levan, J. W.
Sir F. A. Denning, T.
Sir George W. Patton, R.
Sir Hays Hamilton, St. B.
Sir J. L. Reifsnyder, Sw. B.
Rev. Sir A. B. Clarke, W.
Sir H. L. Smith, S.

MARCH 23, 1859, A. O. 741, A. O. E. P. 62.

Sir Edmund H. Turner, E. C.
Sir John McConnel, G.
Sir Archibald H. Maxwell, C. G.
Rev. Sir R. W. Oliver, P.
Sir J. J. Crane, S. W.
Sir J. P. Levan, J. W.
Sir John Shoemaker, T.
Sir Robert A. O. Kerr, R.
Sir George Potts, St. B.
Sir Robert Rodgers, Sw. B.
Sir J. L. Reifsnyder, W.
Sir G. B. Cramer, S.

MARCH 24, 1860, A. O. 742, A. O. E. P. 63.

Sir Edmund H. Turner, E. C.
Sir Archibald H. Maxwell, G.
Sir John P. Levan, C. G.
Rev. Sir R. W. Oliver, P.
Sir C. R. Hostetter, S. W.
Sir John L. Piper, J. W.
Sir C. C. Mason, T.
Sir Robert A. O. Kerr, R.

Sir Robert Rodgers, St. B.
Sir Anthony Vowinkle, Sw. B.
Sir W. W. Barker, W.
Sir Joshua Kelley, S.

MARCH 26, 1861, A. O. 743, A. O. E. P. 64.

Sir Archibald H. Maxwell, E. C.
Sir John P. Levan, G.
Sir C. R. Hostetter, C. G.
Rev. Sir R. W. Oliver, P.
Sir John L. Piper, S. W.
Sir Charles J. Mann, J. W.
Sir C. C. Mason, T.
Sir Robert A. O. Kerr, R.
Sir William R. Findley, St. B.
Sir B. F. Rose, Sw. B.
Sir Robert Rodgers, W.
Sir Joshua Kelley, S.

MARCH 25, 1862, A. O. 744, A. O. E. P. 65.

Sir John P. Levan, E. C.
Sir C. R. Hostetter, G.
Sir John L. Piper, C. G.
Rev. Sir George Guyer, P.
Sir Charles J. Mann, S. W.
Sir Robert Pitcairn, J. W.
Sir J. L. Reifsnyder, T.
Sir Robert A. O. Kerr, R.
Sir M. W. Owens, St. B.
Sir A. Odenwalder, Sw. B.
Sir Robert Rodgers, W.
Sir Joshua Kelley, S.

MARCH 26, 1863, A. O. 745, A. O. E. P. 66.

Sir Robert Pitcairn, E. C.
Sir Robert Rodgers, G.
Sir Charles J. Mann, C. G.
Rev. Sir R. W. Oliver, P.,
Sir W. R. Findley, S. W.
Sir Isaac Fox, J. W.
Sir J. L. Reifsnyder, T.
Sir John McConnel, R.
Sir Adam Odenwalder, St. B.
Sir Joshua Kelley, Sw. B.
Sir R. A. O. Kerr, W.
Sir C. C. Mason, S.

MARCH 24, 1864, A. O. 746, A. O. E. P. 67.

Sir Charles J. Mann, E. C.
Sir R. A. O. Kerr, G.
Sir William R. Findley, C. G.
Rev. Sir George Guyer, P.
Sir John P. Levan, S. W.
Sir A. H. Maxwell, J. W.
Sir J. L. Reifsnyder, T.
Sir A. C. Vauclain, R.
Sir Samuel H. Bell, St. B.
Sir Robert Pitcairn, Sw. B.
Sir William Boyden, W.
Sir C. C. Mason, S.

MARCH 25, 1865, A. O. 747, A. O. E. P. 68.

Sir Robert A. O. Kerr, E. C.
Sir William R. Findley, G.
Sir John L. Piper, C. G.
Sir Edmund H. Turner, P.
Sir J. L. Reifsnyder, S. W.

Sir Isaac Fox, J. W.
Sir Adam Odenwalder, T.
Sir William Boyden, R.
Sir A. Vowinkle, St. B.
Sir A. C. Vauclain, Sw. B.
Sir Charles J. Mann, W.
Sir C. C. Mason, S.

MARCH 24, 1866, A. O. 748, A. O. E. P. 69.

Sir William R. Findley, E. C.
Sir J. L. Reifsnyder, G.
Sir E. B. McCrum, C. G.
Sir E. H. Turner, P.
Sir W. C. Keller, S. W.
Sir H. C. Dern, J. W.
Sir A. Odenwalder, T.
Sir William Boyden, R.
Sir King McLanahan, St. B.
Sir Isaac Fox, Sw. B.
Sir R. A. O. Kerr, W.
Sir C. C. Mason, S.

MEMBERS.

NAME.	DATE OF KNIGHTING.
Ale, Lemuel, (No. 8), Ch. Mem.,	August 31, 1854.
Baker, Rev. Henry R., (No. 8), C. M.,	August 13, 1855.
Boyden, William,	April 26, 1859.
Bell, James,	June 15, 1859.
Bell, Samuel H.,	June 23, 1859.
Barker, Matthew W.,	January 26, 1860.
Bond, Robert M.,	February 16, 1861.
Bell, B. F.,	February 19, 1861.
Clarke, Rev. A. B., (No. 8), Ch. M.,	August 13, 1855.
Crawford, Jesse R.,	September 20, 1855.
Crane, Irvine I.,	September 20, 1855.

NAME.	DATE OF KNIGHTING.
Cramer, George B.,	September 20, 1855.
Clink, Rev. C. M.,	February 14, 1856.
Cunningham, James A.,	December 16, 1856.
Courter, David,	May 11, 1857.
Cresswell, John,	July 16, 1857.
Clark, Rowan,	September 26, 1865.
Chamberlain, W. H.,	May 28, 1866.
Denning, F. A.,	November 15, 1855.
Dailey, J. B.,	October 27, 1857.
Dosh, Rev. J. C. H.,	October 15, 1858.
Dare, George,	June 15, 1859.
Dern, H. C.,	July 25, 1865.
Funk, James,	July 27, 1858.
Findley, Dr. William R.,	February 28, 1860.
Fox, Isaac,	November 26, 1860.
Gilmore, John M.,	September 20, 1855.
Gibson, A. E.,	January 10, 1856.
Gray, Henry E.,	February 14, 1856.
Gardner, James,	December 16, 1856.
Guyer, Rev. George,	December 28, 1858.
Greenwood, Ralph,	July 26, 1859.
Graham, D. L.,	September 25, 1860.
Hamilton, Hays,	November 24, 1857.
Hostetter, C. R.,	June 1, 1859.
Hughes, W. R.,	February 16, 1861.
Hess, Albert E.,	May 28, 1866.
Jackson, W. W.,	August 26, 1856.
Kerr, Robert A. O.,	February 22, 1859.
Kelley, Joshua,	July 23, 1859.
Keller, W. C.,	August 26, 1865.
King, Robert,	August 28, 1866.
Lloyd, A. M., (No. 8), Ch. Mem.,	July 23, 1855.
Lombart, Herman J.,	September 20, 1855.
Levan, John P.,	May 14, 1856.

NAME	DATE OF KNIGHTING.
Long, William J.,	May 18, 1859.
Leathead, Rev. John,	September 22, 1863.
Long, George H.,	June 26, 1860.
McKinney, A. F.,	September 20, 1855.
McMillan, John A.,	September 20, 1855.
Mowrey, George R., (No. 11),	November 15, 1855.
McKee, J. C.,	August 26, 1856.
Maxwell, Archibald H.,	October 27, 1857.
McConnel, John,	July 16, 1857.
Mason, C. C.,	July 23, 1859.
Mann, Charles J.,	November 26, 1860.
Mendenhall, Jesse,	September 22, 1863.
McLanahan, King,	May 29, 1865.
McCrum, E. B.,	July 25, 1865.
Miller, R. Allison,	April 25, 1865.
Miller, Graffus,	October 27, 1865.
O'Donnell, C. W.,	September 20, 1855.
Osterloh, John C.,	July 27, 1858.
Oliver, Rev. R. W.,	July 28, 1858.
Odenwalder, Adam,	November 10, 1859.
Owens, Matthew W.,	November 10, 1860.
Patton, Geo. W., (No. 1), Ch. Mem.,	August 13, 1855.
Potts, George,	October 15, 1858.
Pitcairn, Robert,	November 10, 1858.
Piper, John L.,	March 31, 1860.
Ross, John,	May 29, 1856.
Reifsnyder, Joshua L.,	September 20, 1856.
Rogers, Robert,	January 29, 1859.
Rose, B. F.,	April 26, 1859.
Robison, D. P.,	September 22, 1863.
Sellars, H. A., (No. 8), Ch. Mem.,	August 13, 1855.
Stewart, A. R., (No. 8), Ch. Mem.,	August 13, 1855.
Sargent, C. F.,	February 14, 1856.
Sink, C. B.,	May 14, 1856.

NAME.	DATE OF KNIGHTING.
Smith, H. L.,	May 29, 1856.
Shoemaker, John,	December 23, 1857.
Simons, John B.,	May 9, 1859.
Swartz, George W.,	August 28, 1866.
Terry, James,	March 24, 1857.
Turner, Edmund H.,	October 26, 1858.
Traugh, O. A.,	August 26, 1865.
Vowinkle, Anthony,	May 24, 1859.
Vauclain, A. C.,	September 10, 1859.
Wright, John A., (No. 8), Ch. Mem.,	August 13, 1855.
Wright, Archibald W.,	September 20, 1855.
Willson, Rev. S. A.,	February 1, 1859.
Woods, John,	June 10, 1859.
Wills, William,	October 27, 1863.
Wood, D. D.,	October 24, 1865.

23

PARKE COMMANDERY, No. 11.

Parke Commandery, No. 11, located at Harrisburg, Dauphin County, Pennsylvania. This Commandery, when it received a Dispensation from the R. E. Charles E. Blumenthal, Grand Commander, on the 15th December, 1855, was No. 7, but at the reunion of the two Grand Encampments of the State, became No. 11.

It was organized December 28, 1855. The Petitioners for the Dispensation, were Sir Knights Benjamin Parke, John T. Wilson, John Edwards, George W. McCalla, Theodore F. Scheffer, N. R. Sturdivant, Rev. Beverly R. Waugh, John Wallower, and George R. Mowrey.

The Charter was granted, June 11, 1856.

OFFICERS OF PARKE COMMANDERY, No. 11, FROM ITS ORGANIZATION.

DECEMBER 28, 1855, A. O. 737, A. O. E. P. 58.

Sir Benjamin Parke, E. C.
Sir John T. Wilson, G.
Sir John Edwards, C. G.
Rev. Sir Beverly R. Waugh, P.
Sir Robert A. Lamberton, S. W.
Sir William T. Bishop, J. W.
Sir William H. Kepner, T.
Sir Theodore F. Scheffer, R.
Sir Thomas J. Jordan, St. B.
Sir John Wallower, Sw. B.

Sir William H. Egle, W.
Sir Michael Bender, S.

JUNE 18, 1856, A. O. 738, A. O. E. P. 59.

Sir Benjamin Parke, E. C.
Sir John T. Wilson, G.
Sir John Edwards, C. G.
Rev. Sir Beverly R. Waugh, P.
Sir Robert A. Lamberton, S. W.
Sir William T. Bishop, J. W.
Sir William H. Kepner, T.
Sir Theodore F. Scheffer, R.
Sir Thomas J. Jordan, St. B.
Sir John Wallower, Sw. B.
Sir William H. Egle, W.
Sir Michael Bender, S.

MARCH 15, 1857, A. O. 739, A. O. E. P. 60

Sir Robert A. Lamberton, E. C.
Rev. Sir Beverly R. Waugh, G.
Sir William T. Bishop, C. G.
Sir Amos W. Young, P.
Sir Thomas J. Jordan, S. W.
Sir Robert L. Muench, J. W.
Sir William H. Kepner, T.
Sir Theodore F. Scheffer, R.
Sir John W. Glover, St. B.
Sir John Wallower, Sw. B.
Sir William H. Egle, W.
Sir Michael Bender, S.

MARCH 12, 1858, A. O. 740, A. O. E. P. 61.

Rev. Sir Beverly R. Waugh, E. C.
Sir William T. Bishop, G.

Sir F. W. Boley, C. G.
Sir Amos W. Young, P.
Sir Thomas J. Jordan, S. W.
Sir William O. Hickok, J. W.
Sir William H. Kepner, T.
Sir Theodore F. Scheffer, R.
Sir John W. Glover, St. B.
Sir John Wallower, Sw. B.
Sir William H. Egle, W.
Sir Michael Bender, S.

MARCH 13, 1859, A. O. 741, A. O. E. P. 62.

Sir William T. Bishop, E. C.
Sir Samuel D. Inghram, G.
Sir John W. Glover, C. G.
Rev. Sir Beverly R. Waugh, P.
Sir Thomas J. Jordan, S. W.
Sir C. C. Bombaugh, J. W.
Sir William H. Kepner, T.
Sir Theodore F. Scheffer, R.
Sir William O. Hickok, St. B.
Sir David Mayer, Sw. B.
Sir William H. Egle, W.
Sir Michael Bender, S.

MARCH 18, 1860, A. O. 742, A. O. E. P. 63.

Sir William T. Bishop, E. C.
Sir John W. Glover, G.
Sir William O. Hickok, C. G.
Rev. Sir Beverly R. Waugh, P.
Sir Thomas J. Jordan, S. W.
Sir William Garret, J. W.
Sir J. Brisbane Boyd, T.

Sir Theodore F. Scheffer, R.
Sir Samuel D. Inghram, St. B.
Sir David Mayer, Sw. B.
Sir William H. Egle, W.
Sir Michael Bender, S.

MARCH 19, 1861, A. O. 743, A. O. E. P. 64.

Sir William T. Bishop, E. C.
Sir William O. Hickok, G.
Sir John W. Glover, C. G.
Rev. Sir Beverly R. Waugh, P.
Sir Thomas J. Jordan, S. W.
Sir William H. Egle, J. W.
Sir J. Brisbane Boyd, T.
Sir Theodore F. Scheffer, R.;
Sir David Mayer, St. B.
Sir Samuel D. Inghram, Sw. B.
Sir William Garret, W.
Sir Michael Bender, S.

MARCH 20, 1862, A. O. 744, A. O. E. P. 65.

Sir William T. Bishop, E. C.
Sir John W. Glover, G.
Sir William O. Hickok, C. G.
Rev. Sir Beverly R. Waugh, P.
Sir Thomas J. Jordan, S. W.
Sir William Garret, J. W.
Sir J. Brisbane Boyd, T.
Sir Theodore F. Scheffer, R.
Sir Samuel D. Inghram, St. B.
Sir David Mayer, Sw. B.
Sir William H. Egle, W.
Sir Michael Bender, S.

MARCH 13, 1863, A. O. 745, A. O. E. P. 66.

Sir Charles A. Bannvart, E. C.
Sir William O. Hickok, G.
Sir J. Brisbane Boyd, C. G.
Sir John W. Glover, P.
Sir Samuel H. Colestock, S. W.
Sir J. A. Blattenberger, J. W.
Sir John T. Wilson, T.
Sir Theodore F. Scheffer, R.
Sir Samuel D. Inghram, St. B.
Sir John Edwards, Sw. B.
Sir William H. Egle, W.
Sir Michael Bender, S.

MARCH 12, 1864, A. O. 746, A. O. E. P. 67.

Sir John J. Clyde, E. C.
Sir J. Brisbane Boyd, G.
Sir Theodore F. Scheffer, C. G.
Sir Amos W. Young, P.
Sir Samuel H. Colestock, S. W.
Sir J. A. Blattenberger, J. W.
Sir John T. Wilson, T.
Sir Charles A. Bannvart, R.
Sir John W. Glover, St. B.
Sir David Mayer, Sw. B.
Sir William H. Egle, W.
Sir Michael Bender, S.

MARCH 17, 1865, A. O. 747, A. O. E. P. 68.

Sir Charles A. Bannvart, E. C.
Sir Charles H. Mann, G.
Sir William O. Hickok, C. G.
Sir Valentine Hummel, P.
Sir Samuel H. Colestock, S. W.

Sir John Edwards, J. W.
Sir John T. Wilson, T.
Sir Isaac D. Lutz, R.
Sir Theodore F. Scheffer, St. B.
Sir David Mayer, Sw. B.
Sir John A. Smull, W.
Sir Michael Bender, S.

MARCH 16, 1866, A. O. 748, A. O. E. P. 69.

Sir Theodore F. Scheffer, E. C.
Sir J. Brisbane Boyd, G.
Sir Isaac D. Lutz, C. G.
Sir John J. Clyde, P.
Sir Samuel H. Colestock, S. W.
Sir Jackson Sheaffer, J. W.
Sir John T. Wilson, T.
Sir John Ringland, R.
Sir William K. Alricks, St. B.
Sir Thomas J. Jordan, Sw. B.
Sir William H. Egle, W.
Sir Michael Bender, S.

MEMBERS.

NAME.	DATE OF KNIGHTING.
Auchmuty, S. P.,	April 8, 1864.
Alricks, William K.,	February 6, 1866.
Boyd, J. Brisbane,	December 28, 1855.
Bishop, William T., Sr.,	December 28, 1855.
Bender, Michael,	December 28, 1855.
Bladen, Washington L.,	April 4, 1856.
Boley, F. W.,	April 22, 1857.
Bombaugh, C. C.,	April 16, 1858.
Bannvart, Charles A.,	January 29, 1862.
Blattenberger, Julius A.,	February 26, 1863.

NAME.	DATE OF KNIGHTING.
Clyde, John J.,	June 17, 1859.
Colestock, Samuel H.,	March 13, 1863.
Clement, John Jay,	August 29, 1864.
Clapp, Austin F.,	August 29, 1864.
Delancey, William A.,	June 23, 1857.
Dewitt, William R.,	June 17, 1859.
Edwards, John, (No. 8), Ch. Mem.,	November 8, 1855.
Egle, William H.,	December 28, 1855.
Edwards, A.,	February 14, 1856.
Ebur, Francis H., (No. 13),	April 5, 1856.
Finney, Isaac S.,	August 6, 1866.
Finney, Thomas J.,	August 6, 1866.
Glover, John W.,	January 4, 1856.
Garret, William,	February 23, 1860.
Harrison, F. C., (No. 12),	March 5, 1856.
Howell, Charles M., (No. 13),	April 5, 1856.
Herr, Daniel, (No. 13),	April 5, 1856.
Himes, B.,	February 10, 1857.
Hickok, W. O.,	June 10, 1857.
Hummel, Valentine, Jr.,	December 22, 1863.
Inghram, Samuel D.,	February 14, 1856.
Jordan, Thomas J.,	January 4, 1856.
James, J. Y.,	March 14, 1856.
Junkin, R. H.,	January 29, 1862.
Kepner, William H.,	January 4, 1856.
Knapp, Christian F., (No. 12),	March 5, 1856.
Kauffman, Christian S., (No. 13),	April 5, 1856.
Keim, Beverly R.,	February 21, 1862.
Knipe, Joseph F.,	August 6, 1866.
Lamberton, Robert A.,	January 4, 1856.
Lutz, Isaac D.,	December 22, 1863.
McCalla, George W., (No. 8), C. M.,	November 22, 1855.
Mowrey, Geo. R., (No. 10), Ch. M.,	September 12, 1855.
McCalla, Stephen D.,	December 28. 1855.

NAME.	DATE OF KNIGHTING.
Morris, George S.,	February 14, 1856.
Mason, Gordon F., (No. 16),	March 4, 1856.
Melick, Jacob, (No. 12),	March 5, 1856.
McKelvy, J. B., (No. 12),	March 5, 1856.
Muench, Robert Leyburn,	December 12, 1856.
Mayer, David,	April 16, 1856.
McVey, John W.,	June 3, 1858.
Mann, Charles H., (Admitted),	February 17, 1865.
Parke, Benj., (No. 8, No. 12), C. M.,	July 13, 1855.
Pettibone, Henry,	March 4, 1856.
Parker, N. De Forrest,	February 14, 1862.
Richards, S. R.,	February 14, 1856.
Royal, Isaiah S.,	February 14, 1856.
Rees, John, (No. 13),	April 5, 1856.
Rakestraw, Rev. George,	April 8, 1864.
Ringland, John,	February 6, 1866.
Scheffer, Theodore F., (No. 8), C. M.,	November 22, 1855.
Sturdivant, N. R., (No. 8), Ch. M.,	September 6, 1856.
Schriner, C. F., (No. 13),	April 5, 1856.
Smull, John A.,	December 22, 1863.
Sheaffer, Jackson,	February 17, 1865.
Turner, Edmund H.,	June 10, 1857.
Thomas, Harry,	February 26, 1863.
Unger, Elias J.,	February 23, 1860.
Waugh, Rev. Beverly R., (No. 8, No. 12), Charter Member,	December 28, 1855.
Wilson, John T., (No. 8), Ch. Mem.,	November 22, 1855.
Wallower, John, (No. 8), Ch. Mem.,	November 8, 1855.
Wright, John A., (No. 8),	August 13, 1855.
Walters, Henry J.,	June 23, 1857.
Young, Amos W.,	April 4, 1856.
Ziegler, Jacob;	March 13, 1863.

M *

CRUSADE COMMANDERY, No. 12, located at Bloomsburg, Columbia County, Pennsylvania.
The R. E. Sir Charles E. Blumenthal granted a Dispensation for the establishment of this Commandery on the
5th day of March, 1856, on the application of the following petitioners, viz.: Sir Knights Christian Frederick
Knapp, Francis C. Harrison, J. B. McKelvy, Jacob
Melick, John W. Schriner, Benjamin Parke, Theodore
F. Scheffer, Rev. B. R. Waugh, and John Edwards, who
were organized March 26, 1856. This Commandery was
originally No. 8. The Charter was granted June 11,
1856.

OFFICERS OF CRUSADE COMMANDERY, No. 12,
SINCE ITS ORGANIZATION.

MARCH 26, 1856, A. O. 738, A. O. E. P. 59.

Sir Christian Frederick Knapp, E. C.
Sir James B. McKelvy, G.
Sir Francis C. Harrison, C. G.
Rev. Sir John A. De Moyer, P.
Sir Conrad Bittenbender, S. W.
Sir George S. Gilbert, J. W.
Sir Jacob Melick, T.
Sir Ephraim P. Lutz, R.
Sir Lewis Enke, St. B.
Sir Isaiah W. McKelvy, Sw. B.

Sir T. A. Thornton, W.
Sir George Guinn, S.

MARCH 6, 1857, A. O. 739, A. O. E. P. 60.

Sir Christian Frederick Knapp, E. C.
Sir James B. McKelvy, G.
Sir F. C. Harrison, C. G.
Rev. Sir John A. De Moyer, P.
Sir C. Bittenbender, S. W.
Sir George S. Gilbert, J. W.
Sir Jacob Melick, T.
Sir Ephraim P. Lutz, R.
Sir Lewis Enke, St. B.
Sir Isaiah W. McKelvy, Sw. B.
Sir J. W. Schriner, W.
Sir George Guinn, S.

MARCH 22, 1858, A. O. 740, A. O. E. P. 61.

Sir James B. McKelvy, E. C.
Sir F. C. Harrison, G.
Rev. Sir John A. De Moyer, C. G.
Sir C. Bittenbender, P.
Sir George S. Gilbert, S. W.
Sir J. D. Strawbridge, J. W.
Sir Jacob Melick, T.
Sir Christian F. Knapp, R.
Rev. Sir Isaiah Bahl, St. B.
Sir J. Sharpless, Sw. B.
Sir E. C. Smeed, W.
Sir George Guinn, S.

MARCH 28, 1859, A. O. 741, A. O. E. P. 62.

Sir Francis C. Harrison, E. C.
Rev. Sir John A. De Moyer, G.

Sir George S. Gilbert, C. G.
Sir C. Bittenbender, P.
Sir E. C. Smeed, S. W.
Sir John Sharpless, J. W.
Sir E. P. Lutz, T.
Sir Christian Frederick Knapp, R.
Rev. Sir Isaiah Bahl, St. B.
Sir Isaiah W. McKelvy, Sw. B.
Sir Peter M. Traugh, W.
Sir George Gwinn, S.

MARCH 5, 1860, A. O. 742, A. O. E. P. 63.

Rev. Sir John A. De Moyer, E. C.
Sir E. S. Gilbert, G.
Sir Jacob Melick, C. G.
Rev. Sir J. Kelly, P.
Sir E. C. Smeed, S. W.
Sir John Sharpless, J. W.
Sir E. P. Lutz, T.
Sir Christian Frederick Knapp, R.
Sir C. C. Stroub, St. B.
Rev. Sir Isaiah Bahl, Sw. B.
Sir P. M. Traugh, W.
Sir George Gwinn, S.

MARCH 25, 1861, A. O. 743, A. O. E. P. 64.

Sir E. C. Smeed, E. C.
Sir H. Stanley Goodwin, G.
Sir C. Bittenbender, C. G.
Rev. Sir J. Kelly, P.
Sir A. Ricketts, S. W.
Sir G. M. Hagenbuch, J. W.
Sir E. P. Lutz, T.

Sir C. F. Knapp, R.
Sir William V. Higgins, St. B.
Sir V. S. Doebler, Sw. B.
Sir C. R. Doebler, W.
Sir George Gwinn, S.

MARCH 21, 1862, A. O. 744, A. O. E. P. 65.

Sir H. Stanley Goodwin, E. C.
Sir C. Bittenbender, G.
Sir C. C. Stroub, C. G.
Rev. Sir J. Kelly, P.
Sir J. W. Schriner, S. W.
Sir G. M. Hagenbuch, J. W.
Sir E. P. Lutz, T.
Sir C. F. Knapp, R.
Sir P. M. Traugh, St. B.
Sir W. V. Higgins, Sw. B.
Sir V. S. Doebler, W.
Sir George Gwinn, S.

MARCH 24, 1863, A. O. 745, A. O. E. P. 66.

Sir C. Bittenbender, E. C.
Rev. Sir David C. John, G.
Rev. Sir J. R. Dimm, C. G.
Rev. Sir M. P. Crosthwaite, P.
Sir S. V. Polk, S. W.
Sir Palemon John, J. W.
Sir E. P. Lutz, T.
Sir C. F. Knapp, R.
Sir P. M. Traugh, St. B.
Sir C. C. Stroub, Sw. B.
Sir W. V. Higgins, W.
Sir John Penman, S.

MARCH 27, 1864, A. O. 746, A. O. E. P. 67.

Rev. Sir David C. John, E. C.
Rev. Sir J. R. Dimm, G.
Sir Palemon John, C. G.
Sir W. V. Higgins, P.
Sir John Vallerchamp, S. W.
Sir J. K. Robbins, J. W.
Sir E. P. Lutz, T.
Sir C. F. Knapp, R.
Sir A. J. Polk, St. B.
Sir C. M. Hill, Sw. B.
Sir Charles C. Shorkley, W.
Sir John Penman, S.

MARCH 9, 1865, A. O. 747, A. O. E. P. 68

Sir John Vallerchamp, E. C.
Rev. Sir J. R. Dimm, G.
Sir Palemon John, C. G.
Rev. Sir J. F. Porter, P.
Sir J. K. Robbins, S. W.
Sir E. C. Wadhams, J. W.
Sir E. P. Lutz, T.
Sir C. F. Knapp, R.
Sir A. J. Polk, St. B.
Sir Ogden H. Ostrander, Sw. B.
Sir S. V. Polk, W.
Sir John Penman, S.

MARCH 10, 1866, A. O. 748, A. O. E. P. 6.

Sir Palemon John, E. C.
Rev. Sir J. R. Dimm, G.
Rev. Sir D. A. Beckley, C. G.
Rev. Sir R. E. Wilson, P.
Rev. Sir John Thomas, S. W.

Sir Philip Conrad, J. W.
Sir E. P. Lutz, T.
Sir C. F. Knapp, R.
Sir M. P. Fowler, St. B.
Sir M. S. Ridgway, Sw. B.
Sir E. W. M. Low, W.
Sir Rudolph H. Ringler, S.

MEMBERS.

NAME.	DATE OF KNIGHTING.
Arthur, Henry S.,	February 21, 1861.
Aurand, Rev. Simon,	May 11, 1865.
Aker, Rev. J. M.,	April 26, 1866.
Bittenbender, Conrad,	March 26, 1856.
Barnhart, Rev. Thomas,	August 11, 1856.
Bahl, Rev. Isaiah,	February 11, 1857.
Boone, W. E.,	February 9, 1860.
Beckley, Rev. David A.,	July 2, 1863.
Berry, George S., (No. 22),	September 24, 1863.
Brown, Hiram,	December 30, 1863.
Blair, Bryce R.,	June 30, 1864.
Bowman, Rev. S. L.,	July 26, 1864.
Bennet, S. G.,	October 6, 1864.
Beach, John A.,	November 10, 1864.
Bryden, James A.,	December 8, 1864.
Buckalew, John M.,	December 8, 1864.
Baily, H. F.,	January 12, 1865.
Beede, Alexander,	January 12, 1865.
Barton, H. C.,	February 9, 1865.
Boyd, J. A.,	February 9, 1865.
Brewer, G. W.,	April 6, 1865.
Blair, B. S.,	April 6, 1865.
Bulkley, J. E.,	November 3, 1865.
Bricker, J. L.,	January 25, 1866.
Billman, J. W.,	April 26, 1866.

NAME.	DATE OF KNIGHTING.
Burkhard, J. S.,	April 26, 1866.
Born, Rev. P.,	April 26, 1866.
Boyer, D. C.,	April 26, 1866.
Bloom, D. S.,	August 23, 1866.
Brooks, William,	August 23, 1866.
Crosthwaite, Rev. M. P.,	March 24, 1863.
Chapman, J. W., (No. 22),	September 24, 1863.
Clarke, Henry James,	December 30, 1863.
Creveling, Alfred,	December 30, 1863.
Church, A. H.,	April 27, 1864.
Creasy, H. W.,	July 26, 1864.
Connor, Joseph P.,	December 8, 1864.
Case, Rev. W. W.,	December 8, 1864.
Crawford, A. S., (No. 22),	January 12, 1865.
Carothers, Rev. M. J.,	March 9, 1865.
Cauley, Charles,	April 13, 1865.
Christ, Theodore S.,	May 11, 1865.
Cremer, Rev. W. C.,	June 8, 1865.
Cadwallader, J. M.,	June 8, 1865.
Camp, Samuel,	October 5, 1865.
Conrad, Philip,	January 25, 1866.
Carter, Frank,	January 25, 1866.
Curtin, Constance, (No. 22),	March 1, 1866.
Colburn, Rev. A. W.,	April 26, 1866.
Campbell, H. R.,	April 26, 1866.
Conner, H. J.,	December 20, 1866.
De Moyer, Rev. John A.,	March 26, 1856.
Doebler, Valentine S., (No. 22),	August 10, 1860.
Doebler, Charles R.,	March 8, 1861.
Davis, Charles B.,	May 8, 1862.
Dimm, Rev. J. R.,	October 2, 1862.
Doctor, G. W.,	November 10, 1864.
Drumm, J. R.,	January 12, 1865.
Deifenderfer, James H.,	March 9, 1865.

NAME.	DATE OF KNIGHTING.
Dimmick, A., (No. 23),	April 13, 1865.
Derr, Nathaniel H.,	April 26, 1866.
Derr, F. C.,	April 26, 1866.
De Long, Daniel,	April 26, 1866.
Enke, Lewis,	March 26, 1856.
Ellis, B. Morris, (No. 22),	November 25, 1863.
Ent, Wellington H.,	February 9, 1864.
Eckman, Rev. John G.,	June 30, 1864.
Elliott, John A.,	August 3, 1865.
Eckbert, H. P.,	April 26, 1866.
Eckert, W. F.,	April 26, 1866.
Ferguson, F. A.,	November 29, 1861.
Feltwell, Rev. W. V.,	August 28, 1863.
Fowler, A. P.,	June 30, 1864.
Fowler, Charles S.,	July 26, 1864.
French, S. Livingston,	September 15, 1864.
French, H. W.,	March 9, 1865.
Fowler, S. S.,	November 3, 1865.
Fowler, M. P.,	January 25, 1866.
Gilbert, George S.,	March 26, 1856.
Gwinn, George,	December 28, 1857.
Guyer, Rev. John,	January 30, 1860.
Garman, Samuel, (No. 22),	March 8, 1861.
Goodwin, H. Stanley, (Admitted),	March 26, 1861.
Green, F. D., (No. 22),	May 8, 1862.
Goodwin, Leonard,	February 18, 1864.
Gorham, Lewis,	April 6, 1865.
Garson, William,	August 3, 1865.
Goodlander, James, (No. 22),	November 3, 1865.
Green, Joseph Miles,	March 1, 1866.
Goben, J. P. S.,	March 29, 1866.
Gilchrist, M. H.,	December 20, 1866.
Harrison, Francis C., (No. 11), C. M.,	March 5, 1866.
Hill, Charles M.,	August 6, 1857.

24 *

NAME.	DATE OF KNIGHTING.
Higgins, W. V.,	August 16, 1860.
Hagenbuch, G. M.,	February 21, 1861.
Hoffman, Rev. Francis C.,	April 10, 1861.
Heilner, Rev. J. A.,	November 25, 1863.
Heilner, H. C.,	December 30, 1863.
Hayden, Henry,	March 29, 1864.
Hood, William,	May 23, 1864.
Hamlin, Mahlon,	November 10, 1864.
Hutchinson, Charles,	November 10, 1864.
Henn, Rev. Jacob,	March 9, 1865.
Hutton, Rev. J. B.,	May 11, 1865.
Heiser, Daniel,	October 5, 1865.
Heiser, David,	January 25, 1866.
Helfrich, G. H.,	January 25, 1866.
Hering, Michael B.,	March 1, 1866.
Hill, George H.,	April 26, 1866.
Harman, J. B.,	April 26, 1866.
Haas, John,	April 26, 1866.
Hibshman, Rev. W. H.,	April 26, 1866.
Harman, Jacob M.,	December 20, 1866.
John, Rev. David C.,	July 10, 1862.
John, Palemon,	October 2, 1862.
John, George W.,	July 2, 1863.
John, Nelson P.,	December 8, 1864.
Jones, W. N., (No. 22),	November 3, 1865.
Johnston, M. L.,	January 25, 1866.
Jacoby, William J.,	November 22, 1866.
Johnson, James,	December 20, 1866.
Knapp, Christian F.,(No.11),Ch.M.,	March 5, 1856.
Kelly, Rev. Joshua,	February 21, 1861.
Kinney, Peter,	November 29, 1861
Koons, William B.,	March 24, 1863.
Koons, B. D.,	April 22, 1864.
Kohr, Rev. Emanuel,	March 9, 1865.

NAME.	DATE OF KNIGHTING.
Klotz, Robert, (No. 23),	April 13, 1865.
Knittle, J. B.,	April 26, 1866.
Lutz, Ephraim P.,	March 26, 1856.
Low, E. W. M.,	July 10, 1862.
Logan, William F., (No. 22),	March 24, 1863.
Laycock, Rev. W. J.,	June 8, 1865.
Lenker, J. B.,	June 8, 1865.
Lewis, David,	April 26, 1866.
L'Velle, Martin M.,	December 20, 1866.
McKelvy, J. B., (No. 11), Ch. Mem.,	March 5, 1856.
Melick, Jacob, (No. 11), Ch. Mem.,	March 5, 1856.
Moorehead, Rev. John,	March 26, 1856.
McKelvy, Isaiah W.,	March 26, 1856.
McNair, Thomas S., (No. 23)	June 13, 1858.
Mensch, Andrew C.,	August 16, 1860.
McGhee, Thomas,	February 5, 1861.
Matthews, E. W.,	March 24, 1863.
Monroe, Washington M.,	February 9, 1864.
McNinish, J. S.,	September 15, 1864.
Marchbank, J. D.,	December 8, 1864.
McFarlane, Thomas P.,	April 6, 1865.
McCollum, I. K., (No. 23),	April 13, 1865.
Morris, Rev. Thomas M.,	May 11, 1865.
Morgan, Thomas,	May 11, 1865.
Moyer, L. N.,	August 3, 1865.
Martin, Warren,	March 1, 1866.
Mullin, Rev. James,	April 26, 1866.
Morgan, Daniel,	April 26, 1866.
Millard, Reece J.,	August 23, 1866.
Norcross, Rev. William H.,	April 26, 1866.
Ohl, John G.,	June 14, 1860.
Ostrander, Ogden H.,	February 9, 1865.
Olewine, Rev. J. W.,	August 23, 1866.

NAME.	DATE OF KNIGHTING.
Price, Rev. S. W.,	February 5, 1861.
Polk, Simon V., (No. 22),	April 10, 1862.
Penman, John,	April 30, 1863.
Parmley, J. W., (No. 22),	April 30, 1863.
Polk, A. J.,	July 2, 1863.
Porter, Rev. James F.,	August 28, 1863.
Paxton, B. F.,	December 30, 1863.
Parker, Samuel J., (No. 22),	June 30, 1864.
Parker, Noble,	July 26, 1864.
Pontious, J. D.,	March 9, 1865.
Reiff, D. H., (No. 15),	April 23, 1856.
Ricketts, Agib,	February 5, 1861.
Robbins, J. K.,	May 8, 1862.
Ricketts, R. B.,	March 24, 1863.
Ridgway, M. S.,	December 30, 1863.
Reitze, Jonathan,	April 22, 1864.
Reilly, Thomas A.,	December 8, 1864.
Rishel, L. Kauffman,	January 12, 1865.
Rearick, Rev. Adam,	March 9, 1865.
Robison, J. B.,	July 6, 1865.
Robinson, Thomas W.,	November 3, 1865.
Ringler, Rudolph H.,	January 25, 1866.
Rhorbach, D. C.,	April 26, 1866.
Rhodes, Rev. M.,	April 26, 1866.
Schriner, Jos. W., (No. 8), Ch. Mem.,	February 28, 1856.
Stout, Solomon A., (No. 15),	April 22, 1856.
Strawbridge, J. D.,	September 28, 1857.
Sharpless, John,	December 28, 1857.
Smeed, E. C.,	March 22, 1858.
Stroub, C. C.,	September 20, 1858.
Shorkley, Charles C.,	February 9, 1864.
Shorkley, George,	February 9, 1864.
Saunders, Rev. C. W.,	February 9, 1864.
Shannon, Rev. Samuel,	May 26, 1864.

NAME.	DATE OF KNIGHTING.
Stroub, S. D.,	June 30, 1864.
Sharpless, Loyd T.,	June 30, 1864.
Swallow, Rev. S. C.,	September 15, 1864.
Stroh, Samuel,	November 10, 1864.
Sharrets, Rev. E. A.,	November 10, 1864.
Shanafelt, Rev. Thomas M.,	November 10, 1864.
Sherlock, Rev. Thomas,	December 8, 1864.
Swineford, H.,	January 12, 1865.
Smith, D. Webster,	January 12, 1865.
Smith, D. Wilbur,	January 12, 1865.
Seely, William T.,	February 9, 1865.
Smith, Rev. Samuel,	March 9, 1865.
Sibbett, J. P.,	April 6, 1865.
Salmon, John P., (No. 22),	October 5, 1865.
Snyder, C. W.,	July 6, 1865.
Salmon, Joseph P., (No. 23),	April 12, 1865.
Shoemaker, Michael,	October 5, 1865.
Schwallenberg, F. H., (No. 22),	October 5, 1865.
Stevens, Rev. B. F.,	April 26, 1866.
Shipman, Jacob,	April 26, 1866.
Slaymaker, Jasper,	April 26, 1866.
Spear, Nathaniel,	November 22, 1866.
Sands, Joseph E.,	December 20, 1866.
Stewart, A. B.,	December 20, 1866.
Thornton, Thomas A. H.,	March 26, 1856.
Tobias, John F.,	May 2, 1856.
Tippin, Andrew H., (No. 15),	June 1, 1856.
Traugh, Peter M.,	February 26, 1857.
Thomas, Rev. John,	February 9, 1864.
Tubbs, William R.,	April 22, 1864.
Thornton, Thomas C.,	March 1, 1866.
Taylor, James,	October 18, 1866.
Van Horn, Nathan,	June 14, 1860.
Vallerchamp, John,	April 10, 1861.

NAME.	DATE OF KNIGHTING.
Van Gilder, S. G., (No. 22),	January 12, 1865.
Von Neida, John W.,	January 12, 1865.
Vallerchamp, W. F.,	June 8, 1865.
Vanderslice, J. A., (No. 22),	July 6, 1865.
Vandevender, J. M.,	October 5, 1865.
Van Tassel, R. H.,	November 22, 1866.
Weldy, Francis,	June 12, 1860.
White, Allison,	February 5, 1861.
Wilson, Rev. R. E.,	November 25, 1863.
Wadhams, E. C.,	April 22, 1864.
Wells, E. C.,	July 26, 1864.
Willetts, I. W.,	September 15, 1866.
Wilder, C. S.,	January 25, 1866.
Wiggan, George F.,	March 1, 1866.
Welch, Rev. Benjamin G.,	March 1, 1866.
Wagenseller, George,	April 26, 1866.
Wagenseller, W. F.,	April 26, 1866.
Wagenseller, P. R.,	April 26, 1866.
Wagenseller, M. L.,	April 26, 1866.
Welker, George,	April 26, 1866.
Williams, H. L.,	November 22, 1866.
Williams, M. A.,	December 20, 1866.
Wertman, Daniel K.,	December 20, 1866.
Young, Samuel R.,	July 10, 1862.
Young, Rev. Jacob,	February 9, 1864.
Yetter, J. B.,	September 15, 1864.
Zettlemoyer, B.,	June 8, 1865. ·

COLUMBIA COMMANDERY, No. 13, located at Lancaster City, Pennsylvania.

This Commandery was originally No. 9, but at the union of the two Grand Commanderies. became No. 11, its present number.

The Petitioners for this Commandery were Sir Knights Charles M. Howell, Christian S. Kauffman, Daniel Herr, Francis H. Ebur, Charles F. Shreiner, John Rees, John Herr, H. M. Rawlins, and William Shuler, who made application to R. E. Sir Charles E. Blumenthal, April 18, 1856, who granted the same. Its Charter was granted June 11, 1856.

OFFICERS OF COLUMBIA COMMANDERY, No. 13, FROM ITS ORGANIZATION.

APRIL 18, 1856, A. O. 738, A. O. E. P. 59.

Sir Charles M. Howell, E. C.
Sir Christian S. Kauffmann, G.
Sir Daniel Herr, C. G.
Sir Francis H. Ebur, P.
Sir John L. Reese, S. W.
Sir John Rees, J. W.
Sir Christian F. Schriner, T.
Sir John Herr, R.
Sir John Eckert, St. B.
Sir William Shuler, Sw. B.
Sir Joseph Buchanan, W.
Sir George Lutz, S.

JUNE 24, 1857, A. O. 739, A. O. E. P. 60.

Sir Charles M. Howell, E. C.
Sir Christian S. Kauffman, G.
Sir Daniel Herr, C. G.
Rev. Sir William E. Locke, P.
Sir Joseph Buchanan, S. W.
Sir Francis H. Ebur, J. W.
Sir Christian F. Schriner, T.
Sir Jacob M. Westhœffer, R.
Sir J. A. Wolfe, St. B.
Sir Franklin Hinkle, Sw. B.
Sir John Herr, W.
Sir William Shuler, S.

MARCH 20, 1858, A. O. 740, A. O. E. P. 5.

Sir Christian S. Kauffman, E. C.
Sir Francis H. Ebur, G.
Sir John A. Wolfe, C. G.
Sir Charles M. Howell, P.
Sir Joseph Buchanan, S. W.
Sir John Herr, J. W.
Sir Charles F. Shreiner, T.
Sir Jacob M. Westhœffer, R.
Sir Franklin Hinkle, St. B.
Sir F. S. Albright, Sw. B.
Sir S. F. Eberlin, W.
Sir George Lutz, S.

MARCH 22, 1859, A. O. 741, A. O. E. P. 60

Sir Christian S. Kauffman, E. C.
Sir Francis H. Ebur, G.
Sir John A. Wolfe, C. G.
Sir Charles M. Howell, P.
Sir John Herr, S. W.

Sir S. F. Eberlin, J. W.
Sir Charles F. Shreiner, T.
Sir Jacob M. Westhœffer, R.
Sir E. B. Herr, St. B.
Sir F. S. Albright, Sw. B.
Sir Jacob S. Snyder, W.
Sir George Lutz, S.

MARCH 21, 1860, A. O. 742, A. O. E. P. 63.

Sir Christian S. Kauffman, E. C.
Sir Francis H. Ebur, G.
Sir John A. Wolfe, C. G.
Sir Charles M. Howell, P.
Sir John Herr, S. W.
Sir S. F. Eberlin, J. W.
Sir Charles F. Shreiner, T.
Sir Jacob M. Westhœffer, R.
Sir F. S. Albright, St. B.
Sir E. B. Herr, Sw. B.
Sir John Rees, W.
Sir George Lutz, S.

This Commandery suspended operations and resumed
EFFICIENT labor in 1864.

JANUARY 29, 1864, A. O. 746, A. O. E. P. 67

Sir Charles M. Howell, E. C.
Sir F. S. Albright, G.
Sir Edward W. Swentzel, C. G.
Sir Wyatt W. Miller, P.
Sir Thomas Grieves, S. W.
Sir William Augustus Morton, J. W.
Sir Henry Blinckensderfer, T.
Sir Hugh S. Gara, R.
Sir Joseph Schoch, St. B.

25   N

Sir Henry Carpenter, Sw. B.
Sir Abner D. Campbell, W.
Sir George Lutz, S.

MARCH 16, 1865, A. O. 747, A. O. E. P. 68.

Sir Charles M. Howell, E. C. •
Sir F. S. Albright, G.
Sir David W. Patterson, C. G.
Sir Henry Carpenter, P.
Sir A. J. Kauffman, S. W.
Sir William Augustus Morton, J. W.
Sir Henry Blinckensderfer, T.
Sir Hugh S. Gara, R.
Sir Thomas Grieves, St. B.
Sir Levi Ellmaker, Sw. B.
Sir John B. Albright, W.
Sir George Lutz, S.

MARCH 15, 1866, A. O. 748, A. O. E. P. 69.

Sir Charles M. Howell, E. C.
Sir Jacob M. Westhœffer, G.
Sir Levi Ellmaker, C. G.
Sir Henry Baumgardner, P.
Sir John McCalla, S. W.
Sir William Augustus Morton, J. W.
Sir Henry Blinckensderfer, T.
Sir Hugh S. Gara, R.
Sir Thomas Grieves, St. B.
Sir Herman Miller, Sw. B.
Sir Charles E. Wentz, W.
Sir George Lutz, S.

MEMBERS.

NAME.	DATE OF KNIGHTING.
Albright, F. S.,	February 27, 1857.
Adams, John B.,	November 30, 1860.
Albright, John B.,	January 26, 1865.
Buchanan, Joseph,	February 27, 1857.
Blinckensderfer, Henry,	February 27, 1857.
Brubaker, John C.,	September 15, 1857.
Boyd, Stephen W. P.,	January 29, 1864.
Bushong, Israel,	February 28, 1864.
Boardman, Harris,	September 23, 1864.
Bentz, Peter, (No. 21),	October 27, 1864.
Bear, Jacob W.,	February 23, 1865.
Baumgardner, Henry,	May 25, 1865.
Blinckensderfer, William,	July 27, 1865.
Bair, John,	August 24, 1865.
Bucher, John C.,	September 28, 1865.
Best, John,	April 26, 1866.
Carl, Jeremiah, (No. 21),	February 28, 1864.
Campbell, Abner D.,	February 28, 1861.
Carpenter, Henry, M. D.,	February 28, 1861.
Crane, Robert,	October 26, 1865.
Cromlish, Rev. John,	April 26, 1866.
Carter, Samuel,	April 26, 1866.
Clark, Franklin,	May 24, 1866.
Derringer, M. S.,	February 27, 1857.
Dale, Abner,	July 27, 1860.
Davis, Joseph R., (No. 21),	November 24, 1864.
Deaner, John,	November 24, 1864.
Dorr, Henry,	May 25, 1865.
Davis, Thomas J.,	June 9, 1865.
Davis, Caleb S.,	November 23, 1865.
Dillon, Samuel H.,	December 28, 1865.
Davis, William,	February 22, 1866.
Dunlap, Dr. John N.,	March 22, 1866.

NAME.	DATE OF KNIGHTING.
Douglas, James L.,	September 27, 1866.
Ebur, Francis H., (No. 11), Ch. Mem.,	April 5, 1856.
Eckert, John,	February 26, 1857.
Eberlin, Samuel F.,	February 27, 1857.
Evans, Fitz James, (No. 21),	February 26, 1864.
Ellmaker, Levi,	December 22, 1864.
Edwards, Richard C.,	February 22, 1866.
Ernst, D. B.,	July 27, 1860.
Elliott, Rev. William H.,	November 30, 1860.
Fahnestock, H. R.,	December 22, 1864.
Fralick, Daniel R.,	March 22, 1866.
Fisher, Michael,	April 26, 1866.
Green, Arthur N., (No. 21),	January 29, 1864.
Gara, Hugh S.,	February 28, 1864.
Grieves, Thomas,	February 28, 1864.
Garber, Davis,	September 23, 1864.
Gilberthorpe, William, (No. 21),	October 27, 1864.
Geiger, George,	April 27, 1865.
Greider, Benjamin M.,	July 27, 1865.
Garret, Edwin,	October 26, 1865.
Ginder, Philip,	April 26, 1866.
Geiger, Elisha,	May 24, 1866.
Graham, Dana,	May 24, 1866.
Gorrecht, Peter W.,	October 25, 1866.
Howell, Chas. M., (No. 11), Ch. M.,	April 5, 1856.
Herr, Daniel, (No. 11), Ch. Mem.,	April 5, 1856.
Herr, John, Charter Member,	April 18, 1856.
Hinckle, Franklin,	June 16, 1857.
Herr, E. B.,	June 25, 1858.
Hartman, Henry F.,	July 27, 1860.
Heiges, Jacob D., (No. 21),	October 27, 1864.
Huber, John F.,	February 23, 1865.
Hurst, Elam D.,	July 27, 1865.
Hambright, Henry A.,	October 26, 1865.

NAME.	DATE OF KNIGHTING.
Haines, Samuel B.,	December 28, 1865.
Huber, Samuel,	December 28, 1865.
Heinitsh, Charles A.,	January 25, 1866.
Hess, Daniel D.,	April 26, 1866.
Herr, Daniel H.,	October 25, 1866.
Johnson, William,	February 23, 1865.
Jeffries, Joseph,	January 25, 1866.
Kauffman, Chris. S., (No. 11), C. M.,	April 5, 1856.
Kauffman, A. J.,	January 29, 1864.
Killian, H. R.,	April 29, 1864.
Krause, Conrad A.,	January 26, 1865.
Knotwell, Henry R.,	February 23, 1865.
Kready, Benjamin C.,	April 27, 1865.
Keller, Samuel E.,	April 27, 1865.
Kerns, Horatio S.,	August 24, 1865.
Keplinger, John S.,	September 28, 1865.
Knotwell, Joseph,	November 23, 1865.
Kuhn, William D.,	December 28, 1865.
Kelly, John M.,	January 25, 1866.
Locke, Rev. William E.,	June 16, 1857.
Lutz, George,	September 15, 1857.
Laverty, John D.,	December 28, 1865.
Morton, William Augustus,	January 29, 1864.
Martin, Peter,	January 29, 1864.
Miller, Wyatt W.,	February 28, 1864.
Miller, Philip,	October 27, 1864.
Miller, Herman,	December 22, 1864.
Muller, John B.,	December 22, 1864.
McConkey, J. Q. A., ˙	April 27, 1865.
Myers, Samuel M.,	July 27, 1865.
Martin, John, M. D.,	October 26, 1865.
Miller, Robert,	October 26, 1865.
Miller, William H.,	November 23, 1865.
McClellan, Robert L.,	December 28, 1865.

25 *

NAME.	DATE OF KNIGHTING.
McCalla, John,	January 25, 1866.
McCaskey, William S.,	April 26, 1866.
Oblender, Adam,	May 24, 1866.
Patterson, Samuel,	March 22, 1861.
Patterson, David W.,	April 29, 1864.
Prince, D. O., (No. 21),	April 29, 1864.
Pownall, George,	July 27, 1865.
Peters, Jacob G.,	November 23, 1865.
Rawlins, Henry M., Charter Mem.,	April 18, 1856.
Rees, John, (No. 11), Ch. Mem.,	April 5, 1856.
Reese, John L.,	February 27, 1857.
Rambo, A. M.,	June 15, 1860.
Rathvon, Simon S.,	April 29, 1864.
Richardson, William,	November 24, 1864.
Reed, George K.,	February 23, 1865.
Rotharmel, Jacob,	February 23, 1856.
Ringwalt, A. Z.,	February 23, 1865.
Roberts, Jacob,	March 23, 1865.
Raub, J. Miller,	May 25, 1865.
Rhodes, Charles J.,	August 24, 1865.
Russel, David N.,	September 28, 1865.
Reed, Joseph A. E.,	September 27, 1866.
Shreiner, Chas. F., (No. 11), Ch. M.,	April 5, 1856.
Shuler, William, Charter Member,	April 18, 1856.
Snyder, Jacob S.,	June 25, 1858.
Saeger, James,	July 27, 1860.
Smith, John H.,	November 30, 1860.
Sheaffer, Joseph H.,	September 27, 1861.
Shœffer, John,	January 29, 1864.
Slokum, Samuel J.,	January 29, 1864.
Schoch, Joseph,	February 28, 1864.
Swentzel, Edward W.,	February 28, 1864.
Shultz, John Andrew,	September 23, 1864.
Smith, William, (No. 21),	October 27, 1864.

NAME.	DATE OF KNIGHTING.
Spahr, Michael B., (No. 21),	October 27, 1864.
Springer, John Jacob,	January 26, 1865.
Stetzel, George,	March 23, 1865.
Sample, Samuel R.,	April 27, 1865.
Strickler, Matthew M.,	May 25, 1865.
Schurenbrand, John A.,	May 25, 1865.
Stoner, Jacob S.,	July 27, 1865.
Sheer, William C. F.,	July 27, 1865.
Shaeffer, Josiah H.,	August 24, 1865.
Sener, J. Frederick,	August 24, 1865.
Samson, Joseph,	October 26, 1865.
Shirk, Henry S.,	December 28, 1865.
Sanderson, George L.,	February 22, 1866.
Springer, George F.,	February 22, 1866.
Scheaffer, Christian,	April 26, 1866.
Seibert, George,	May 24, 1866.
Sides, Abraham,	May 24, 1866.
Umstead, Rev. J. T.,	February 22, 1866.
Wentz, Charles E., (Admitted),	August 26, 1850.
Westhaeffer, Jacob M.,	February 27, 1857.
Wolfe, John A.,	February 27, 1857.
Woodcock, William,	March 22, 1861.
Weise, John P.,	September 23, 1864.
White, Thomas, (No. 21),	October 27, 1864.
Winter, C. F., (No. 21),	November 24, 1864.
Whittaker, Washington,	December 22, 1864.
Wittinger, John,	January 26, 1865.
Williamson, John G.,	May 25, 1865.
Widmyer, Christian,	November 23, 1865.
Warfel, Silas N.,	February 22, 1866.
Wilson, William A.,	October 25, 1866.
Zook, Abner H.,	March 23, 1865.

PALESTINE COMMANDERY, No. 14, (originally No. 10), meets at Carbondale, Luzerne County, Pennsylvania. Application was made to the R. E. Sir Charles E. Blumenthal, Grand Commander, who granted on the 1st day of May, 1856, a Dispensation to open Palestine Commandery. The Petitioners to constitute the Commandery were Sir Knights John L. Gore, Philo C. Gritman, William N. Moonies, William R. Baker, S. E. Bilger, William Root, William W. Davies, Washington Burr, G. L. Dickson, A. Crocker, and Alfred Dart.

On the 11th day of June, 1856, the Charter was granted by the Grand Commandery.

OFFICERS OF PALESTINE COMMANDERY, No. 14,
SINCE ITS ORGANIZATION.

MAY 1, 1856, A. O. 738, A. O. E. P. 59.

Sir John L. Gore, E. C.
Sir Philo C. Gritman, G.
Sir William N. Moonies, C. G.
Sir William R. Baker, P.
Sir S. E. Bilger, S. W.
Sir Alfred Dart, J. W.
Sir William W. Davies, T.
Sir A. Crocker, R.
Sir Washington Burr, St. B.
Sir G. L. Dickson, Sw. B.
Sir William Root, W.

JUNE 16, 1856, A. O. 738, A. O. E. P. 59.

Sir John L. Gore, E. C.
Sir Philo C. Gritman, G.
Sir William N. Moonies, C. G.
Sir William R. Baker, P.
Sir S. E. Bilger, S. W.
Sir Alfred Dart, J. W.
Sir William W. Davies, T.
Sir A. Crocker, R.
Sir Washington Burr, St. B.
Sir G. L. Dickson, Sw. B.
Sir William Root, W.

MARCH 16, 1857, A, O. 739, A. O. E. P. 60.

Sir Philo C. Gritman, E. C.
Sir Robert C. Simpson, G.
Sir William N. Moonies, C. G.
Sir William R. Baker, P.
Sir George L. Dickson, S. W.
Sir Samuel E. Bilger, J. W.
Sir John L. Gore, T.
Sir David G. Smith, R.
Sir Washington Burr, St. B.
Sir George S. Kingsbury, Sw. B.
Sir W. W. Davies, W.
Sir William Root, S.

MARCH 15, 1858, A. O. 740, A. O. E. P. 61.

Sir William R. Baker, E. C.
Sir George L. Dickson, G.
Sir William N. Moonies, C. G.
Sir H. L. Freeman, P.
Sir W. W. Davies, S. W.
Sir J. W. Hughes, J. W.

N *

Sir Washington Burr, T.
Sir David G. Smith, R.
Sir Alfred Dart, St. B.
Sir Samuel E. Bilger, Sw. B.
Sir A. Crocker, W.
Sir William Root, S.

MARCH 14, 1859, A. O. 741, A. O. E. P. 62.

Sir George L. Dickson, E. C.
Sir James Hosie, G.
Sir William N. Moonies, C. G.
Sir William R. Baker, P.
Sir Alfred Dart, S. W.
Sir W. W. Davies, J. W.
Sir John L. Gore, T.
Sir Washington Burr, R.
Sir Philo C. Gritman, St. B.
Sir Samuel E. Bilger, Sw. B.
Sir John W. Hughes, W.
Sir William Root, S.

MARCH 13, 1860, A. O. 742, A. O. E. P. 63.

Sir Samuel E. Bilger, E. C.
Sir James Hosie, G.
Sir William N. Moonies, C. G.
Sir William R. Baker, P.
Sir David G. Smith, S. W.
Sir J. W. Hughes, J. W.
Sir John L. Gore, T.
Sir Washington Burr, R.
Sir Thomas Voyle, St. B.
Sir Jacob Smithers, Sw. B.
Sir H. L. Freeman, W.
Sir William Root, S.

MARCH 12, 1861, A. O. 743, A. O. E. P. 64.

Sir Samuel E. Bilger, E. C.
Sir James Hosie, G.
Sir William N. Moonies, C. G.
Sir William R. Baker, P.
Sir David G. Smith, S. W.
Sir John W. Hughes, J. W.
Sir John L. Gore, T.
Sir Washington Burr, R.
Sir Thomas Voyle, St. B.
Sir Jacob Smithers, Sw. B.
Sir H. L. Freeman, W.
Sir William Root, S.

MARCH 11, 1862, A. O. 744, A. O. E. P. 65.

Sir Samuel E. Bilger, E. C.
Sir James Hosie, G.
Sir John W. Hughes, C. G.
Sir William R. Baker, P.
Sir Philo C. Gritman, S. W.
Sir William N. Moonies, J. W.
Sir John L. Gore, T.
Sir Washington Burr, R.
Sir Amos Nichols, St. B.
Sir James E. Howe, Sw. B.
Sir Thomas Voyle, W.
Sir William Root, S.

MARCH 10, 1863, A. O. 745, A. O. E. P 66.

Sir Samuel E. Bilger, E. C.
Sir James Hosie, G.
Sir John W. Hughes, C. G.
Sir William R. Baker, P.
Sir Philo C. Gritman, S. W.

Sir E. B. Burnham, J. W.
Sir William N. Moonies, T.
Sir Washington Burr, R.
Sir Amos Nichols, St. B.
Sir James E. Howe, Sw. B.
Sir Thomas Voyle, W.
Sir William Root, S.

MARCH 19, 1864, A. O. 746, A. O. E. P. 67.

Sir William R. Baker, E. C.
Sir George L. Dickson, G.
Sir William N. Moonies, C. G.
Sir J. B. Van Bergen, P.
Sir James Hosie, S. W.
Sir Philo C. Gritman, J. W.
Sir Thomas Orchard, T.
Sir Washington Burr, R.
Sir E. B. Burnham, St. B.
Sir James E. Howe, Sw. B.
Sir Thomas Voyle, W.
Sir William Root, S.

MARCH 18, 1865, A. O. 747, A. O. E. P, 68.

Sir J. B. Van Bergen, E. C.
Sir Hiram Marsh, G.
Sir William N. Moonies, C. G.
Sir Thomas Orchard, P.
Sir Philo C. Gritman, S. W.
Sir A. Hubbard, J. W.
Sir Washington Burr, T.
Sir William R. Baker, R.
Sir Thomas Voyle, St. B.
Sir A. E. Burr, Sw. B.
Sir E. B. Burnham, W.
Sir William Root, S.

MARCH 17, 1866, A. O. 748, A. O. E. P. 69.

Sir J. B. Van Bergen, E. C.
Sir Hiram Marsh, G.
Sir William N. Moonies, C. G.
Sir Thomas Orchard, P.
Sir Philo C. Gritman, S. W.
Sir A. Hubbard, J. W.
Sir Washington Burr, T.
Sir William R. Baker, R.
Sir Thomas Voyle, St. B.
Sir A. E. Burr, Sw. B.
Sir E. B. Burnham, W.
Sir William Root, S.

MEMBERS.

NAME.	DATE OF KNIGHTING.
Baker, William R., Charter Member,	May 1, 1856.
Bilger, Samuel E., Charter Member,	May 1, 1856.
Burr, Washington, Charter Member,	May 1, 1856.
Blanding, V. M.,	July 23, 1858.
Burnham, E. B.,	March 17, 1863.
Burr, A. E.,	October 6, 1863.
Crocker, A., Charter Member,	May 1, 1856.
Davies, William W., Charter Mem.,	May 1, 1856.
Dickson, George L., Charter Mem.,	May 1, 1856.
Dart, Alfred, Charter Member,	May 1, 1856.
Dickson, Thomas,	June 12, 1857.
Decker, Isaac,	March 18, 1864.
Freeman, H. L.,	November 20, 1857.
Gore, John L., (Morton Encamp't., N. Y., No. 4), Charter Member,	May 1, 1856.
Gritman, Philo C., Charter Member,	May 1, 1856.
Harvey, E. B.,	September 19, 1856.
Hums, E. B.,	May 16, 1857.
Hosie, James,	August 16, 1857.

NAME.	DATE OF KNIGHTING.
Hughes, John W.,	August 16, 1857.
Howe, James E.,	February 17, 1860.
Hubbard, Alonzo,	March 18, 1864.
Kingsbury, G. S.,	May 15, 1857.
Moonies, William N., Charter Mem.,	May 1, 1856.
Marsh, Hiram,	August 16, 1857.
Nichols, Amos,	July 6, 1860.
Orchard, Thomas,	October 6, 1863.
Perkins, William H.,	May 15, 1857.
Root, William, Charter Member,	May 1, 1856.
Rowson, W. S.,	October 27, 1856.
Reynolds, L. D.,	May 15, 1857.
Simpson, Robert C.,	May 15, 1857.
Smith, David G.,	May 15, 1857.
Smithers, Jacob,	April 16, 1858.
Voyle, Thomas,	February 19, 1858.
Van Bergen, J. B.,	March 25, 1863.
Walker, Rev. T. D.,	June 20, 1856.
Wade, G. B. R.,	July 6, 1860.

JERUSALEM COMMANDERY, No. 15, (originally No. 11), was located at Pottstown, Montgomery County, Pennsylvania.

The Dispensation for constituting Jerusalem Commandery was issued on the 5th day of May, 1856, by the R. E. Sir Charles E. Blumenthal, Grand Commander. The Petitioners were Sir Knights Solomon A. Stout, Andrew H. Tippin, D. H. Reiff, Charles Moore, W. A. Van Buskirk, G. S. Snyder, H. C. Feger, George R. Clarke, A. L. Custer, and Alexander Malsberger.

The Charter was granted June 11, 1856.

By a unanimous vote of the Commandery and the approbation of the R. E. Sir Robert Pitcairn, on January 4, 1867, the meetings of this Commandery were changed to Phœnixville, Pennsylvania.

OFFICERS OF JERUSALEM COMMANDERY, No. 15, SINCE ITS ORGANIZATION.

MAY 15, 1856, A. O. 738, A. O. E. P. 59.

Sir Solomon A. Stout, E. C.
Sir Andrew H. Tippin, G.
Sir D. H. Reiff, C. G.
Sir C. Moore, P.
Sir H. C. Feger, S. W.
Sir W. A. Van Buskirk, J. W.
Sir A. L. Custer, T.
Sir W. C. Rutter, R.
Sir George R. Clarke, St. B.

Sir S. R. Ellis, Sw. B.
Sir Elias Kitchen, W.
Sir Daniel McCormick, S.

MARCH 14, 1857, A. O. 739, A. O. E. P. 60.

Sir Andrew H. Tippin, E. C.
Sir Hiram C. Feger, G.
Sir George R. Clarke, C. G.
Sir William C. Rutter, P.
Sir William A. Van Buskirk, S. W.
Sir John H. Seltzer, J. W.
Sir Charles Moore, T.
Sir Alexander Malsberger, R.
Sir Elias Kitchen, St. B.
Sir S. R. Ellis, Sw. B.
Sir A. L. Custer, W.
Sir Daniel McCormick, S.

MARCH 21, 1858, A. O. 740, A. O. E. P. 61.

Sir Andrew H. Tippin, E. C.
Sir Hiram C. Feger, G.
Sir George R. Clarke, C. G.
Sir A. L. Custer, P.
Sir Alexander Malsberger, S. W.
Sir H. F. Yohn, J. W.
Sir Solomon A. Stout, T.
Sir William C. Rutter, R.
Sir W. A. Van Buskirk, St. B.
Sir Samuel R. Ellis, Sw. B.
Sir J. Weaver, W.
Sir Daniel McCormick, S.

MARCH 20, 1859, A. O. 741, A. O. E. P. 62.

Sir Andrew H. Tippin, E. C.
Sir Hiram C. Feger, G.

Sir George R. Clarke, C. G.
Sir A. L. Custer, P.
Sir Alexander Malsberger, S. W.
Sir H. F. Yohn, J. W.
Sir Solomon A. Stout, T.
Sir William C. Rutter, R.
Sir W. A. Van Buskirk, St. B.
Sir S. R. Ellis, Sw. B.
Sir Elias Kitchen, W.
Sir Daniel McCormick, S.

MARCH 19, 1860, A. O. 742, A. O. E. P. 63.

Sir William C. Rutter, E. C.
Sir Hiram C. Feger, G.
Sir George R. Clarke, C. G.
Sir Joseph Umstead, P.
Sir Henry F. Yohn, S. W.
Sir W. A. Van Buskirk, J. W.
Sir Solomon A. Stout, T.
Sir Alexander Malsberger, R.
Sir A. L. Custer, St. B.
Sir Jeremiah Weaver, Sw. B.
Sir Henry Christian, W.
Sir Daniel McCormick, S.

MARCH 18, 1861, A. O. 743, A. O. E. P. 64.

Sir William C. Rutter, E. C.
Sir Hiram C. Feger, G.
Sir George R. Clarke, C. G.
Sir Joseph Umstead, P.
Sir Henry F. Yohn, S. W.
Sir W. A. Van Buskirk, J. W.
Sir Solomon A. Stout, T.
Sir Alexander Malsberger, R.
Sir A. L. Custer, St. B.

Sir Jeremiah Weaver, Sw. B.
Sir Henry Christian, W.
Sir Daniel McCormick, S.

MARCH 17, 1862, A. O. 744, A. O. E. P. 65.

Sir Hiram C. Feger, E. C.
Sir George R. Clarke, G.
Sir W. A. Van Buskirk, C. G.
Sir William C. Rutter, P.
Sir Aaron L. Custer, S. W.
Sir Henry F. Yohn, J. W.
Sir Solomon A. Stout, T.
Sir Alexander Malsberger, R.
Sir Jeremiah Weaver, St. B.
Sir D. H. Brittain, Sw. B.
Sir Henry Christian, W.
Sir Daniel McCormick, S.

MARCH 16, 1863, A. O. 745, A. O. E. P. 66.

Sir Ernest Knapp, E. C.
Sir George Walters, G.
Sir J. Vanderslice, C. G.
Sir William C. Rutter, P.
Sir Hiram C. Feger, S. W.
Sir W. A. Van Buskirk, J. W.
Sir Solomon A. Stout, T.
Sir Alexander Malsberger, R.
Sir Henry F. Yohn, St. B.
Sir Aaron L. Custer, Sw. B.
Sir D. H. Brittain, W.
Sir Daniel McCormick, S.

MARCH 15, 1864, A. O. 746, A. O. E. P. 67.

Sir George Walters, E. C.
Sir John Vanderslice, G.

Sir George C. Nichols, C. G.
Sir Isaac S. Clegg, P.
Sir George Clegg, S. W.
Sir George W. Fromfield, J. W.
Sir Solomon A. Stout, T.
Sir Alexander Malsberger, R.
Sir Abettis Keely, St. B.
Sir William W. Wisler, Sw. B.
Sir William Clegg, W.
Sir Daniel McCormick, S.

MARCH 22, 1865, A. O. 747, A. O. E. P. 68.

Sir John Vanderslice, E. C.
Sir George C. Nichols, G.
Sir A. S. Vanderslice, C. G.,
Sir Isaac Clegg, P.
Sir George R. Clarke, S. W.
Sir W. A. Van Buskirk, J. W.
Sir Solomon A. Stout, T.
Sir Alexander Malsberger, R.
Sir Samuel Deimer, St. B.
Sir William Clegg, Sw. B.
Sir William C. Rutter, W.
Sir Daniel McCormick, S.

MARCH 21, 1866, A. O. 748, A. O. E. P. 69.

Sir Addison S. Vanderslice, E. C.
Sir Isaac Clegg, G.
Sir Samuel Deimer, C. G.
Sir Levi B. Kaler, P.
Sir W. A. Van Buskirk, S. W.
Sir William C. Rutter, J. W.
Sir Solomon A. Stout, T.
Sir Alexander Malsberger, R.
Sir George Clegg, St. B.

Sir Peter Emery, Sw. B.
Sir Abeltis Keely, W.
Sir Daniel McCormick, S.

MEMBERS.

NAME.	DATE OF KNIGHTING.
Acceret, Jacob,	December 12, 1863.
Brower, Lafayette,	May 15, 1856.
Beckly, Rev. L. V.,	May 15, 1856.
Brittain, Daniel,	November 20, 1856.
Brownback, James,	December 3, 1864.
Bean, Henry,	September 6, 1866.
Clarke, George R., Charter Mem.,	May 15, 1856.
Custer, Aaron L., Charter Mem.,	May 17, 1856.
Christian, Henry,	November 20, 1856.
Clegg, William H.,	June 4, 1861.
Clegg, Isaac,	December 5, 1861.
Clegg, George,	December 5, 1861.
Chalfant, Albert M.,	December 6, 1866.
Deimer, Samuel,	May 14, 1864.
Deimer, Artemus,	June 10, 1865.
Ellis, S. R.,	May 15, 1856.
Emery, Peter,	May 14, 1864.
Feger, Hiram C., Charter Mem.,	May 15, 1856.
Frick, George B.,	February 19, 1857.
Fronefield, George W.,	December 4, 1862.
Kitchen, Elias,	May 15, 1856.
Knapp, Ernest,	June 4, 1861.
Kaler, L. B.,	May 29, 1862.
Keely, Abettis,	December 12, 1863.
Keely, Ephraim P.,	May 14, 1864.
Moore, Charles, Charter Mem.,	May 15, 1856.
Malsberger, Alexander, Ch. Mem.,	May 16, 1856.
McCormick, Daniel,	November 20, 1856.
Morgan, Joseph,	December 6, 1866.

NAME.	DATE OF KNIGHTING.
Nichols, George C.,	May 29, 1862.
Reiff, D. H., (No. 12), Ch. Mem.,	April 23, 1856.
Rutter, William C., Ch. Mem.,	May 15, 1856.
Stout, Solomon A., (No. 12), Ch. M.,	April 23, 1856.
Seltzer, J. H.,	May 15, 1856.
Snyder, George S., Charter Mem.,	May 15, 1856.
Tippin, Andrew H., (No. 12), Ch. M.	April 23, 1856.
Umstead, Joseph,	March 22, 1860.
Van Buskirk, William A., Ch. Mem.,	May 15, 1856.
Vanderslice, John,	May 29, 1862.
Vanderslice, Addison S.,	December 5, 1861.
Weaver, Jeremiah,	May 15, 1856.
Walters, George,	December 5, 1861.
Wisler, W. W.,	December 12, 1863.
Whiteman, Levi,	May 14, 1864.
Yohn, Henry F.,	November 20, 1856.

THIS Commandery is located in Towanda, Bradford County, Pennsylvania, and was originally established as Wivanda Encampment, in that place, on the 20th day of July, 1826, and the Charter authorized it to confer the Orders of 1, *Knights Templar;* 2, *Knights of Malta;* 3, *Knights of the Mediterranean Pass; and* 4, *Knights of the Red Cross.* (See page 114). On application, October 3, 1857, to R. E. Sir Benjamin Parke, Grand Commander, he granted a new Dispensation, under the name of Northern Commandery, No. 16. The Petitioners for the Commandery were Sir Knights George H. Bull, (the former E. C., of Wivanda Commandery), Sidney Hayden, Gordon F. Mason, Sevillon W. Alden, Abram Edwards, George P. Tracy, W. Patton, J. D. Goodenough, and John Edwards.

This Commandery was established December 4, 1857, and received its Charter June 23, 1858.

OFFICERS OF NORTHERN COMMANDERY, No. 16, SINCE ITS ORGANIZATION.

DECEMBER 4, 1857, A. O. 739, A. O. E. P. 60.

Sir Sidney Hayden, E. C.
Sir H. Lawrence Scott, G.
Sir H. C. Porter, C. G.
Sir E. O. Goodrich, P.
Sir H. B. McKean, S. W.

Sir George E. Fox, J. W.
Sir James H. Webb, T.
Sir E. H. Mason, R.
Sir George H. Bull, St. B.
Sir Gordon F. Mason, Sw. B.
Sir G. P. Tracy, W.
Sir James Harris, S.

MARCH 16, 1858, A. O. 740, A. O. E. P. 61.

Sir H. Lawrence Scott, E. C.
Sir H. C. Porter, G.
Sir George E. Fox, C. G.
Sir E. O. Goodrich, P.
Sir H. B. McKean, S. W.
Sir George D. Montanye, J. W.
Sir James H. Webb, T.
Sir E. H. Mason, R.
Sir George H. Bull, St. B.
Sir Gordon F. Mason, Sw. B.
Sir George P. Tracy, W.
Sir James Harris, S.

MARCH 15, 1859, A. O. 741, A. O. E. P. 62.

Sir George E. Fox, E. C.
Sir H. C. Porter, G.
Sir E. B. Coolbaugh, C. G.
Sir E. O. Goodrich, P.
Sir H. B. McKean, S. W.
Sir George D. Montanye, J. W.
Sir James H. Webb, T.
Sir E. H. Mason, R.
Sir P. D. Morrow, St. B.
Sir W. H. H. Gore, Sw. B.
Sir E. S. Benedict, W.
Sir James Harris, S.

MARCH 14, 1860, A. O. 742, A. O. E. P. 63.

Sir George E. Fox, E. C.
Sir H. C. Porter, G.
Sir E. B. Coolbaugh, C. G.
Sir E. O. Goodrich, P.
Sir H. B. McKean, S. W.
Sir George D. Montanye, J. W.
Sir Allen McKean, T.
Sir E. S. Benedict, R.
Sir D. C. Hall, St. B.
Sir Jeremiah Culp, Sw. B.
Sir W. H. H. Gore, W.
Sir James Harris, S.

MARCH 13, 1861, A. O. 743, A. O. E. P. 64.

Sir George E. Fox, E. C.
Sir H. C. Porter, G.
Sir E. B. Coolbaugh, C. G.
Sir E. O. Goodrich, P.
Sir G. D. Montanye, S. W.
Sir P. D. Morrow, J. W.
Sir G. F. Mason, T.
Sir C. S. Russell, R.
Sir D. C. Hall, St. B.
Sir Stephen Strickland, Jr., Sw. B.
Sir Ira H. Smith, W.
Sir James Harris, S.

MARCH 12, 1862, A. O. 744, A. O. E. P. 65.

Sir George E. Fox, E. C.
Sir E. H. Mason, G.
Sir H. B. McKean, C. G.
Sir E. O. Goodrich, P.

Sir C. B. Patch, S. W.
Sir J. W. Means, J. W.
Sir James Harris, T.
Sir C. S. Russell, R.
Sir Henry Mercur, St. B.
Sir S. Strickland, Jr., Sw. B.
Sir Ira H. Smith, W.
Sir Patrick Phelan, S.

MARCH 11, 1863, A. O. 745, A. O. E. P. 66.

Sir H. B. McKean, E. C.
Sir S. Strickland, Jr., G.
Sir C. B. Patch, C. G.
Sir E. O. Goodrich, P.
 ᐟSir J. W. Means, S. W.
Sir G. D. Montanye, J. W.
Sir E. B. Coolbaugh, T.
Sir C. S. Russell, R.
Sir H. W. Noble, St. B.
Sir Patrick Phelan, Sw. B.
Sir Henry Mercur, W.
Sir James Harris, S.

MARCH 10, 1864, A. O. 746, A. O. E. P. 67.

Sir H. B. McKean, E. C.
Sir J. W. Means, G.
Sir C. B. Patch, C. G.
Sir E. O. Goodrich, P.
Sir Henry Mercur, S. W.
Sir W. H. H. Gore, J. W.
Sir E. B. Coolbaugh, T.
Sir C. S. Russell, R.
Sir H. W. Noble, St. B.
Sir A. G. Craumer, Sw. B.

Sir Patrick Phelan, W.
Sir James Harris, S.

MARCH 15, 1865, A. O. 747, A. O. E. P. 68.

Sir H. B. McKean, E. C.
Sir J. W. Means, G.
Sir C. B. Patch, C. G.
Sir E. O. Goodrich, P.
Sir Henry Mercur, S. W.
Sir W. H. H. Gore, J. W.
Sir E. B. Coolbaugh, T.
Sir C. S. Russell, R.
Sir H. W. Noble, St. B.
Sir A. G. Cranmer, Sw. B.
Sir Patrick Phelan, W.
Sir James Harris, S.

MARCH 14, 1866, A. O. 748, A. O. E. P. 69.

Sir H. B. McKean, E. C.
Sir G. D. Montanye, G.
Sir J. W. Means, C. G.
Sir E. T. Elliott, P.
Sir William A. Peck, S. W.
Sir A. G. Cranmer, J. W.
Sir E. B. Coolbaugh, T.
Sir C. S. Russell, R.
Sir Stephen Strickland, Jr., St. B.
Sir D. H. Barston, Sw. B.
Sir R. H. Patch, W.
Patrick Phelan, S.

MEMBERS.
NAME.   DATE OF KNIGHTING.

Alden, S. W., (Monroe + Rochester,
    N. Y.,) Ch. Mem., Admitted,   December 4, 1857.

NAME.	DATE OF KNIGHTING.
Bull, George H., Charter Member,	July 20, 1826.
Brownson, W. A.,	April 16, 1858.
Benedict, E. S.,	January 7, 1859.
Boyden, Thomas B.,	December 9, 1861.
Bishop, William T., Jr.,	September 16, 1864.
Barston, D. H.,	December 16, 1864.
Blackman, Lyman,	March 6, 1865.
Coolbaugh, Edwin B.,	December 4, 1857.
Culp, Jeremiah,	March 19, 1858.
Camochan, S. G.,	November 16, 1863.
Cranmer, A. G.,	December 16, 1864.
Christian, John,	April 14, 1865.
Collins, J. M.,	May 12, 1865.
Coon, G. W.,	August 11, 1865.
Dusenberry, John H.,	March 18, 1859.
Edwards, Abram, (No. 11), Ch. Mem.,	February 14, 1856.
Edwards, John, (No. 11), Ch. Mem.,	November 8, 1855.
Elliott, E. T.,	September 16, 1864.
Fox, George E.,	December 4, 1857.
Goodenough, J. D., Ch. M., Admit'd,	December 4, 1857.
Goodrich, E. O.,	December 4, 1857.
Gore, W. H. H.,	December 5, 1857.
Goodrich, H. P.,	December 5, 1857.
Griffis, William,	January 7, 1859.
Gaulner, David,	February 8, 1860.
Hayden, Sidney, (St. Omer's, Elmira, N. Y.), Ch. M., Admit'd,	December 4, 1857.
Harris, James,	December 4, 1857.
Hall, D. C.,	June 10, 1858.
Hinman, J. Y.,	February 17, 1865.
Kendall, R. C.,	April 14, 1865.
Lawshe, R. H.,	May 7, 1858.
Laning, R. H.,	August 11, 1865.
Mason, Gordon F., (No. 11), Ch. M.,	March 4, 1856.

NAME.	DATE OF KNIGHTING.
Mason, E. Hastings,	December 4, 1857.
McKean, H. B.,	December 5, 1857.
Montanye, F. D.,	December 5, 1857.
McKean, Allen,	March 17, 1859.
Montanye, George D.,	April 22, 1859.
Morrow, P. D.,	April 22, 1859.
Means, J. F.,	February 5, 1862.
Means, John W.,	February 27, 1863.
Mercur, Henry,	February 27, 1863.
McMillan, A. R.,	April 3, 1863.
Mercur, Charles,	June 25, 1864.
Montanye, Leston D.,	March 6, 1865.
Mason, A. G.,	May 12, 1865.
Mason, J. H.,	August 11, 1865.
Northrop, O. W.,	February 3, 1862.
Noble, H. W.,	September 18, 1863.
Newall, E. M.,	September 15, 1865.
Overton, D. A.,	July 8, 1859.
Patton, William, (Washington City, D. C.), Ch. Mem., Admitted,	December 4, 1857.
Porter, H. C.,	December 4, 1857.
Patton, J. G.,	April 6, 1860.
Phelan, Patrick,	February 27, 1863.
Patch, C. B.,	January 10, 1862.
Peck, William A.,	September 16, 1864.
Patch, R. H.,	September 16, 1864.
Russell, C. S.,	March 28, 1859.
Roberts, William,	May 9, 1865.
Scott, H. Lawrence,	December 4, 1857.
Strickland, Stephen, Jr.,	February 5, 1858.
Smith, Ira H.,	June 15, 1860.
Smith, C. J.,	December 16, 1865.
Tracy, Geo. P., (No. 3), Ch. Mem.,	September 13, 1855.
Webb, James H.,	December 4, 1857.

NAME.	DATE OF KNIGHTING.
Walker, David,	May 20, 1858.
Wakeman, B. E.,	March 17, 1859.
Watkins, G. H.,	July 11, 1863.
Woodruff, O. H.,	August 11, 1865.

27 *

CŒUR DE LION COMMANDERY, No. 17, was established
by Dispensation on the 28th day of April, 1858, in
Scranton, Luzerne County, Pennsylvania, by the R. E.
Sir Benjamin Parke, Grand Commander, on the appli-
cation of Sir Knights Robert C. Simpson, George S.
Kingsbury, William H. Perkins, Thomas Dickson, A.
Crocker, E. O. Goodrich, F. D. Montanye, H. P. Good-
rich, and John L. Gore.
The Charter is dated June 23, 1858.

OFFICERS OF CŒUR DE LION COMMANDERY, No. 17, SINCE ITS ORGANIZATION.

APRIL 28, 1858, A. O. 740, A. O. E. P. 61.

Sir R. C. Simpson, E. C.
Sir Thomas Dickson, G.
Sir Joseph Godfrey, C. G.
Sir William H. Perkins, P.
Sir George S. Kingsbury, S. W.
Sir Edward Kingsbury, J. W.
Sir E. H. Kulin, T.
Sir W. P. Carling, R.
Sir R. J. Searle, St. B.
Sir A. E. Hunt, Sw. B.
Sir N. F. Marsh, W.
Sir Hezekiah Fisher, S.

MARCH 13, 1859, A. O. 741, A. O. E. P. 62.

Sir Robert C. Simpson, E. C.
Sir Thomas Dickson, G.
Sir Joseph Godfrey, C. G.
Sir William H. Perkins, P.
Sir George S. Kingsbury, S. W.
Sir Edward Kingsbury, J. W.
Sir E. H. Kulin, T.
Sir W. P. Carling, R.
Sir R. J. Searle, St. B.
Sir A. E. Hunt, Sw. B.
Sir N. F. Marsh, W.
Sir Hezekiah Fisher, S.

MARCH 12, 1860, A. O. 742, A. O. E. P. 63.

Sir William H. Perkins, E. C.
Sir George S. Kingsbury, G.
Sir Sidney Broadbent, C. G.
Sir Joseph Godfrey, P.
Sir Edward Kingsbury, S. W.
Sir Thomas Dickson, J. W.
Sir A. E. Hunt, T.
Sir W. P. Carling, R.
Sir R. J. Searle, St. B.
Sir E. H. Kulin, Sw. B.
Sir N. F. Marsh, W.
Sir Hezekiah Fisher, S.

MARCH 11, 1861, A. O. 743, A. O. E. P. 64.

Sir Joseph Godfrey, E. C.
Sir George S. Kingsbury, G.
Sir Sidney Broadbent, C. G.
Sir Edward P. Kingsbury, P.
Sir Thomas Dickson, S. W.

Sir William P. Carling, J. W.
Sir William H. Perkins, T.
Sir H. C. Rogers, R.
Sir E. H. Kulin, St. B.
Sir N. F. Marsh, Sw. B.
Sir R. J. Searle, W.
Sir Hezekiah Fisher, S.

MARCH 10, 1862, A. O. 744, A. O. E. P. 65

Sir Joseph Godfrey, E. C.
Sir George S. Kingsbury, G.
− Sir Sidney Broadbent, C. G.
Sir Edward P. Kingsbury, P.
Sir Thomas Dickson, S. W.
Sir William P. Carling, J. W.
Sir William H. Perkins, T.
Sir H. C. Rogers, R.
Sir E. H. Kulin, St. B.
Sir N. F. Marsh, Sw. B.
Sir R. J. Searle, W.
Sir George P. McMillan, S.

MARCH 9, 1863, A. O. 745, A. O. E. P. 66.

Sir Joseph Godfrey, E. C.
Sir George S. Kingsbury, G.
Sir B. S. Kellogg, C. G.
Sir Edward P. Kingsbury, P.
Sir J. N. Van Vechten, S. W.
Sir J. G. Sanderson, J. W.
Sir William H. Perkins, T.
Sir H. C. Rogers, R.
Sir Thomas Dickson, St. B.
Sir O. L. Hallstead, Sw. B.

Sir Sidney Broadbent, W.
Sir George P. McMillan, S.

MARCH 8, 1864, A. O. 746, A. O. E. P. 67.

Sir Joseph Godfrey, E. C.
Sir John Van Vechten, G.
Sir Edward P. Kingsbury, C. G.
Sir Charles A. Stevens, P.
Sir John Koch, S. W.
Sir Sidney Broadbent, J. W.
Sir William H. Perkins, T.
Sir William P. Carling, R.
Sir Thomas Dickson, St. B.
Sir O. L. Hallstead, Sw. B.
Sir Sidney Broadbent, W.
Sir George P. McMillan, S.

MARCH 16, 1865, A. O. 747, A. O. E. P. 68.

Sir Joseph Godfrey, E. C.
Sir William A. Chittenden, G.
Sir Edward P. Kingsbury, C. G.
Sir Charles A. Stevens, P.
Sir J. N. Van Vechten, S. W.
Sir J. G. Sanderson, J. W.
Sir William H. Perkins, T.
Sir William P. Carling, R.
Sir O. L. Hallstead, St. B.
Sir Thomas Dickson, Sw. B.
Sir Sidney Broadbent, W.
Sir George P. McMillan, S.

MARCH 15, 1866, A. O. 748, A. O. E. P. 69.

Sir Joseph Godfrey, E. C.
Sir Charles A. Stevens, G.

O *

Sir Thomas E. Geddis, C. G.
Sir F. L. Hiller, P.
Sir A. B. Stevens, S. W.
Sir A. Davis, J. W.
Sir William H. Perkins, T.
Sir William P. Connell, R.
Sir M. May, St. B.
Sir S. E. Shick, Sw. B.
Sir J. Bryant, W.
Sir George P. McMillan, S.

MEMBERS.

NAME.	DATE OF KNIGHTING.
Amsden, F. J.,	June 13, 1866.
Broadbent, Sidney,	June 16, 1858.
Bryant, J.,	December 16, 1865.
Crocker, A., (No. 14), Ch. Mem.,	June 10, 1856.
Carling, William P.,	April 28, 1858.
Chittenden, William A.,	November 16, 1864.
Clark, Myron J.,	March 30, 1865.
Connell, William P.,	November 23, 1865.
Dickson, Thomas, (No. 14), Ch. M.,	June 10, 1856.
Dickson, George L.,	July 12, 1865.
Davis, A.,	September 21, 1865.
Drinker, C. M.,	November 23, 1865.
Drinker, C. G.,	January 3, 1866.
Dale, M. H.,	February 28, 1866.
Engle, M. D.,	November 23, 1865.
Fisher, Hezekiah,	April 28, 1858.
Goodrich, E. O., (No. 16), Ch. Mem.,	December 4, 1857.
Goodrich, H. P., (No. 16), Ch. Mem.,	December 5, 1857.
Gore, John L., (No. 14), Ch. Mem.,	June 10, 1856.
Godfrey, Joseph,	April 28, 1858.
Geddis, Thomas L.,	September 21, 1865.
Hunt, A. E.,	June 16, 1858.
Hallstead, O. L.,	March 4, 1863.

NAME.	DATE OF KNIGHTING.
Hollister, H.,	March 30, 1865.
Hiller, F. L.,	November 23, 1865.
Jackson, A. Reeves,	November 23, 1865.
Judd, W. J.,	February 28, 1866.
Kingsbury, Geo. S., (No. 14), C. M.,	June 10, 1856.
Kulin, E. H.,	April 28, 1858.
Kingsbury, Edward,	April 28, 1858.
Kingsbury, Edward P.,	June 16, 1858.
Kellogg, B. S.,	May 7, 1862.
Koch, John,	February 18, 1863.
Luce, R. W.,	November 16, 1864.
Lynde, E. C.,	November 16, 1864.
Loderick, Jonas P.,	February 28, 1866.
Montanye, F. D., (No. 16), Ch. M.,	December 5, 1857.
Marsh, N. F.,	April 28, 1858.
Meylert, Michael,	September 1, 1858.
McMillan, George P.,	December 20, 1862.
Matthews, William,	March 30, 1865.
May, M.,	November 23, 1865.
Perkins, Wm. H. (No. 14), Ch. M.,	June 10, 1856.
Postens, J. J.,	February 28, 1866.
Price, John A.,	June 13, 1866.
Rogers, H. C.,	February 1, 1861.
Ruthven, James,	December 20, 1865.
Simpson, Robert C., (No. 14), C. M.,	June 10, 1856.
Searle, R. S.,	June 16, 1858.
Sanderson, J. Gardner,	December 20, 1862.
Stevens, Charles A.,	October 6, 1863.
Shopland, Samuel,	April 17, 1865.
Stevens, A. B.,	September 21, 1865.
Shick, S. E.,	December 20, 1865.
Scranton, William H.,	January 3, 1866.
Van Vechten, John N.,	July 2, 1862.
Weston, Charles T.,	April 17, 1865.

KEDRON COMMANDERY, No. 18, was instituted in Greensburg, Westmoreland County, Pennsylvania. The Dispensation was issued by R. E. Sir William Henry Allen, Grand Commander, March 19, 1860.

The following Sir Knights composed the Petitioners, viz.: Richard Coulter, William R. Terry, William J. Long, John W. Geary, Rev. William H. Locke, J. R. Weldin, S. F. Northam, Benjamin F. Rose, and C. F. Sargent.

The Charter was granted June 23, 1860.

LIST OF OFFICERS.

MARCH 19, 1860, A. O. 742, A. O. E. P. 63.

Sir Richard Coulter, E. C.
Sir William R. Terry, G.
Sir William J. Long, C. G.
Rev. Sir William H. Locke, P.
Sir John W. Geary, S. W.
Sir J. R. Weldin, J. W.
Sir S. F. Northam, T.
Sir Benjamin F. Rose, R.
Sir C. F. Sargent, St. B.
Sir Samuel Rock, Sw. B.
Sir Daniel Welty, W.
Sir James Hunter, S.

324

MARCH 28, 1860, A. O. 742, A. O. E. P. 63.

Sir Richard Coulter, E. C.
Sir William R. Terry, G.
Sir William J. Long, C. G.
Rev. Sir William H. Locke, P.
Sir Z. P. Bierer, S. W.
Sir William S. Brown, J. W.
Sir D. W. Shryock, T.
Sir William Robinson, R.
Sir Samuel Rock, St. B.
Sir George L. Potts, Sw. B.
Sir Daniel Welty, W.
Sir James Hunter, S.

MARCH 24, 1861, A. O. 743, A. O. E. P. 64.

Sir Richard Coulter, E. C.
Sir William R. Terry, G.
Sir William J. Long, C. G.
Rev. Sir William H. Locke, P.
Sir Z. P. Bierer, S. W.
Sir William S. Brown, J. W.
Sir D. W. Shryock, T.
Sir William Robinson, R.
Sir Samuel Rock, St. B.
Sir George L. Potts, Sw. B.
Sir Daniel Welty, W.
Sir James Hunter, S.

MARCH 23, 1862, A. O. 744, A. O. E. P. 65.

Sir Z. P. Bierer, E. C.
Sir William S. Brown, G.
Sir George L. Potts, C. G.
Rev. Sir William H. Locke, P.
Sir Samuel Rock, S. W.

28

Sir R. Zimmerman, J. W.
Sir D. W. Shryock, T.
Sir William Robinson, R.
Sir A. Lobaugh, St. B.
Sir Richard Coulter, Sw. B.
Sir Daniel Welty, W.
Sir James Hunter, S.

MARCH 22, 1863, A. O. 745, A. O. E. P. 66.

Sir William S. Brown, E. C.
Sir George L. Potts, G.
Sir Samuel Rock, C. G.
Rev. Sir William H. Locke, P.
Sir Daniel Welty, S. W.
Sir R. Zimmerman, J. W.
Sir D. W. Shryock, T.
Sir William Robinson, R.
Sir R. W. Turney, St. B.
Sir John W. Geary, Sw. B.
Sir Richard Coulter, W.
Sir James Hunter, S.

MARCH 21, 1864, A. O. 746, A. O. E. P. 67.

Sir George L. Potts, E. C.
Sir D. W. Shryock, G.
Sir Henry Kettering, C. G.
Rev. Sir William H. Locke, P.
Sir Daniel Welty, S. W.
Sir R. W. Turney, J. W.
Sir Z. P. Bierer, T.
Sir William Robinson, R.
Sir Samuel Rock, St. B.
Sir R. Zimmerman, Sw. B.
Sir William S. Brown, W.
Sir James Hunter, S.

MARCH 20, 1865, A. O. 747, A. O. E. P. 68.

Sir George L. Potts, E. C.
Sir D. W. Shryock, G.
Sir Henry Kettering, C. G.
Rev. Sir William H. Locke, P.
Sir Daniel Welty, S. W.
Sir R. W. Turney, J. W.
Sir Z. P. Bierer, T.
Sir William Robinson, R.
Sir Samuel Rock, St. B.
Sir R. Zimmerman, Sw. B.
Sir William S. Brown, W.
Sir James Hunter, S.

MARCH 19, 1866, A. O. 748, A. O. E. P. 69.

Sir D. W. Shryock, E. C.
Sir Henry Kettering, G.
Sir Samuel Rock, C. G.
Rev. Sir William H. Locke, P.
Sir Augustus Row, S. W.
Sir R. W. Turney, J. W.
Sir Z. P. Bierer, T.
Sir William Robinson, R.
Sir George L. Potts, St. B.
Sir R. Zimmerman, Sw. B.
Sir William S. Brown, W.
Sir James Hunter, S.

MEMBERS.

NAME.	DATE OF KNIGHTING.
Bierer, Zachariah P.,	April 11, 1860.
Brown, William S.,	April 11, 1860.
Coulter, Richard, (No. 1), Ch. Mem.,	May 11, 1858.
Geary, John W., (No. 1), Ch. Mem.,	October 2, 1846.

NAME.	DATE OF KNIGHTING.
Hunter, James,	April 11, 1860.
Kettering, Henry,	March 1, 1864.
Long, W. J., (No. 10), Ch. Mem.,	May 18, 1859.
Locke, Rev. W. H., (No. 1), Ch. M.,	September 26, 1859.
Lobaugh, Arnold,	April 11, 1860.
Long, George H.,	May 1, 1860.
Northam, Stephen F., (No. 1), Ch. M.,	January 5, 1859.
Potts, George L.,	April 11, 1860.
Rose, Benj. F., (No. 10), Ch. Mem.,	April 26, 1859.
Rock, Samuel,	April 11, 1860.
Robinson, William,	April 11, 1860.
Rowe, Augustus,	March 20, 1865.
Robinson, D. S.,	March 20, 1865.
Sargent, C. F., (No. 10), Ch. Mem.,	February 14, 1856.
Shryock, David W.,	May 1, 1860.
Terry, Wm. R., (No. 3), Ch. Mem.,	September 30, 1854.
Turney, Robert W.,	June 4, 1860.
Weldin, J. R., (No. 1), Ch. Mem.,	August 23, 1850.
Welty, Daniel,	April 11, 1860.
Zimmerman, Reuben,	April 11, 1860.

HUGH DE PAYENS COMMANDERY, No. 19, was established at Easton, Northampton County, Pennsylvania, by Dispensation issued by the R. E. Sir William H. Allen, Grand Commander, on the 12th day of April, 1860.

The Petitioners for the Commandery were Sir Knights Herbert Thomas, John Green, William B. Semple, Abraham Miller, (C), Josiah Cole, Samuel Freeman, C. Pomp, Lewis H. Stout, and James M. Porter, Jr.

The Charter was granted June 23, 1860.

OFFICERS OF HUGH DE PAYENS COMMANDERY, No. 19, SINCE ITS ORGANIZATION.

APRIL 12, 1860, A. O. 742, A. O. E. P. 63.

Sir Herbert Thomas, E. C.
Sir John Green, G.
Sir William B. Semple, C. G.
Rev. Sir Joseph J. Elsegood, P.
Sir Lewis H. Stout, S. W.
Sir Samuel Freeman, J. W.
Sir Charles Pomp, T.
Sir George W. Wagner, R.
Sir Josiah Cole, St. B.
Sir Abraham Miller, (C.), Sw. B.
Sir James M. Porter, Jr., W.
Sir Enos Werkheisser, S.

JUNE 28, 1860, A. O. 742, A. O. E. P. 63.

Sir Herbert Thomas, E. C.
Sir John Green, G.
Sir William B. Semple, C. G.
Rev. Sir Joseph J. Elsegood, P.
Sir Lewis H. Stout, S. W.
Sir Samuel Freeman, J. W.
Sir Charles Pomp, T.
Sir George W. Wagner, R.
Sir Josiah Cole, St. B.
Sir Abraham Miller, (C.), Sw. B.
Sir James M. Porter, Jr., W.
Sir Enos Werkheisser, S.

MARCH 27, 1861, A. O. 743, A. O. E. P. 64.

Sir John Green, E. C.
Sir Abraham Miller, (C.), G.
Sir William B. Semple, C. G.
Rev. Sir Joseph J. Elsegood, P.
Sir Lewis H. Stout, S. W.
Sir Samuel Freeman, J. W.
Sir Charles Pomp, T.
Sir George W. Wagner, R.
Sir Josiah Cole, St. B.
Sir Thomas D. Conyngham, Sw. B.
Sir Martin Fry, W.
Sir Enos Werkheisser, S.

MARCH 26, 1862, A. O. 744, A. O. E. P. 65.

Sir Abraham Miller, (C.), E. C.
Sir William B. Semple, G.
Sir James M. Porter, Jr., C. G.
Rev. Sir Joseph J. Elsegood, P.
Sir Lewis H. Stout, S. W.

Sir Samuel Freeman, J. W.
Sir Charles Pomp, T.
Sir George W. Wagner, R.
Sir Josiah Cole, St. B.
Sir William Young, Sw. B.
Sir Martin Fry, W.
Sir Enos Werkheisser, S.

MARCH 25, 1863, A. O. 745, A. O. E. P. 66.

Sir William B. Semple, E. C.
Sir James M. Porter, Jr., G.
Sir Lewis H. Stout, C. G.
Rev. Sir Joseph J. Elsegood, P.
Sir William Mutchler, S. W.
Sir George Sweeny, J. W.
Sir Charles Pomp, T.
Sir George W. Wagner, R.
Sir Josiah Cole, St. B.
Sir William Young, Sw. B.
Sir Martin Fry, W.
Sir Enos Werkheisser, S.

MARCH 24, 1864, A. O. 746, A. O. E. P. 67.

Sir James M. Porter, Jr., E. C.
Sir Lewis H. Stout, G.
Rev. Sir Joseph J. Elsegood, C. G.
Sir William Mutchler, P.
Sir Uriah Sandt, S. W.
Sir Francis V. Barnet, J. W.
Sir Abraham Miller, (C.), T.
Sir George W. Wagner, R.
Sir Gamble Young, St. B.
Sir John H. Heckman, Sw. B.
Sir Martin Fry, W.
Sir Jeremiah Dietrich, S.

MARCH 23, 1865, A, O. 747, A. O. E. P. 68.

Sir Lewis H. Stout, E. C.
Rev. Sir Joseph J. Elsegood, G.
Sir William Mutchler, C. G.
Sir James M. Porter, Jr., P.
Sir Uriah Sandt, S. W.
Sir Francis V. Barnet, J. W.
Sir Abraham Miller, (C.), T.
Sir George W. Wagner, R.
Sir Enos Werkheisser, St. B.
Sir Gamble Young, Sw. B.
Sir John H. Heckman, W.
Sir John Konn, S.

MARCH 22, 1866, A. O. 748, A. O. E. P. 69

Rev. Sir Joseph J. Elsegood, E. C.
Sir William Mutchler, G.
Sir Uriah Sandt, C. G.
Sir James Madison Porter, P.
Sir Francis Vogle Barnet, S. W.
Sir Jacob Breckenridge Clemens, J. W.
Sir Abraham Miller, T.
Sir John Frederick Thompson, R.
Sir Enos Werkheisser, St. B.
Sir James Young, Sw. B.
Sir Gamble Young, W.
Sir John Young, S.

MEMBERS.

NAME.	DATE OF KNIGHTING.
Ackerman, William Carty,	November 6, 1865.
Benedict, Isbon,	June 14, 1860.
Barnet, Francis Vogle,	December 7, 1863.
Brinker, George,	February 1, 1864.

NAME.	DATE OF KNIGHTING.
Bender, George H.,	February 6, 1865.
Brunner, Augustus Grove,	April 16, 1866.
Borheck, Frederick Raphael,	April 16, 1866.
Beckel, Louis Frederick,	April 30, 1866.
Brening, Peter Benjamin,	May 21, 1866.
Cole, Josiah, (No. 4), Charter Mem.,	April 11, 1860.
Conyngham, Thomas D.,	December 16, 1860.
Clader, Franklin,	January 7, 1861.
Cummings, Samuel Morton,	August 7, 1865.
Clemens, Jacob Breckenridge,	August 7, 1865.
Detwiler, John J.,	December 10, 1860.
Dean, John W.,	October 30, 1863.
Davis, W. H.,	December 7, 1863.
Dietrick, Edward,	February 1, 1864.
Dietrick, Jeremiah,	February 1, 1864.
Durling, John Nye,	November 20, 1865.
Desh, Owen Heisler,	June 4, 1866.
Elsegood, Rev. Joseph J.,	December 3, 1860.
Eilenberger, Peter F.,	May 1, 1865.
Erwin, Ambrose John,	May 21, 1866.
Freeman, Samuel, (No. 4), Ch. M.,	April 11, 1860.
Fry, Martin,	June 14, 1860.
Fried, George L.,	September 2, 1861.
Forman, Lawrence,	April 3, 1865.
Fetter, Marcus Christman,	February 5, 1866.
Finley, George,	April 2, 1866.
Finley, Herman Marcus,	April 2, 1866.
Green, John, (No. 4), Ch. Mem.,	March 23, 1860.
Green, Edward H.,	June 14, 1860.
Garis, David,	June 14, 1860.
Gillespie, Samuel,	April 6, 1863.
Gilligan, John M.,	January 4, 1864.
Gaynor, Edward John,	April 2, 1866.
Geissinger, Jacob Freeman,	June 4, 1866.

NAME.	DATE OF KNIGHTING.
Hoff, William A.,	June 14, 1860.
Hecht, C. Edward,	June 14, 1860.
Heckman, John H.,	April 7, 1862.
Huff, Moses,	October 30, 1863.
Hay, Jacob,	November 2, 1863.
Haviland, William K.,	January 4, 1864.
Hill, Frederick,	April 2, 1866.
Heiney, Augustus Frederick,	June 8, 1866.
Johnston, Joseph,	January 4, 1864.
Knauss, C. Henry,	February 11, 1861.
Kitchen, Samuel C.,	April 21, 1863.
Konn, John,	May 2, 1864.
Kutz, John,	August 1, 1864.
Knauss, Cornelius Marcus,	February 5, 1866.
Kellogg, William,	April 2, 1866.
Leibert, Richard W.,	February 4, 1861.
Lewis, Samuel Seymour,	October 5, 1863.
Lehman, Bernard Eugene,	March 19, 1866.
Lehner, William,	June 6, 1866.
Miller, Abr'm., (C.), (No. 4), C. M.,	March 23, 1860.
Moore, Rev. S. T.,	November 12, 1860.
Mitchell, James Y.,	December 3, 1860.
Mutchler, William,	April 7, 1862.
Morrison, Joseph,	December 5, 1864.
Mingle, James Lane,	August 7, 1865.
Mutchler, James,	June 4, 1866.
Neiman, Daniel Hilner,	June 4, 1866.
Oliver, Theodore,	October 1, 1866.
Pomp, Charles, (No. 4), Ch. Mem.,	April 11, 1860.
Porter, J. Madison, Jr., (No. 4), C. M.,	March 23, 1860.
Pyle, Robert C.,	November 2, 1863.
Rice, William,	September 12, 1864.
Ramsden, Robert,	August 7, 1865.
Rockwell, Egbert,	August 7, 1865.

NAME.	DATE OF KNIGHTING.
Reich, Owen,	January 1, 1866.
Semple, Wm. B., (No. 4), Ch. Mem.,	March 23, 1860.
Stout, Lewis H., (No. 4), Ch. Mem.,	March 23, 1860.
Sitgreaves, Theodore R.,	June 14, 1860.
Savitz, Joseph,	November 5, 1860.
Sweeny, George,	November 30, 1860.
Sandt, Uriah,	April 6, 1863.
Slater, Gabriel H.,	November 9, 1863.
Schug, Amandus,	February 1, 1864.
Schimmel, George,	August 1, 1864.
Thomas, Herbert, (No. 4), Ch. Mem.,	April 11, 1860.
Tombler, Henry G.,	February 6, 1865.
Thompson, J. Frederick,	April 3, 1865.
Vanarsdale, Samuel B.,	September 7, 1863.
Veile, Xavier,	July 3, 1865.
Wagner, George W.,	November 30, 1860.
Werkheisser, Enos,	December 12, 1860.
White, Henry K.,	September 7, 1863.
Wilson, W. R.,	March 7, 1864.
Young, William,	April 11, 1861.
Young, Gamble,	March 10, 1862.
Young, James,	December 5, 1864.
Yohe, Caleb,	April 16, 1866.

ALLEN COMMANDERY, No. 20, was instituted by Dispensation, granted April 21, 1860, by the R. E. Sir William Henry Allen, Grand Commander.

This Commandery is located at Allentown, Lehigh County, Pennsylvania. The Petitioners were Sir Knights William Lilly, William R. Otis, George B. Schall, James Houston, J. B. McCreary, John Y. Bechtel, L. F. Chapman, Solomon Griesemer, David O. Moser, and Simeon H. Price.

The Charter was granted June 23, 1860.

OFFICERS OF ALLEN COMMANDERY, No. 20, SINCE ITS ORGANIZATION.

APRIL 21, 1860, A. O. 742, A. O. E. P. 63.

Sir William Lilly, E. C.
Sir William R. Otis, G.
Sir George B. Schall, C. G.
Sir L. F. Chapman, P.
Sir James Houston, S. W.
Sir David O. Moser, J. W.
Sir Solomon Griesemer, T.
Sir John Y. Bechtel, R.
Sir J. B. McCreary, St. B.
Sir Simeon H. Price, Sw. B.
Sir R. T. Kreider, W.
Sir J. G. Odenheimer, S.

MARCH 12, 1861, A. O. 743, A. O. E. P. 64

Sir William R. Otis, E. C.
Sir George B. Schall, G.
Sir L. F. Chapman, C. G.
Sir David O. Moser, P.
Sir J. D. Lowall, S. W.
Sir Simeon H. Price, J. W.
Sir Solomon Griesemer, T.
Sir John Y. Bechtel, R.
Sir Charles Kline, St. B.
Sir James Houston, Sw. B.
Sir R. T. Kreider, W.
Sir J. G. Odenheimer, S.

MARCH 11, 1862, A. O. 744, A. O. E. P. 65.

Sir George B. Schall, E. C.
Sir John D. Lawall, G.
Sir Joseph H. Dubbs, C. G.
Sir A. J. G. Dubbs, P.
Sir Simeon H. Price, S. W.
Sir Henry Conell, J. W.
Sir Solomon Griesemer, T.
Sir John Y. Bechtel, R.
Sir Daniel Clader, St. B.
Sir Charles Kline, Sw. B.
Sir J. G. Odenheimer, W.
Sir H. J. Herman, S.

MARCH 10, 1863, A. O. 745, A. O. E. P. 66.

Sir George B. Schall, E. C.
Sir John D. Lawall, G.
Sir Joseph H. Dubbs, C. G.
Sir A. J. G. Dubbs, P.
Sir Simeon H. Price, S. W.

Sir Henry Conell, J. W.
Sir Solomon Griesemer, T.
Sir John Y. Bechtel, R.
Sir J. G. Odenheimer, St. B.
Sir John H. Fogle, Sw. B.
Sir Charles Kline, W.
Sir William B. Fogle, S.

MARCH 9, 1864, A. O. 746, A. O. E. P. 67.

Sir George B. Schall, E. C.
Sir John D. Lawall, G.
Sir J. H. Dubbs, C. G.
Sir A. J. G. Dubbs, P.
Sir Simeon H. Price, S. W.
Sir Henry Conell, J. W.
Sir Solomon Griesemer, T.
Sir John Y. Bechtel, R.
Sir J. G. Odenheimer, St. B.
Sir John H. Fogle, Sw. B.
Sir Charles Kline, W.
Sir William B. Fogle, S.

MARCH 8, 1865, A. O. 747, A. O. E. P. 68.

Sir John D. Lawall, E. C.
Sir John Y. Bechtel, G.
Sir E. B. Young, C. G.
Sir John H. Fogle, P.
Sir Benjamin Lochman, S. W.
Sir Charles Kline, J. W.
Sir Solomon Griesemer, T.
Sir Dewees J. Martin, R.
Sir Henry J. Saeger, St. B.
Sir William B. Fogle, Sw. B.
Sir Simeon J. Price, W.
Sir George B. Schall, S.

MARCH 13, 1866, A. O. 748, A. O. E. P. 69.

Sir Edward B. Young, E. C.
Sir Dewees J. Martin, G.
Sir John H. Fogle, C. G.
Sir Henry S. Clemens, P.
Sir Benjamin Lochman, S. W.
Sir Charles Kline, J. W.
Sir Solomon Griesemer, T.
Sir William C. Lichtenwalner, R.
Sir James Houston, St. B.
Sir John B. Moser, Sw. B.
Sir C. F. Schultz, W.
Sir Daniel Clader, S.

MEMBERS.

NAME.	DATE OF KNIGHTING.
Bechtel, John Y., (No. 9), Ch. Mem.,	February 28, 1860.
Babcock, Charles B.,	December 11, 1860.
Blumer, Jacob A.,	May 1, 1866.
Bear, Peter,	June 28, 1866.
Chapman, L. F., (No. 9), Ch. Mem.,	February 28, 1860.
Conell, Henry,	February 12, 1861.
Clader, Daniel,	May 14, 1861.
Clemens, Henry S.,	April 13, 1864.
Cooper, C. W.,	May 1, 1866.
Dubbs, Joseph H.,	March 12, 1861.
Dubbs, A. J. G.,	May 28, 1861.
Dillinger, J. S.,	May 1, 1866.
Fogle, John H.,	February 12, 1861.
Fogle, William B.,	May 28, 1861.
Fogel, A. J.,	May 1, 1866.
Fogel, Willoughby,	June 28, 1866.
Faust, Owen,	June 28, 1866.
Griesemer, Solomon, (No. 9), Ch. M.,	February 28, 1860.

NAME.	DATE OF KNIGHTING.
Houston, James, (No. 9), Ch. Mem.,	February 28, 1860.
Herman, A. J.,	May 14, 1861.
Hoffman, William H.,	May 17, 1866.
Holstein, Julius,	May 17, 1866.
Heller, Jacob,	June 28, 1866.
Kline, Charles,	May 2, 1860.
Kreider, R. T.,	May 15, 1860.
Kessler, Tobias,	May 1, 1866.
Lilly, William, (No. 9), Ch. Mem.,	March 25, 1854.
Lawall, John D.,	May 2, 1860.
Lichtenwalner, W. C.,	March 24, 1862.
Lochman, Benjamin,	December 22, 1864.
Longnecker, H. C.,	May 1, 1866.
Lewis, Joseph,	May 17, 1866.
Moser, David O., (No. 9), Ch. Mem.,	May 25, 1858.
McCreary, J. B., (No. 4), Ch. Mem.,	March 25, 1853.
Mink, T. H.,	March 24, 1862.
Mink, B. H.,	March 24, 1862.
Martin, Dewees J.,	December 22, 1864.
Moser, John B.,	February 8, 1866.
Morgan, Joseph C.,	May 17, 1866.
Otis, William R., (No. 9), Ch. Mem.,	February 28, 1860.
Odenheimer, J. G.,	May 2, 1860.
Oliver, John H.,	May 1, 1866.
Price, Simeon H., (No. 9), Ch. Mem.,	April 16, 1860.
Reichert, C. Frank,	March 8, 1866.
Roeder, J. B.,	May 1, 1866.
Rehrig, Esaias,	May 1, 1866.
Ritter, Oliver A.,	May 1, 1866.
Ruhr, Thomas,	May 17, 1866.
Raudenbush, A. W.,	May 17, 1866.
Rupp, Herman,	May 17, 1866.
Raudenbush, M. W.,	May 17, 1866.
Schall, Geo. B., (No. 9), Ch. Mem.,	February 28, 1860.

NAME.	DATE OF KNIGHTING.
Saeger, Henry J.,	December 22, 1864.
Schultz, Christian F.,	February 8, 1866.
Stetler, John G.,	May 1, 1866.
Schuler, Elias,	May 17, 1866.
Seip, Peter,	June 28, 1866.
Stein, Henry,	June 28, 1866.
Troxell, Aaron,	May 1, 1866.
Troxell, Alexander,	May 1, 1866.
Weiser, Nelson,	May 1, 1866.
Young, Edward B.,	December 24, 1864.
Artman, Willoughby,	December 13, 1866.
Bastian, Daniel H.,	May 10, 1866.
Balliet, Joseph E.,	December 13, 1866.
Hartzell, George W.,	December 13, 1866.
Laubach, Thomas H.,	December 13, 1866.
Shantz, A. M.,	December 13, 1866.

29 *

YORK COMMANDERY, No. 21, was constituted in York, York County, Pennsylvania, January 19, 1865, the Dispensation having been issued by the R. E. Sir H. Stanley Goodwin, Grand Commander, on January 13, 1865.

The Petitioners for York Commandery were Sir Knights Fitz James Evans, Arthur N. Green, Jeremiah Carl, David O. Prince, William Gilberthorpe, Jacob D. Heiges, M. B. Spahr, Thomas White, Charles F. Winter, Peter Bentz, J. R. Davis, and William Smith.

The Charter was granted June 14, 1865.

OFFICERS OF YORK COMMANDERY, No. 21, SINCE ITS ORGANIZATION.

JANUARY 19, 1865, A. O. 747, A. O. E. P. 68.

Sir Fitz James Evans, E. C.
Sir Arthur N. Green, G.
Sir Jeremiah Carl, C. G.
Sir Michael B. Spahr, P.
Sir David O. Prince, S. W.
Sir J. R. Davis, J. W.
Sir George H. Maish, T.
Sir William Gilberthorpe, R.
Sir Charles Winter, St. B.
Sir Thomas White, Sw. B.
Sir Jacob D. Heiges, W.
Sir A. E. Fahs, S.

JUNE 24, 1865, A. O. 747, A. O. E. P. 68.

Sir Fitz James Evans, E. C.
Sir Arthur N. Green, G.
Sir Jacob D. Heiges, C. G.
Sir M. B. Spahr, P.
Sir David O. Prince, S. W.
Sir J. R. Davis, J. W.
Sir George H. Maish, T.
Sir D. P. Shultz, R.
Sir Jacob Hay, St. B.
Sir William H. Stahle, Sw. B.
Sir Henry E. Passmore, W.
Sir A. E. Fahs, S.

MARCH 15, 1866, A. O. 748, A. O. E. P. 69.

Sir Arthur N. Green, E. C.
Sir J. D. Heiges, G.
Sir D. O. Prince, C. G.
Sir John Gibson, P.
Sir J. R. Davis, S. W.
Sir Samuel H. Spangler, J. W.
Sir George H. Maish, T.
Sir O. C. Brickley, R.
Sir Charles F. Winter, St. B.
Sir George A. Heckert, Sw. B.
Sir George P. Smyser, W.
Sir A. E. Fahs, S.

MEMBERS.

NAME.	DATE OF KNIGHTING.
Bentz, Peter, (No. 13), Ch. Mem.,	October 27, 1864.
Brickley, O. C.,	January 19, 1865.
Baugher, George F.,	January 19, 1865.
Bressler, Charles H.,	January 19, 1865.

NAME.	DATE OF KNIGHTING.
Berg, Andrew, Rev.,	May 18, 1865.
Beck, Emanuel C.,	June 12, 1865.
Burnham, N. F.,	October 18, 1866.
Carl, Jeremiah, (No. 13), Ch. Mem.,	February 28, 1864.
Davis, J. R., (No. 13), Ch. Mem.,	November 24, 1864.
Demarest, George W.,	December 21, 1865.
Dieterich, David,	December 21, 1865.
Dubs, William,	January 18, 1866.
Doty, G. S.,	June 8, 1866.
Evans, Fitz James, (No. 13), Ch. M.,	February 28, 1864.
Emmet, Jacob, Jr.,	January 19, 1865.
Elliott, A. W.,	February 16, 1865.
Ettele, Henry,	April 20, 1865.
Fahs, Augustus E.,	January 19, 1865.
Fields, Charles O.,	April 20, 1865.
Fox, Charles J.,	October 18, 1866.
Frank, John P.,	November 19, 1866.
Green, Arthur N., (No. 13), Ch. M.,	January 29, 1864.
Gilberthorpe, Wm., (No. 13), Ch. M.,	October 27, 1864.
Gibson, John,	May 18, 1865.
Gross, Israel F.,	November 16, 1865.
Gerry, James, Jr.,	November 19, 1866.
Heiges, Jacob D., (No. 13), Ch. M.,	October 27, 1864.
Heckert, George A.,	January 19, 1865.
Hay, Jacob, Jr.,	February 16, 1865.
Hay, George Lauman,	April 20, 1865.
Herman, John C.,	November 16, 1865.
Heiges, John M.,	November 16, 1865.
Jordan, W. H.,	June 12, 1865.
Karg, George A.,	January 19, 1865.
Klinefelter, Charles A.,	May 18, 1865.
Keech, William L.,	May 18, 1865.
Latimer, Henry,	May 18, 1865.
Loucks, Isaac,	December 21, 1865.

NAME.	DATE OF KNIGHTING.
Logan, James J.,	February 15, 1865.
Maish, George H.,	January 19, 1865.
Minsker, John,	January 19, 1865.
Myers, Samuel R.,	May 18, 1865.
Mintzer, S. J. W.,	July 20, 1865.
Myers, Thomas S.,	September 21, 1865.
Myers, William A.,	June 8, 1866.
Maish, Levi,	November 19, 1866.
Prince, David O., (No. 13), Ch. Mem.,	April 29, 1864.
Passmore, Henry E.,	January 19, 1865.
Rosenmiller, J. F.,	June 12, 1865.
Riesker, John J.,	January 18, 1866.
Ryan, Eli,	March 12, 1866.
Smith, Wm., (No. 13), Charter Mem.,	October 27, 1864.
Spahr, Michael B., (No. 13), Ch. M.,	October 27, 1864.
Stallman, Frederick,	January 19, 1865.
Smyser, Edward G.,	January 19, 1865.
Spangler, Samuel H.,	January 19, 1865.
Stahle, William A.,	January 19, 1865.
Strayer, Lewis,	January 19, 1865.
Schall, Michael,	January 19, 1865.
Schall, Jacob D.,	February 16, 1865.
Small, James B.,	March 16, 1865.
Shultz, D. P.,	March 16, 1865.
Smyser, Emanuel D.,	April 20, 1865.
Stine, John R.,	May 18, 1865.
Smyser, George P.,	September 21, 1865.
Seaton, Edward A.,	October 5, 1865.
Sproutt, J. Dewitt,	October 5, 1865.
Souder, William,	December 21, 1865.
Shatzburger, William,	June 8, 1866.
Tanger, David S.,	May 18, 1865.
White, Thomas, (No. 13), Ch. Mem.,	October 27, 1864.
Winter, Charles F., (No. 13), Ch. M.,	November 24, 1864.

NAME.	DATE OF KNIGHTING.
Weigle, Nathaniel,	January 19, 1865.
Weiser, Charles S.,	March 16, 1865.
Wheeler, Edward,	July 20, 1865.
Weinrich, Charles,	July 20, 1865.

An application was presented to the Right Eminent Grand Commandery of the State of Pennsylvania, which assembled at Lancaster City, June 12, 1866, praying for a Charter, and signed by the following Sir Knights, viz.: William F. Logan, James Goodlander, Joseph W. Chapman, Samuel G. Van Gilder, B. Morris Ellis, Constance Curtin, Valentine S. Doebler, Simon V. Polk, George S. Berry, F. D. Greene, John P. Salmon, Samuel J. Parker, John W. Parmley, D. W. Smith, S. Garman, William N. Jones, F. H. Schwallenberg, John A. Vanderslice, and A. S. Crawford. The Commandery to be located in Williamsport, Lycoming County, and to be known as BALDWIN II. COMMANDERY, No. 22.

On the recommendation of the Committee on Charters, (viz.: Sir Knights H. B. McKean, John Vallerchamp, and J. L. Hutchinson), the Charter was granted June 12, 1866.

OFFICERS OF BALDWIN II. COMMANDERY, No. 22.

JUNE 13, 1866, A. O. 748, A. O. E. P. 69.

Sir William F. Logan, E. C.
Sir James Goodlander, G.
Sir Joseph W. Chapman, C. G.
Sir Samuel G. Van Gilder, P.
Sir B. Morris Ellis, S. W.

Sir Constance Curtin, J. W.
Sir Valentine S. Doebler, T.
Sir Simon V. Polk, R.
Sir George S. Berry, St. B.
Sir F. D. Greene, Sw. B.
Sir John P. Salmon, W.
Sir Samuel J. Parker, S.

MEMBERS.

NAME.	DATE OF KNIGHTING.
Berry, George S., (No. 12), Ch. Mem.,	September 24, 1863.
Beard, W. W.,	September 13, 1866.
Bush, D. G.,	September 13, 1866.
Beard, Henry,	September 14, 1866.
Bryant, R. E.,	October 16, 1866.
Chapman, Jos. W., (No. 12), Ch. M.,	September 24, 1863.
Curtin, Constance, (No. 12), Ch. M.,	March 1, 1866.
Crawford, A. S., (No. 12), Ch. Mem.,	January 12, 1865.
Clay, M. L.,	September 13, 1866.
Cornell, E. A.,	September 14, 1866.
Cook, J. R.,	September 14, 1866.
Doebler, Valentine S., (No. 12), C. M.,	August 16, 1860.
Doebler, C. R., (No. 12), Admitted,	September 13, 1866.
Ellis, B. Morris, (No. 12), Ch. Mem.,	November 25, 1863.
Embick, F. E.,	September 13, 1866.
Fisher, J. S.,	October 16, 1866.
Goodlander, Jas., (No. 12), Ch. Mem.,	November 3, 1865.
Greene, F. D., (No. 12), Ch. Mem.,	May 8, 1862.
Garman, Samuel, (No. 12), Ch. Mem.,	March 8, 1861.
Greene, J. Miles, (No. 12), Admitted,	September 13, 1866.
Hays, Frank,	September 13, 1866.
Hays, J. W.,	September 13, 1866.
Hastings, H. S.,	September 13, 1866.
Hagenbuch, G. M., (No. 12), Admit'd,	September 13, 1866.
Herring, M. B., (No. 12), Admitted,	September 13, 1866.

NAME.	DATE OF KNIGHTING.
Humes, H. B.,	November 20, 1866.
Humes, J. Harvey,	November 20, 1866.
Higgins, W. V., (Admitted),	November 20, 1866.
Jones, Wm. N., (No. 12), Ch. Mem.,	November 3, 1865.
Logan, Wm. F., (No. 12), Ch. Mem.,	March 24, 1863.
Ligget, John,	December 18, 1866.
Martin, Warren, (No. 12), Admitted,	September 13, 1866.
Mason, John S.,	November 20, 1866.
Moltz, Philip A.,	November 20, 1866.
Polk, Simon V., (No. 12), Ch. Mem.,	April 10, 1862.
Parker, Sam'l. J., (No. 12), Ch. Mem.,	June 30, 1864.
Parmly, John W., (No. 12), Ch. Mem.,	April 30, 1863.
Parsons, H. C.,	September 13, 1866.
Prior, W. R.,	September 14, 1866.
Quiggle, R. C.,	October 16, 1866.
Richardson, B. B.,	September 13, 1866.
Roberts, A. P.,	October 16, 1866.
Salmon, John P., (No. 12), Ch. Mem.,	April 13, 1865.
Smith, D. W., (No. 12), Ch. Mem.,	January 12, 1865.
Schwallenberg, F. H., (No. 12), C. M.,	October 5, 1865.
Sweeney, C. W.,	September 13, 1866.
Snyder, Geo. S., (No. 15), Admitted,	September 13, 1866.
Schiesley, Casimir,	September 14, 1866.
Snyder, Henry F.,	December 18, 1866.
Van Gilder, S. G., (No. 12), Ch. M.,	January 12, 1865.
Vanderslice, John A., (No. 12), C. M.,	July 6, 1865.
Young, S. R., (No. 12), Admitted,	September 13, 1866.

30

THIS Commandery is located at Mauch Chunk, Carbon County, Pennsylvania. An application was made August 30, 1866, to the R. E. Sir Robert Pitcairn, Grand Commander, by the following Sir Knights, viz.: William Lilly, James Houston, Anthony W. Raudenbush, Milton W. Raudenbush, Robert Klotz, Thomas S. McNair, Joseph P. Salmon, A. Dimmick, and I. K. McCollum.

Sir Robert Pitcairn, Grand Commander, granted a Dispensation on the 28th day of September, 1866, and the V. E. Sir Jeremiah L. Hutchinson, D. G. Commander, organized the same. The Commandery is named PACKER COMMANDERY, No. 23.

OFFICERS OF PACKER COMMANDERY, No. 23.

A. D. 1866, A. O. 748, A. O. E. P. 69.

Sir Thomas S. McNair, E. C.
Sir James Houston, G.
Sir Robert Klotz, C. G.
Sir Joseph P. Salmon, P.
Sir Anthony W. Raudenbush, S. W.
Sir I. K: McCollum, J. W.
Sir William Lilly, T.
Sir Milton W. Raudenbush, R.
Sir Robert A. Packer, St. B.
Sir Wilson Wright, Sw. B.
Sir A. Dimmick, W.
Sir Josiah W. McCrea, S.

MEMBERS.

NAME.	DATE OF KNIGHTING.
Albright, Charles,	November 20, 1866.
Brown, E. R.,	September 28, 1866.
Butler, R. Q.,	September 28, 1866.
Beisel, Reuben,	November 20, 1866.
Craig, Allen,	November 20, 1866.
Dimmick, A., (No. 12), Ch. Mem.,	April 13, 1865.
Dinkey, James A.,	September 28, 1866.
De Young, Horace,	November 20, 1866.
Houston, James, (No. 9), Ch. Mem.,	February 28, 1860.
Jones, Levi,	November 20, 1866.
Klotz, Robert, (No. 12), Ch. Mem.,	April 13, 1865.
Lilly, William, (No. 9), Ch. Mem.,	March 16, 1854.
McNair, Thomas S., (No. 12), Ch. M.,	June 13, 1858.
McCollum, I. K., (No. 12), Ch. Mem.,	April 13, 1865.
McCrea, Josiah W.,	November 19, 1866.
Markle, George B.,	November 20, 1866.
McNair, J. Sharon,	November 20, 1866.
North, T. C.,	September 28, 1866.
Packer, Robert A.,	September 28, 1866.
Raudenbush, A. W., (No. 20), C. M.,	July 26, 1866.
Raudenbush, M. W., (No. 20), C. M.,	July 26, 1866.
Salmon, Jos. P., (No. 12), Ch. Mem.,	October 5, 1865.
Sites, S. E.,	November 20, 1866.
Wilhelm, James H.,	September 28, 1866.
Walter, T. F.,	November 20, 1866.
Whiston, M. D.,	November 20, 1866.
Wright, Wilson,	November 20, 1866.
Weiss, Charles A.,	November 20, 1866.

CONCLUDING REMARKS.

"The Temple's completed—exalt high each voice."

In the preceding pages of this volume, we have endeavored to give the rise and progress of the Knights Templar, but more especially its introduction into Pennsylvania, and its history to the present time. This has been obtained from memorials in the Archives of the Grand Commandery of Pennsylvania, and through the kindness of many Sir Knights, in the various Subordinate Commanderies, who devoted their time in assisting me to procure truthful historical facts. My attention, however, has been called to a REMARKABLE TEMPLAR FACT, by Sir Sidney Hayden, author of "Washington and his Masonic Compeers," (a work which should be in the hands of every Mason), which I shall make the subject of the concluding chapter of this work, because it demonstrates that Templarism had an earlier origin in Pennsylvania, even than we had claimed, and almost coeval with the Declaration of Independence.

As early as 1782, the R. W. Grand Lodge of Pennsylvania published an edition of the Ahiman Rezon, (of which but few copies are extant), which was compiled by the Rev. Dr. William Smith, and dedicated on the 24th of June, 1782, to His Excellency, George Washington, "in testimony of his exalted services to his country, as well as that noble philanthropy which distinguishes him among Masons." To this work he added a Masonic sermon, preached by himself, at the request of

352

the Grand Lodge on the 28th of December, 1778, on which occasion Washington was present as a Mason, and is also dedicated to Brother Washington, "the friend of his country and mankind—ambitious of no higher title, if higher was possible." This Ahiman Rezon referred to, has a collection of Masonic songs, and among the number—

AN ODE ON MASONRY.

BY BROTHER LT. COL. JOHN PARK, A. M., P. M.

ADDRESSED TO BRO. COL. PROCTOR, K. T.

—— *Ab ipso*
Ducit opes, animumque ferro.—Hor.

FULL CHORUS.

Hail! celestial Masonry,
Craft that makes us wise and free!
Heav'n-born cherub! bring along
The tuneful band, the patriot song:
See WASHINGTON, he leads the train,
'Tis he commands the grateful strain;
See ev'ry crafted son obeys,
And to the god-like Brother homage pays.

SONG.

Then give to merit what is due,
And twine the *mystic bays.*
In joyful strains his deeds renew
And sing the hero's praise.

RECITATIVE.

While time brings mortal honors to decay,
'Tis freedom gives, what time can't steal away.

SONG.

Unbend his brow from martial care,
And give the patriot rest;
Who nobly brav'd the storms of war,
To make his country blest.

RECITATIVE.

Wake from the tomb the souls of martyrs free,
To view this hemisphere of liberty;
Let them with ravish'd eyes look down upon
The glorious work perform'd by WASHINGTON.

SONG.

Then Brethren to my lays attend,
And hail our Father and our Friend;
Let Fame resound him thro' the land,
And echo "*'Tis our Master Grand.*"

RECITATIVE.

Begin, ye sons of Solomon,
Prepare the wreath for WASHINGTON;
'Tis he our ancient craft shall sway,
Whilst we with *three times three* obey.

SONG.

When evening's solemn hours pervade,
We choose the still masonic shade;
With hearts sincere, our *hands upon,*
We bless the *Widow's mystic son.*

RECITATIVE.

For you, my friend, the inspired muses sing,
Thou firm opposer of a tyrant king;
Go imitate in fact our glorious head,
And in the Lodge, O, PROCTOR, take the lead.

AIR.

I.

Support the Craft with honest pride;
   When in the field, our foes confound,
Display your iron thunders wide,
   And strew the bleeding courses round.

II.

Let patriot fire strain ev'ry nerve,
For WASHINGTON upon you smiles;
With him 'tis more than fame to serve,
'Tis fame with him to share his toils.

GRAND CHORUS.

Hail! celestial Masonry!
Craft that makes us wise and free;
Heav'n-born cherub! bring along
The tuneful band, the patriot song;
See WASHINGTON, he leads the train;
'Tis he commands the grateful strain.
See ev'ry Crafted son obeys,
And to the godlike Brother homage pays.

The author of this Ode was Colonel John Park, who
was a native of Delaware, and born about the year
1740, and educated in the University at Philadelphia,
under the care of Rev. Dr. William Smith, who was its
Provost, and at the same time held the office of R. W.
Grand Secretary of the Grand Lodge of Pennsylvania.
Colonel Park served in the Revolutionary War under
Washington, as Colonel; was at Boston and Valley
Forge. He was one of the most active members of the
American Union Military Lodge, which was instituted
by the Grand Lodge of Massachusetts on the 15th of
February, 1776, for the Connecticut line. Colonel Park
had attained the rank of Past Master in this Lodge.
He was a poet, and a volume of his literary productions
was published after the war, comprising translations of
the works of Horace, with original odes and poems of
his own, ascribed to various American worthies.

The dedication of this ode to Colonel Proctor, proves
that he was a Knight Templar as early as the 7th day
of February, 1779, and also Worshipful Master of the
Lodge, of which we shall speak more particularly hereafter. To Pennsylvanians, therefore, it is a subject of

deep interest, because from this fact we can trace Templarism to have existed in our State for a period of eighty-seven years. But the question to the inquiring Mason will naturally arise, who was Colonel Thomas Proctor? and what was his standing as a Patriot and a Mason? I reply, Brother Proctor filled all the prominent military offices from Captain to Major-General—was the intimate friend of Brother Washington, and the Masonic ties which bound them together were the efficient means of preserving their united friendship and brotherly love, which was only terminated by death. We base our remarks upon the facts, which we shall now submit, as sustaining us in our position, which we have derived from Sir Sidney Hayden ; the History of Montgomery Lodge, No. 19, of Philadelphia, written by Brother George Griscom, P. M., and the "Pennsylvania Archives." Brother Thomas Proctor was the son of Francis Proctor, who emigrated to this country from Ireland, and became a member of Lodge No. 3. He was commissioned as a Captain of Artillery on the 25th of October, 1775, having raised the first artillery company in the State. This commission is signed by Brother Benjamin Franklin, President of the Committee of Safety.

October 3, 1776. He was commissioned *Major* to raise a second company of artillery.

January 17, 1777. He presented the State of Pennsylvania with a brass six-pounder which he had captured at Princeton.

February 20, 1777. He was appointed Colonel of a regiment of artillery for Pennsylvania.

May 18, 1779. He was appointed by Congress a Colonel of artillery in the army of the United States.

April 21, 1780. Commissioned by Congress as Colonel of the Fourth Battalion of Artillery.

December 25, 1782. Commissioned by Congress as Major of artillery.

May 17, 1792. Commissioned by Governor Mifflin as Major of an artillery battalion of Philadelphia.

April 12, 1793. Commissioned by Governor Mifflin as Brigadier-General of the Militia of Philadelphia.

June 7, 1796. Commissioned as Major-General of the Militia of the City and County of Philadelphia.

On the 18th of April, 1781, Colonel Proctor resigned his commission in the army—was elected High Sheriff of the County of Philadelphia, and received from General Washington the following letter, showing his estimation of him as a patriot and a soldier:

HEADQUARTERS, NEW WINDSOR, *April* 20, 1781.

SIR:—Your favor of the 9th did not reach me until the 18th. I am sorry to find that the situation of your domestic affairs renders it necessary for you to quit the service. It always gives me pain to part with an officer, but particularly so with one whose experience and attention have made him useful in his profession. I cannot, in justice to you, permit you to leave the army without expressing my approbation of your conduct upon every occasion since you joined me in 1776, wishing you success in the line of life which you have now embraced.

I have signified my acceptance of your resignation which bears date the 18th inst., to the Board of War.

I am, sir,
Your most ob't. and humble serv't.,
G. WASHINGTON.

While Colonel Proctor held the office of High Sheriff, he was appointed by the Grand Lodge, one of a Committee to distribute to distressed prisoners in the jail, funds appropriated by that Grand Body for their relief.

So intimate was the communion between Washington and Proctor, that in the trials of camp life they became endeared to each other; and as the crowning act in Brother Proctor's life, to perpetuate in everlasting remembrance the birthday of the immortal Washington, we find the following letter published in the Pennsylvania Archives:

PHILADELPHIA, *February* 3, 1790.

To HIS EXCELLENCY, THOMAS MIFFLIN—SIR: I have thought it my duty to acquaint your Excellency and the Honorable, the Executive Council, that the 11th inst., (old style), will be the birthday of the Illustrious, the President of the United States of America, and should it be thought expedient by your Honorable Body to announce the same by a certain number of discharges from twelve-pounders, your Excellency will be pleased to signify the same to

Your Excellency's obedient servant,

THOMAS PROCTOR, *Major.*

To this circumstance, therefore, are we indebted for the initiative steps for the celebration of the birthday of Washington.

We have now established his military life, in which he devoted his services to the freedom of his country, and shall examine into his Masonic life.

The Provincial Grand Lodge of Pennsylvania was constituted June 20, 1764, by a Warrant from the Grand Lodge of England. In 1776, Brother Proctor was Worshipful Master of Lodge No. 2, (in which Lodge he received all his Masonic degrees, from Entered Apprentice to Knight Templar), and continued a member thereof, until the 18th of May, 1779, when the Grand Lodge of Pennsylvania granted a Charter to the First Regiment of Pennsylvania Artillery, and was No. 19 on

its Registry, (it being the same day on which he received
his commission as Colonel in the Continental Army), but
subsequently it was called Montgomery Lodge, No. 19,
and is still in existence.

This was the first Military Lodge Warrant granted in
the American Army by Pennsylvania.   Colonel Proctor
bore this Warrant with him in his campaign with General Sullivan against the Indians of Western New York,
in 1779.   And the first account of any work under it,
was at Wilkesbarre, in the Valley of the Wyoming,
where General Sullivan had the bodies of Captain Davis
and Lieutenant Jones, who were slain and scalped by
the Indians, taken up and reinterred with Masonic ceremonies.   This was the first Masonic meeting ever held
in that valley; and the procession of Brethren (says
Hayden in his Life of Washington and his Masonic
Compeers) that bore the bodies of their slain companions
from their first resting-place in the forest, for a more
decent interment at Wyoming, was attended by the
regimental band, which played Roslin Castle on their
march.   This Military Lodge, on that occasion, met at
the Marquee of Colonel Proctor.   In 1794, a Masonic
Lodge was chartered in Wilkesbarre, No. 61, by the R.
W. Grand Lodge of Pennsylvania.

We have referred to the reinterment of Captain Davis
and Lieutenant Jones; it will not be amiss to state that
this service was held on the 18th of August, 1779, where
a sermon was preached by Dr. Rogers, one of the Chap-
lains, from the seventh verse of the seventh chapter of
Job—"Remember that my life is wind."

The progress of Masonry was thus following the foot-
steps of war in its advancement into the American
wilderness, and like the shadows of an angel wing, soft-
ening the outlines of the path of war.

The sound of its gavel was renewed at old Tioga Point,

under a Warrant granted by the R. W. Grand Lodge
of Pennsylvania, in 1796, for Lodge No. 70, which is
still working but a few rods from where this Masonic
service was preached at Fort Sullivan, in 1779.

In the Military Warrant of Lodge No. 19, Thomas
Proctor was named as Worshipful Master, Charles Young
as Senior Warden, and John Melbeck as Junior Warden.
Brother Proctor has been represented as a man of great
moral excellency, of unbending integrity, of pleasing
urbanity of manners, of warm friendship, and possessing
in a pre-eminent degree the Masonic virtues of patience
and perseverance; fervency and zeal. With such quali-
ties of heart and mind, he carried with him not only the
glorious standard of our country, but the insignia of our
Order, and on the tented field opened his Lodge *in due
form.* Around that altar the immortal Washington,
Lafayette, and the Masonic brethren of the army, would
gather and take sweet counsel together as Masons, as
patriots, and as citizens.

As a Mason, we find Brother Proctor addressing the
Grand Master of the Grand Lodge of Massachusetts, as
early as July, 1780, on the propriety of appointing
Brother Washington as General Grand Master.

On December 27, 1796, Brother Proctor, with Brothers
Smith and Duplessis, were appointed a Committee by
the Grand Lodge of Pennsylvania to wait on Brother
Washington, and acquaint him that the Grand Lodge
would present an address to him at whatever time would
be most convenient for him to receive it. Brother
Washington appointed the subsequent day, and the Committee discharged their duty.

When the Grand Lodge of Pennsylvania was invited
by Congress to join in the funeral ceremonies to do
honor to the memory of Brother Washington, Brother
Proctor, on account of the intimacy which always existed

between the Father of his Country and himself, was appointed *Master of Ceremonies.*

Colonel Proctor's name appears often on the records of the Grand Lodge of Pennsylvania. On one occasion, February 10, 1780, the record states, "Brother Proctor, Master of No. 19, has generously paid, as an acknowledgment to this Grand Lodge, £150, the receipt of which is acknowledged by the Grand Secretary. Brother Proctor also offered very satisfactory reasons for not attending the last General Quarterly Communication, having been detained by business of a public nature."

We now retrace our steps to Lodge No. 19.

When the Revolution was ended, and the R. W. Grand Lodge of Pennsylvania, on the 16th of October, 1786, had declared herself a Grand Lodge independent of any Foreign jurisdiction, the subordinate Lodges surrendered their Charters and received new ones in lieu thereof. The officers of No. 19 also petitioned the Grand Lodge for a new Charter, which was granted December 18, 1786, and was regularly constituted January 13, 1787, with Thomas Proctor as its Worshipful Master; Charles Young, Senior Warden, and J. Melbeck, Junior Warden.

Brother Proctor continued a member of Lodge No. 19, until his death, which occurred March 16, 1807, at the age of sixty-seven years, and his remains were buried with the usual Masonic honors in St. Paul's Episcopal Church burying-ground, on Third, below Walnut streets.

In the historical sketch of Lodge No. 19, I find the following interesting Masonic facts with regard to Brother Proctor, which I transcribe as worthy of preservation.

There is enough left to us to show that a full history of Colonel Proctor's connection with our Lodge would be one of rare interest, and full of instruction to the Craft. Information from sources undoubtedly authentic has been received, that while the army under General Washington was in winter quarters at Morristown, New Jersey, in 1779–80, where Colonel Proctor had joined it with his regiment, the Lodge was there opened by him under this Warrant.

It is well known that the Father of our country, like Proctor, was an ardent Mason, as well as soldier, and gave his countenance to this Military Lodge. His friend and companion in arms, the young General and illustrious hero, the Marquis De Lafayette, followed the example of his Chief, and it is said, that he was here initiated into the mysteries of the Craft. There seems no room for reasonable doubt, that both of these illustrious personages were then and there visitors to, and participants in, the work of this Lodge; and the tradition is, that Washington presided at the conferring of degrees on Lafayette.

It is said to have been on this occasion that the jewels and paraphernalia of St. John's Lodge, No. 1, of Newark, New Jersey, were loaned to this Military Lodge under Colonel Proctor, while at Morristown.

The following entries on the oldest book of minutes of St. John's Lodge, are exceedingly important and valuable as the highest kind of evidence in corroboration of this interesting tradition.

"From the most authentic sources it is supposed the list of articles mentioned on the other side, was loaned to the Army Lodge, (No. 19), encamped at Morristown, for the purpose of initiating General Lafayette."

J. H. LANDELL,
Secretary of St. John's Lodge, No. 1.

[COPY.]

"An account of sundry articles taken out of the Lodge chest of Newark, St. John's Lodge, No. 1, by consent of

Brother John Robinson, Brother Lewis Ogden, Brother
John Ogden, and lent unto Brother Thomas Henry and
Brother Jerry Brenin, to carry so far as Morristown;
said Brothers Henry and Brenin promising, on the
word of Brothers, to return the same articles as per in-
ventory below, unto our Brother John Robinson, present
Secretary, when called for.
"Witness our hands, Brothers, below.
    "Signed,   THOMAS HENRY,
                JEREMIAH BRENIN."

ARTICLES.

"24 aprons; 2 ebony truncheons, one tipped with silver,
(the other they are to get, if to be found); 3 large can-
dlesticks; 3 large candle moulds; 1 silk pedestal, cloth
bound, with silver lace, damask cushion; 1 silver key
with a blue ribbon striped with black; do. level, with
do.; do. square; do. plumb. 18 aprons returned.
"NEWARK, *December* 24, 1779."

In a letter dated March 6, 1852, from Brother J. H.
Landell, formerly Secretary of St. John's Lodge, No. 1,
at Newark, New Jersey, are the following passages:
St. John's Lodge, being the oldest in the State, numbers among the members some few of the good and true
men who passed through the fiery ordeal of the dark
age of Masonry unscathed, and are now left to us as the
preservers of the ancient usages and customs of our
ancient and honorable Order. It is true we have but
few of these ancient relics left us, and they are fast
traveling the road "from which no traveler returns."
Seeing the engraving of the tomb of Lafayette in
your last number, calls to mind a statement of Brother
Judson, of that great and good man. It appears when
the American army was at Morristown, in this State, at

the time of the Revolution, Lafayette was Entered, Passed, and Raised to the degree of a Master Mason in the Army Lodge, of which Washington was *then* Master.

In Brother Alexander's History of St. John's Lodge, No. 1, of Newark, published in Brother Hyneman's "Masonic Mirror," vol. 5, it is stated that the work of that Lodge was suspended from 1772 until 1798; and that during this suspension, on motion of a Brother, the Lodge furniture was ordered to be removed to Morristown, for the purpose of holding Camp Lodges in the American army. At one of these Camp Lodges, it is said the immortal Father of his country presided, and during his Mastership, he had the pleasure of conferring the sublime degree of a Master Mason upon his illustrious friend, the Marquis De Lafayette. As there was but one Camp Lodge held at Morristown, the Lodge in which this work is said to have been done, must have been the one for which Colonel Proctor held the Warrant from the Grand Lodge of Pennsylvania, to wit, No. 19, now Montgomery Lodge, No. 19, of Philadelphia.

In truth so well established has the correctness of this account always been considered, that it has passed into history, and has become a part of the annals of the State of New Jersey.

In a volume entitled "Historical Collections of New Jersey, (by Barber and Horne), page 385, after mentioning that the American Army, under Washington, had its winter quarters at Morristown and vicinity on two different occasions, viz., in January, 1777, and 1779–80, the fact (plainly corroborative of our tradition) is stated, that while here, he, (Washington), attended the Masonic Lodge then held in Morris Hotel, in the room where the bar now is."

All honor, therefore, to the Keystone State, within

whose limits the representatives of the thirteen Colonies, on the 4th of July, 1776, promulgated to the nations of the earth, the eternal principles of civil and religious liberty, and declared that we are, and of right ought to be a free and independent people.

All honor to the Keystone State, that the Knights Templar within our jurisdiction has the historic evidence that on the 7th of February, 1779, Sir Thomas Proctor, W. M., of Lodge, No. 19, was acknowledged as a Knight Templar, and as a Pilgrim Warrior, battled manfully not only to protect the Temple of American Liberty, but the principles of Masonry and the Orders of Christian Knighthood.

All honour to the Keystone State, that on the 12th day of May, 1797, the FIRST Grand Encampment, ever organized in America, was duly constituted in Philadelphia, and the Grand Officers of this Grand Encampment, like the three Grand Masters of the Solomonian Temple, "laid the foundation thereof, very deep, not in great stones, costly stones, and hewed stones," but in the affections of every Sir Knight who labors to erect a Temple worthy of the principles of the blessed Immanuel. Realizing the truthfulness of every position we have assumed, conscious of the rectitude of our intentions, by making truth our aim, our object, and our standard, of justice and equity, we commit our work to the Members of the Masonic Fraternity, as well as those who have been taught the mysteries pertaining to the Orders of Christian Knighthood; and in the language of a Most Excellent Master, exclaim

> Thy *Wisdom* inspired the great institution;
>   Thy *Strength* shall support it, till nature expires,
> And when the creation shall fall into ruin,
>   Its *Beauty* shall rise thro' the midst of the fire.

31 *

CONSTITUTION

OF THE

GRAND COMMANDERY OF KNIGHTS TEMPLAR

OF PENNSYLVANIA.

CONSTITUTION.

ARTICLE I.

Of the State Grand Commandery.

SECTION I.—How Constituted.

THE Grand Commandery of Pennsylvania is constituted as follows:

I. The Right Eminent Grand Commander.
II. The Very Eminent Deputy Grand Commander.
III. The Eminent Grand Generalissimo.

IV.	" "	Captain-General.
V.	" "	Prelate.
VI.	" "	Senior Warden.
VII.	" "	Junior Warden.
VIII.	" "	Treasurer.
IX.	" "	Recorder.
X.	" "	Standard Bearer.
XI.	" "	Sword Bearer.
XII.	" "	Warder.
XIII.	" "	Captain of the Guards (or Sentinel).

Likewise,

XIV. All Past Grand Commanders (and Grand Masters).
XV. All Past Deputy Grand Commanders (and Deputy Grand Masters).
XVI. All Past Grand Generalissimos.

xvii. All Past Grand Captain-Generals.

So long as they remain members of the Subordinate Commanderies under this State jurisdiction.

Likewise,

xviii. The Eminent Commander.

xix. The Generalissimo.

xx. The Captain-General.

Of each chartered Subordinate Commandery working under this Grand Commandery.

Likewise,

xxi. All Past Eminent Commanders of the Subordinate Commanderies working under this State Grand Commandery, so long as they remain members of Subordinate Commanderies under this jurisdiction.

Each of the individuals enumerated in this section shall be entitled, when present, to one vote.

No person shall be eligible to office in this State Grand Commandery unless he shall be at the time a member of some Subordinate Commandery, working under this Grand Commandery, and who has filled, or is at the present time filling, one of the first three offices in his Commandery: *Provided,* That no person shall be eligible to either of the first four offices of the Grand Commandery, unless he holds, or has held, the office of Eminent Commander of a Subordinate Commandery. (Amended June 14, 1865).

SECTION II.—Proxies.

Any officer specified in the first section, save and except Past Commanders, may appear and vote by proxy; said proxy being, at the time of service, a member of the same Subordinate Commandery as his principal, and producing a certificate of his appointment.

SECTION III.—MEETINGS.

1. The Annual Conclave of the Grand Commandery shall be holden on the second Tuesday of June, in each and every year, and be opened at eight o'clock, P. M., and shall be held alternately east and west of the Alleghany Mountains, at such place as may be directed at the preceding meeting.

2. *Order of Business at Stated Meetings.*—The minutes of the proceedings of the last Annual Conclave, and of any special Grand Conclaves, are to be read, unless dispensed with.

3. After the minutes are approved, the Grand Commander shall appoint a *Committee on Credentials*, composed of three Sir Knights, who shall report the names of the members present, as soon as practicable.

4. The following Standing Committees, each to consist of *three* Sir Knights, shall also be appointed, who shall report upon the several matters referred to them during the session of the Grand Commandery.

1. On the Doings of the Grand Officers.
2. On Dispensations and Charters.
3. On By-Laws.
4. On Finance.
5. On Grievances.
6. On Designating the next place of meeting.
7. On Unfinished Business.
8. On Mileage and Pay of Representatives.
9. On Landmarks.
10. On Foreign Correspondence, which shall make report at as early a period during the next session as may be practicable. This Committee shall be appointed

by the Grand Commander immediately after his installation.

The election of Grand Officers shall be held on the morning of the second day of the session, after ten o'clock.

The Grand Commander shall exemplify, or cause to be exemplified, the work of the Orders during the meeting of the Grand Conclave.

Special Meetings.—Special meetings may be called by the Grand Commander, at his discretion. No business shall be transacted at the special meetings, save that which was specified in the original summons.

The several Grand Officers shall hold their respective offices until their successors shall be duly elected and installed. All questions shall be determined by a majority of votes, except alterations of this Constitution, which shall require two-thirds present. The presiding officer, for the time being, shall have one vote. In case of the votes being equally divided, he shall also give the casting vote. No appeal shall lie to the Grand Commandery from the decision of the Grand Commander.

This Grand Commandery shall have exclusive jurisdiction over the Templar and Appendant Orders in this State; grant charters, decide appeals, and settle all controversies that may arise between Subordinate Commanderies; authorize a uniform ritual and work, and do all things necessary to promote the good, well-being and perpetuation of Templar Masonry; but subordinate to the Grand Encampment of the United States, so long as this Grand Commandery shall be connected therewith.

SECTION IV.—DUTIES OF OFFICERS.

1st. *The Right Eminent Grand Commander* shall preside over all stated and special meetings, exercise a watchful supervision over all the Subordinate Commanderies, and see that all the constitutional enactments, rules and edicts of the Grand Encampment of the United States, and of this State Grand Commandery, are duly and promptly observed. He shall have power, during the recess, to grant letters of Dispensation to nine or more petitioners, possessing the Constitutional qualifications, empowering them to form and open a Commandery; this Dispensation to cease at the next annual meeting, or continue by order of the Grand Commandery.

No dispensation shall be issued, unless the petition shall be recommended by the nearest Commandery, and the petitioners give satisfactory evidence of good standing, of suitable place of meeting, of possessing or having ability to procure proper furniture and dress for the use of the Commandery, and of being competent to conduct intelligently the ceremonies, work, and government of their Commandery.

He may visit and preside at any Commandery, and give such instructions and directions as the good of the institution may require; but always adhering to the ancient landmarks.

It is his duty, either in person or by proxy, to attend all meetings of the Grand Encampment of the United States.

2d. *The Very Eminent Deputy Grand Commander.*

The Very Eminent Deputy Grand Commander, in the event of the death, removal, or physical incompetency of his superior, shall act as the Grand Commander. At all other times, he shall perform such duties as may be assigned him by the Grand Commandery or the Grand Commander.

It is his duty, either in person or by proxy, to attend all meetings of the Grand Encampment of the United States.

32

3d. *Eminent Grand Generalissimo and Grand Captain-General.*

In the absence of their respective superiors, they shall severally act as Grand Commanders, in order according to rank. At all other times they shall perform such duties as may be assigned them by the Grand Commander, or such as are traditionally appropriate to their respective stations.

4th. *Eminent Grand Recorder.*

The Grand Recorder shall make an annual report to this Grand Commandery of the returns of the Subordinate Commanderies, showing their elected officers, the increase and numbers of each Subordinate, and the amount paid or due by each; also, such other matters as may conduce to the general good of the order.

He shall keep a true record of the proceedings of this Grand Body, and receive and collect all moneys due to this Commandery, and pay the same over to the Grand Treasurer.

He shall mail to the Grand Master and Grand Recorder of the Grand Encampment of the United States; also, to the Grand Commander and Grand Recorder of each State Grand Commandery; also, to the Eminent Commander and Recorder of each subordinate under this jurisdiction, copies of our annual proceedings; also, of all expulsions or rejections within this jurisdiction. Also, shall advise the Recorder of each Commandery within the State of every suspension or expulsion in any subordinate therein. Also, he shall open and keep in a suitable book a register of each Subordinate Commandery—showing the present and past officers and members of each; also, of all rejections, suspensions and expulsions.

5th. *Eminent Grand Treasurer.*

The Grand Treasurer shall receive and keep in charge all the money and property of this Grand Commandery. He shall pay only such orders as may have been passed by vote of this Grand Commandery, signed by the Grand Recorder and countersigned by the Grand Commander. He shall, at each annual or special meeting, present an accurate report of the state of the Treasury.

SECTION V.—FEES, DUES AND FINANCES.

The revenue of the Grand Commandery shall be derived as follows:

For every Dispensation, to be paid before the
   same is issued, ... $90 00
When the Charter is issued, the further sum of . 10 00
   (for the use of the Recorder).
For every Knight Templar, receiving either or
   both orders of Knighthood, . . . 3 00
For annual dues, ... 1 00
For Grand Commandery diploma, . . . 2 00

ARTICLE VII.

ALTERATIONS AND AMENDMENTS.

Every proposed alteration or amendment of this Constitution, shall be made at one session of the Conclave, and acted upon at the next, and that publicity be given it by incorporating the proposed alteration or amendment, with the proceedings. (Amended June 14, 1865).

SUBORDINATE COMMANDERIES.

Subordinate Commanderies shall not confer the Orders of Knighthood upon any one but a Royal Arch Mason, nor for a less sum than twenty dollars.

Every application must be recommended by a member

of the Commandery, and inclose the whole amount of fee.

Applicants for the Orders of Knighthood must reside within the jurisdiction of this Grand Commandery; or, if sojourners, they must have the consent of the Commandery nearest to their place of residence.

Every Commandery shall meet at least quarterly for business.

Each Commandery shall hold its annual election at the stated meeting in March, and the installation of officers shall take place on or before the second Tuesday of June.

No dispensation for constituting a Commandery of Knights Templar shall issue, except upon the petition of nine Sir Knights of the Order, which petition shall be recommended by the Commandery nearest to the place where such new Commandery is proposed to be established.

Every Commandery shall, before the 9th day of May in every year, transmit to the Grand Recorder, in such form as shall be furnished, its annual returns, accompanied by the fees and dues to the Grand Commandery.

Any Commandery neglecting or refusing to make its annual returns, accompanied by fees and dues, shall be notified thereof; and if, after three months' notice, it fails to pay, it shall be suspended until restored by the edict of the Grand Commander.

Any Commandery which shall have omitted to make its annual returns and payments on or before the second Tuesday of June, shall thereby be deprived of its representative in the Grand Commandery.

When a Commandery is disbanded, or dissolved, by neglecting to make its returns, or neglecting to pay its dues, or by unknightly conduct, or by the death or resignation of its members, it is the duty of the last Commander and Recorder, within three months after its dissolution, to surrender to the Grand Recorder, the Warrant, books and papers, jewels, furniture, and funds of such Commandery; and the last Commander is to transmit to the Grand Recorder an inventory thereof. No Sir Knight of such Commandery shall be admitted into any other Commandery, nor entitled to the benefits of Templar Masonry, until he shall have paid to the Grand Recorder all arrears due from him to such Commandery.

ARTICLE IX.

The Rules of Order and general regulations of the United States Grand Encampment shall govern the proceedings of this Grand Commandery.

ARTICLE X.

In all cases of degradation or suspension, an appeal shall lie to the Grand Commandery.

DECISIONS.

MADE BY R. E. SIR BENJAMIN PARKE, GRAND COMMANDER.

PETITIONERS.

1857, *July* 16.—In Masonry, by Constitutional regulations in Pennsylvania, the petitioners for a *new* Lodge must "not be members of any Lodge" at the time of petitioning. In Knighthood there is no such law. Any Sir Knight, being a resident of this State, may be one of the petitioners for a new Commandery, and act in it, while it is under dispensation. When such new Com-

mandery obtains a charter, the petitioner should with-
draw from one or the other; though I know of no law
requiring him to do so.

CONFERRING ORDERS.

1857, *August* 24.—There is no Statute in our Order
giving power to the Grand Commander to issue dispensations for conferring the Orders of Knighthood, out of
the usual course, or waiving the provisions of By-Laws.
A reason for this may be that no such power is necessary
to accomplish the object you seek. There is no law of
our Order which prohibits conferring the Orders *at the
time of the application*, with the unanimous consent of all
the members present. Unless, therefore, your By-Laws
prohibit it, you can confer the Orders at the time you
desire.

MEMBERSHIP.

1857, *September* 21.—It is not necessary to a membership in a Commandery, that a Sir Knight should belong
to either a Blue Lodge or Chapter in Masonry. Templarism, or Christian Masonic Knighthood, *as an organization*, is entirely independent of Masonry. Its only
constitutional alliance therewith, is the requisition that
the Orders of Knighthood shall not be conferred upon
any but a Royal Arch Mason.

BALLOTING.

1857, *December* 11.—There is no law in Masonic
Knighthood *prescribing or requiring the "ballot box,"* or
even a *"ballot,"* as *the* mode of ascertaining the opinions
of the members of a Commandery, upon a proposition
or petition for the Orders of Knighthood. Neither was
there any such law in Masonry under the "ancient
charges," which simply provided that the members "are
to signify their *consent* or *dissent*, in their own prudent

way, either virtually or in form, but with *unanimity*." The Constitutions or regulations of Grand Lodges generally prescribe the "ballot," and general usage, in both Masonry and Knighthood, is in favor of the use of the "ballot box," with white and black balls; which, being so well understood and so convenient, I recommend to be used in our Commanderies, especially and in *all cases* when it is asked for by any member present. But if, when the applicant was proposed, unanimous *consent* was given by all the members present, no one expressing a *dissent*, or asking for a ballot, he was legally elected, and you were right in conferring the Orders upon him.

PAYMENT OF DUES.

1858, *April* 6.—The dues to be paid by the Subordinate Commanderies to the Grand Commandery, are the sum of *two dollars* (now $3), for each initiation, and the further sum of *one dollar* for every member of said Subordinate Commandery. The number of members are taken at the time the return is made. No difference between those made twelve months or twelve days before the return day. So, if any members had withdrawn, or been suspended, or degraded, at any time before the return day, they are not counted in the number of members for whom dues are to be paid.

OFFICERS UNDER DISPENSATION.

1858, *April* 28.—A petition for dispensation need not nominate officers, though it is usually done. The officers of a Commandery under dispensation are the appointment of the R. E. Grand Commander. The usage, in this State, has been for Commanderies under dispensation to adopt By-Laws and elect officers, to be named in their charter when granted. These By-Laws, together with all their proceedings, are returned to the next Grand

Commandery. If they are *approved*, and a charter granted, the officers named therein, if present, are installed, and take their seats in the Grand Commandery as members thereof.

CHARGES AGAINST A SIR KNIGHT.

1858, *June* 2.—Neither charges preferred against a Sir Knight in a Masonic Lodge or Chapter of which he is a member, nor his suspension or expulsion therefrom, upon a trial of those charges, will, of *themselves*, without a trial by his Commandery, deprive him of membership therein; nor do I think the legal doctrine of *"res judicata"* can be admitted in its full extent, in regard to the judgment of such Lodge or Chapter, so as to preclude the necessity or bar the right of a full investigation by the Commandery, upon the merits of the case. The strong presumption in regard to the proceedings should probably be that the trial was regular and the judgment right; but as it might turn out there was a mistake, or that some extraneous or undue bias had influenced or colored the proceedings, they ought not to be considered conclusive. Every Sir Knight is entitled to a fair trial by his *peers in Knighthood*, the social and moral code of which is, that of the highest style of Christian morality, a conformity to the whole moral law and the precepts of Him who gave us the great central rule of moral action, "As ye would that men do to you, do ye even so to them."

MADE BY R. E. SIR WILLIAM H. ALLEN, GRAND COMMANDER.

DUES AND FEES.

1860, *June* 22.—Commanderies *under dispensation* owe no annual dues to the Grand Commandery, but must pay the usual fees for persons receiving the Orders of Knighthood in them before receiving their charters.

HERMAN YERKES.

1860, *June* 22.—That Sir Herman Yerkes cannot visit Commanderies under this jurisdiction, until he shall be formally healed.

MADE BY R. E. SIR E. H. TURNER.

SUSPENDED SIR KNIGHTS.

1863, *June* 10.—That when a Sir Knight is suspended for non-payment of dues, the Grand Recorder being notified of it, the payment of his dues will restore him to good financial position in his Commandery; but to restore him to membership, he must make application in writing, which application shall take the usual course, and by a majority vote he shall be restored to membership.

MADE BY R. E. SIR H. STANLEY GOODWIN.

1864, *June* 13.—That it is right and proper to confer the Orders of Knighthood upon any number of applicants at one and the same time.

MADE BY R. E. SIR WILLIAM H. STRICKLAND.

1866, *June* 12.—On application from an E. C. for permission to re-ballot in case of several applicants for the Orders of Knighthood, who had been rejected, I decided that reference to the Grand Commandery was not necessary, as it is the privilege of the E. C. of each Subordinate Commandery to order or refuse a ballot at his discretion.

RESOLUTIONS.

REPRESENTATIVE.

1857, *June* 22.—*Resolved*, That hereafter no representative from any Commandery under this jurisdiction, unless their returns are made to the Grand Recorder, agreeably to the Constitution, shall be entitled to speak or vote in this Commandery.

MEMBERSHIP.

1858, *June* 22.—*Resolved*, That while this Grand Commandery recognizes the right of a Sir Knight, while a member of a Subordinate Commandery, to assist, with his name and presence, in the formation of another Commandery, *while under Dispensation*, without losing his membership in the former; yet, upon the reception of a warrant by the Second Commandery, the Sir Knight should ELECT in which Commandery he will maintain his membership.

DIPLOMAS.

1858, *June* 22.—*Resolved*, That the Grand Recorder is hereby authorized to issue a Grand Commandery certificate to any Sir Knight, upon the production and filing with him the certificate, in proper form, of the Subordinate Commandery to which such Sir Knight is attached, and on the payment of the usual fee.

PAY OF REPRESENTATIVES.

1858, *June* 24.—*Resolved*, That hereafter this Grand Commandery will pay but ONE Representative from each Commandery, (together with the actual expenses of the Grand Officers, when in attendance on each Annual Conclave).   .

P. GRAND COMMANDERS.

1859, *June* 22.—*Resolved*, That the necessary expenses of Past Grand Commanders, incurred in attending the meetings of the Annual Conclave, be hereafter paid out of the funds of the Grand Commandery.

OFFICERS ENTITLED TO VOTE.

1862, *June* 10.—*Resolved*, That P. Grand Commanders Allen and Knapp be instructed to report whether an E. Commander, who is a Past Commander, is entitled to two votes; and, also, whether a Grand Officer can cast a vote as such, and another for Past Eminent Commander, at the same time.

P. R. E. G. C. Allen made the following report on Masonic Law, which was affirmed by the vote of the Grand Commandery:

To the R. E. Grand Commander and Eminent Sir Knights of the Grand Commandery of Pennsylvania:

Two questions of law have been referred to the undersigned, and an opinion requested.

1st, Whether a Commander, voting as the representative of a Subordinate Commandery in this Grand Commandery, can lawfully cast another vote as a Past Commander.

2d. Whether an officer of this Grand Commandery, after voting as such, may lawfully cast another vote as Past Commander of a Subordinate Commandery.

The first section of the Constitution of this Grand Commandery contains a list of all the classes of persons who constitute this Grand Commandery. These are the Grand and Past Officers, the Commanders, Generalissimos, and Captain-Generals; and the Past Commanders of Subordinate Commanderies under this Grand Commandery.

It is expressly declared, that each of the *individuals* enumerated in this Section, shall be entitled, when present, to *one vote*.

As the word *individual* was evidently intended by the framers of the Constitution to apply to *persons* and not to *officers* as such, the undersigned are of opinion that no officer or member of this Grand Commandery can lawfully cast more than one vote, except as holding one or more proxies for officers of his Commandery, or when the Grand Commander decides a tie vote.

The undersigned answer both questions in the negative.

The undersigned have found the Constitution so plain on these points, that they have deemed it, unnecessary to fortify their opinion by referring to the usage of other Masonic bodies, all of which, it is believed, allow but one vote to one member.

Respectfully submitted,

WILLIAM H. ALLEN,

C. F. KNAPP,

P. G. Commanders.

TEMPLAR YEAR.

1864, *June* 13.—*Resolved*, That the 1st day of May shall be designated as the commencement of the Templar year.

PROXIES.

1864, *June* 13.—*Resolved*, That the Officers of Subordinate Commanderies in sending of a Proxy be required to conform to the prescribed forms.

SUSPENSION OR EXPULSION.

1865, *June* 14.—*Resolved*, That the Expulsion or Suspension of a Knight Templar by the Lodge to which he belongs, deprives him of all the privileges of Knighthood. Upon receiving official notice of the action of the Lodge, the Commandery to which he belongs should strike his name from its rolls.

FINANCES.

1866, *June* 13.—*Resolved*, That the Grand Treasurer be directed to purchase a book, in which he shall keep full and correct accounts of the receipts and disbursements of the Grand Commandery, and that said book shall be the property of the Grand Commandery, and shall with the funds and other property of the Grand Commandery, be delivered to his successor immediately after installation.

Form of Petition for Dispensation to establish a Commandery.

To the Right Eminent Grand Commander of the Grand Commandery of Knights Templar of the State of Pennsylvania:

The petition of the undersigned respectfully represents, that they are severally Knights of the Red Cross, Knights Templar, and Knights of Malta, residing in the Commonwealth of Pennsylvania. That they are in good standing as Knights of those illustrious Orders, and among them there are, in their opinion, a competent number well qualified to form and open a Commandery of Knights Templar and the appendant Orders, and to properly discharge the various duties thereof, according to ancient usage. That they have a suitable place of meeting and ability to procure proper furniture and dress for conducting the ceremonies and work of a Commandery. Having the good of the Order at heart, and desirous to extend the benefits and blessings thereof to worthy companions, they pray for a DISPENSATION, empowering them to form, open, and hold a regular Commandery of Knights Templar, and the appendant Orders, in the   of   County of   and State of Pennsylvania, to be named   Commandery, subordinate to, under the jurisdiction of, and to be conducted in accordance with the Constitution, Rules, and Edicts of the Grand Commandery of Pennsylvania, of the Grand Encampment of the United States, and the general principles, landmarks, and usages of the Order. And they beg leave respectfully to recommend Sir Knight   as the first Eminent Commander, Sir Knight   as the first Generalissimo, Sir Knight   as the first Captain-General.

Dated at   A. D. 18   A. O. 7   A. O. E. P. 7

33   R

ƒorm of Demit.

To all Sir Knights of the Illustrious Order of the Red Cross, and of the valiant and magnanimous Orders of Knights Templar and Knights of Malta, to whom these presents may come, Greeting:

THIS IS TO CERTIFY, That Sir Knight ——— ——— whose name appears in the margin of this DEMIT, is a Knight Templar, late a member of ——— Commandery, No. —. That he is in good standing in the Order and free from all charges on the books; and as such, we courteously commend him to the fraternal regard of all valiant and magnanimous Sir Knights, wherever dispersed around the globe.

In testimony whereof we have hereunto set our hands and caused the seal of our Commandery to be affixed, this [L. S.] day of   in the year of our Lord 18   , and of the Order 7   A. O. E. P. 7

ATTEST: ——— ——— E. C.
——— ——— *Recorder.*

———————

ƒorm of Dispensation to elect Officers out of the Warranted Time.

To all true and courteous Sir Knights; but more especially to the Officers and members of   Commandery, No.   in the   of   Greeting:

KNOW YE, That whereas no regular election of the officers of the aforesaid Commandery, under its Charter and By-Laws, took place at the time and place as provided for in such By-Laws, to wit, for the annual election in March last: Now, THEREFORE, I, A. B., Grand Commander of the Grand Commandery of Knights Templar of the State of Pennsylvania, by virtue of the high powers in me vested, do hereby grant and issue this, my especial Dispensation, unto our worthy Subordinate, the aforesaid Commandery, No.   , hereby authorizing the officers and members of such Commandery, at such time and place as may be by them appointed, to wit: at a regular meeting, to proceed and in due order elect suitable Sir Knights of their body and Commandery, to serve in the several offices provided for in their By-Laws; and the Sir Knights so elected, after being duly installed, to serve until the next annual election and installation of its officers, under the said By-Laws; all members to have due and timely notice of such meeting, and for the election aforesaid. And I hereby enjoin it upon the E. Commander and Recorder of such Commandery, to certify, under the seal of said Commandery, to our E. Grand Recorder, within six days after said election, the proceedings had under this Dispensation.

Given under my hand and seal, at   , this   day of
A. D. 18   A. O. 7   A. O. E. P. 7
A. B.,   R. E. G. C., of G. C. of Pa.

𝔉orm of a ℭertificate for ℜroxy.

To the Grand Commandery of the State of Pennsylvania:

THIS IS TO CERTIFY, That in consideration of the confidence I repose in the courtesy and magnanimity of our valiant Sir Knight —— ——, I have nominated and appointed, and by these presents do nominate and appoint the said Sir Knight —— ——, to be my proxy in the Grand Commandery of the State of Pennsylvania, then and there to represent me and to do every act and thing agreeably to the Constitution of the Grand Commandery, as fully and completely as I could do myself, were I personally present.

Witness my hand and seal this   day of   A. D. 18   A. O.
7   A. O. E. P. 7

(Name),   —— ——
(Office),   —— ——

Form of Petition for the Orders of Knighthood.

To the Eminent Commander, Officers, and Sir Knights of   Commandery, No.   of Knights Templar and the appendant Orders: ·

I, the undersigned, hereby declare, that I am a Royal Arch Mason in good standing; a member of   Chapter, No.
under a Charter from the Grand Chapter of   ;
that I have a firm and steadfast belief in the truth of the Christian religion, and the doctrine of the Holy Trinity, as revealed in the New Testament; and respectfully pray that I may be made in your Commandery a Knight of the Order of Knights Templar and appendant Orders, and become a member of your Commandery. Should my request be granted, I promise to conform to all the ceremonies, engagements, rules, and statutes of your Order, as well as those of your Commandery.

Witness my hand, this   day of   A. D. 18
Recommended and vouched for on
  the honor of a Knight, by

THE R. E. Grand Commandery meets Second Tuesday of June, annually, alternate meetings being held East and West of the Mountain.

SUBORDINATE COMMANDERIES.

NAME.	No.	LOCATION.	TIME OF MEETING.
Pittsburg,	1,	Pittsburg,	Second Tuesday.
Philadelphia,	2,	Philadelphia,	Second Tuesday.
Jacques De Molay,	3,	Washington,	First Friday.
St. John's,	4,	Philadelphia,	Fourth Friday.
Hubbard,	5,	Waynesburg,	Third Wednesday.
St. Omer's,	7,	Brownsville,	Third Tuesday.
St. John's,	8,	Carlisle,	Fourth Thursday.
De Molay,	9,	Reading,	Second Tuesday.
Mountain,	10,	Altoona,	Fourth Tuesday.
Parke,	11,	Harrisburg,	First Tuesday.
Crusade,	12,	Bloomsburg,	Second Thursday.
Columbia,	13,	Lancaster,	Fourth Thursday.
Palestine,	14,	Carbondale,	Third Friday.
Jerusalem,	15,	Phenixville,	Friday before Full Moon.
Northern,	16,	Towanda,	Friday after 2d Monday.
Cœur De Lion,	17,	Scranton,	Second Wednesday.
Kedron,	18,	Greensburg,	First Tuesday.
Hugh De Payens,	19,	Easton,	First Monday.
Allén,	20,	Allentown,	Second Thursday.
York,	21,	York,	Third Thursday.
Baldwin II.,	22,	Williamsport,	Fourth Thursday.
Packer,	23,	Mauch Chunk,	Third Tuesday.

33 *

INDEX.

391

R *

394   INDEX.